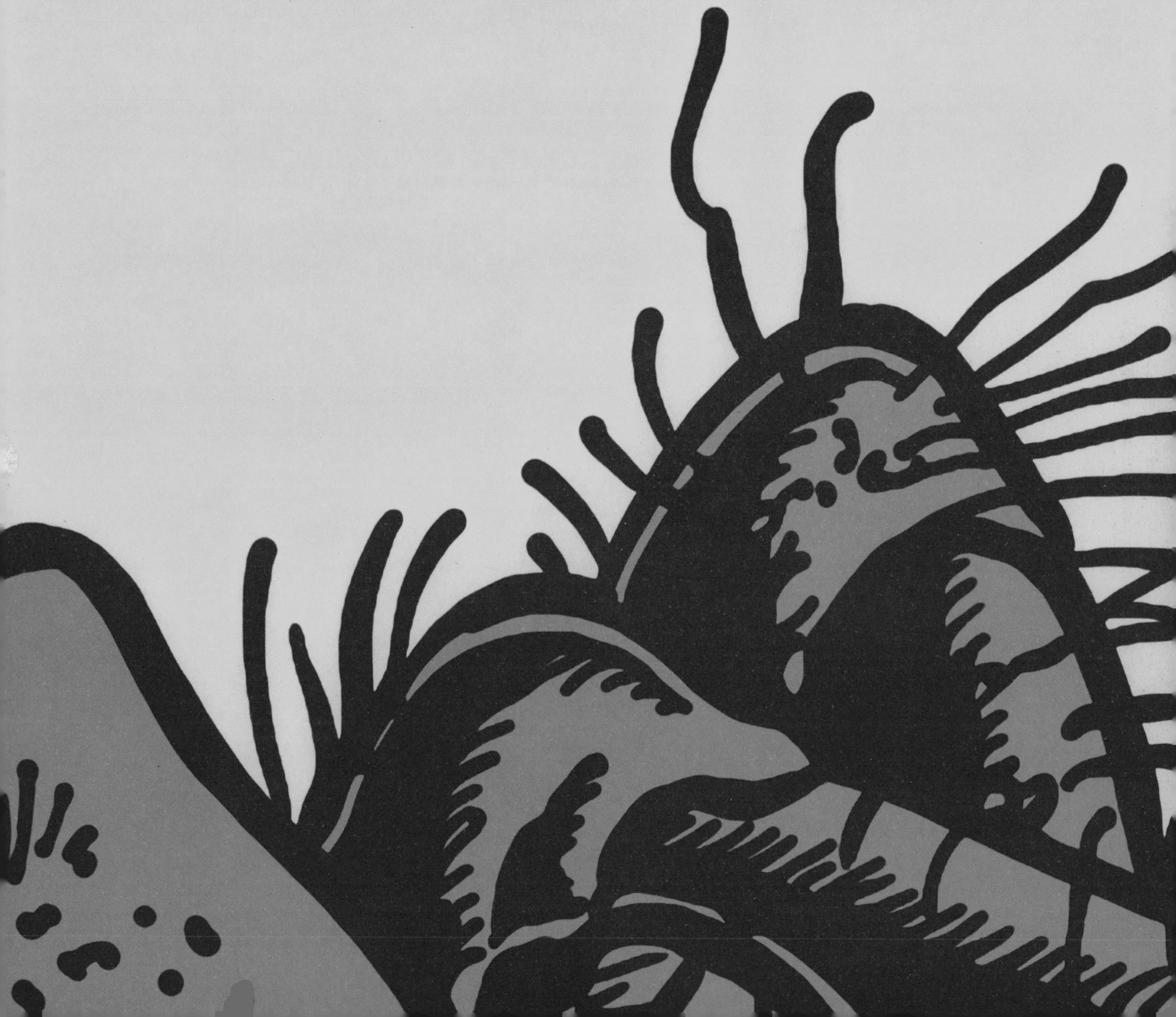

KEN REID
Artist

Also featuring the work of
Reg Parlett & Robert Nixon

Creative Director & CEO:
Jason Kingsley

Chief Technical Officer:
Chris Kingsley

Head of Books & Comics:
Ben Smith

Graphic Novels Editor:
Keith Richardson

Junior Graphic Novels Editor:
Maz Smith

PR:
Michael Molcher

Publishing Assistant:
Owen Johnson

Graphic Design:
Oz Osborne & Sam Gretton

Reprographics:
Joseph Morgan, Richard Tustian
& Emma Denton

ISBN: 9-781-78108-660-5
Published by Rebellion, Riverside House, Osney Mead, Oxford, UK. OX2 0ES
www.rebellion.co.uk

Originally serialised in **Shiver & Shake** from 10th March 1973-5th October 1974.

Special thanks to Irmantas Povilaika and Antony Reid.

Printed in Malta by Gutenberg Press
Manufactured in the EU by Stanton Book Services,
Wellingborough, NN8 3PJ, UK.
Printed on FSC Accredited Paper.

First printing: December 2018
10 9 8 7 6 5 4 3 2 1
A CIP catalogue record for this book is available
from the British Library.

For information on other Rebellion graphic novels
visit **treasuryofbritishcomics.com**, or if you
have any comments on this book, please email
books@2000ADonline.com

CREEPY CREATIONS

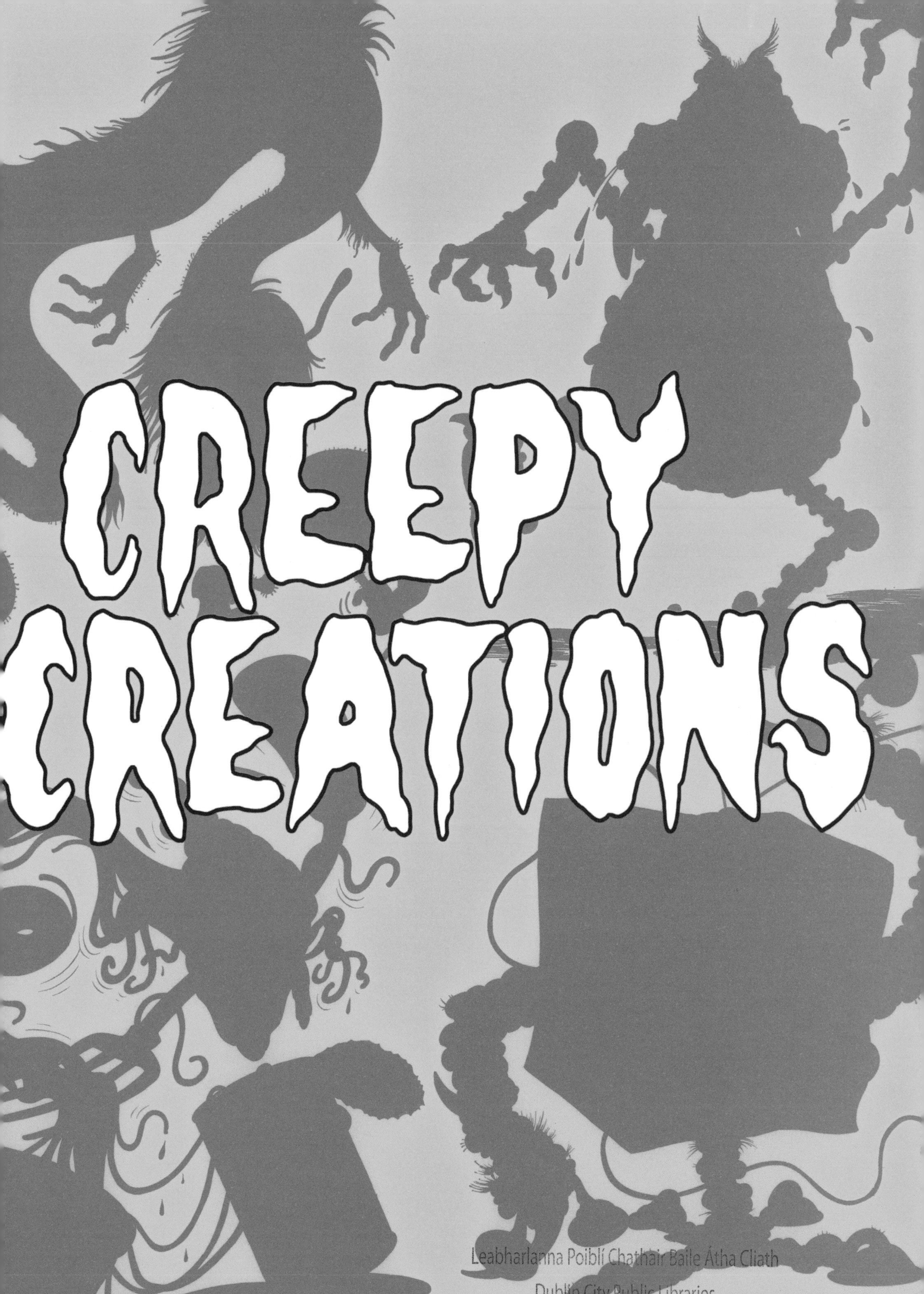

CREEPY CREATIONS

EXTRA CREEPIES

†   Creepy creation by Reg Parlett

*   Creepy creation by Robert Nixon

There maybe other entries where we haven't been able to 100% identify the artist.

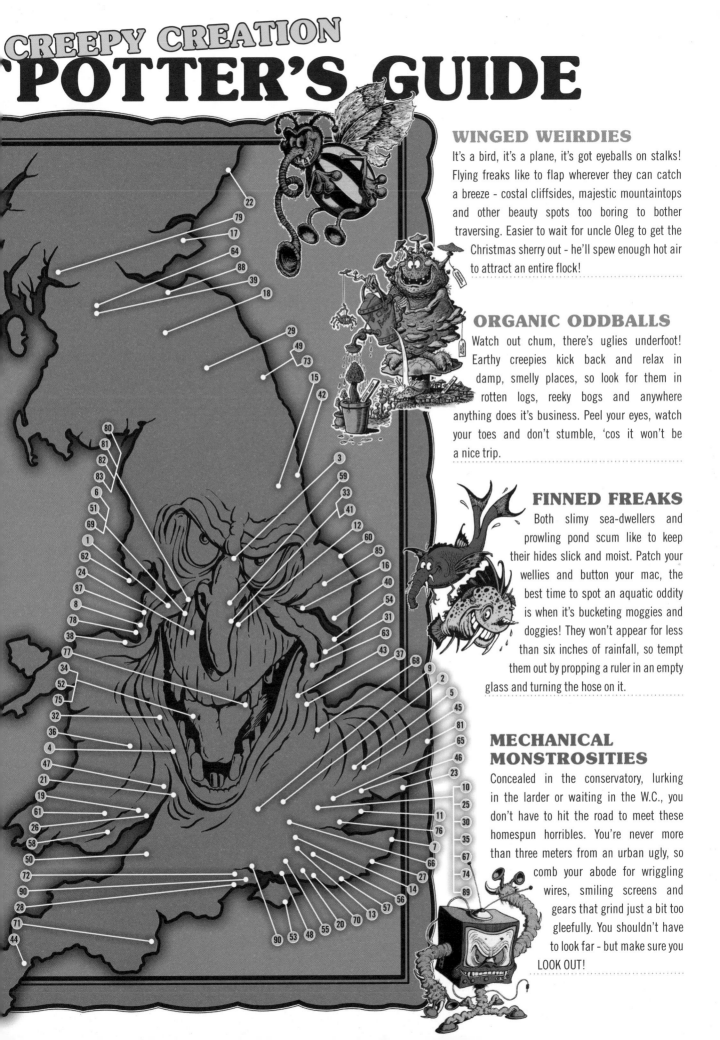

CREEPY CREATION
'POTTER'S GUIDE

WINGED WEIRDIES

It's a bird, it's a plane, it's got eyeballs on stalks! Flying freaks like to flap wherever they can catch a breeze - costal cliffsides, majestic mountaintops and other beauty spots too boring to bother traversing. Easier to wait for uncle Oleg to get the Christmas sherry out - he'll spew enough hot air to attract an entire flock!

ORGANIC ODDBALLS

Watch out chum, there's uglies underfoot! Earthy creepies kick back and relax in damp, smelly places, so look for them in rotten logs, reeky bogs and anywhere anything does it's business. Peel your eyes, watch your toes and don't stumble, 'cos it won't be a nice trip.

FINNED FREAKS

Both slimy sea-dwellers and prowling pond scum like to keep their hides slick and moist. Patch your wellies and button your mac, the best time to spot an aquatic oddity is when it's bucketing moggies and doggies! They won't appear for less than six inches of rainfall, so tempt them out by propping a ruler in an empty glass and turning the hose on it.

MECHANICAL MONSTROSITIES

Concealed in the conservatory, lurking in the larder or waiting in the W.C., you don't have to hit the road to meet these homespun horribles. You're never more than three meters from an urban ugly, so comb your abode for wriggling wires, smiling screens and gears that grind just a bit too gleefully. You shouldn't have to look far - but make sure you LOOK OUT!

THE ERUPTING PRESSURE COOKER OF PRESTON BROOK

A Creepy Creation

THE PUNISHING PRESSURE COOKER
OF PRESTON BROOK

© Antony J Reid June 2018

CREEPY CREATIONS WERE perfectly suited to my Dad's manic monster imagination and style. He enjoyed drawing them as it gave him the freedom to invent these crazy unworldly creatures. A close line between hysterically funny to disturbingly scary. Some were actually rejected for the latter.

For all the *Creepy Creations* he drew I can't recall him doing one of a pressure cooker. Perhaps he did, but the horrible experience he went through in real life caused by one may have put him off. Allow me to relate the tale.

For a number of years my dad owned a boat. **Miss Basset**. She was a 4-berth cabin cruiser he moored on the Bridgewater canal. He sometimes used to work on **Miss Basset**, his floating studio, posting his work off from the local post office.

One weekend we were moored near the entrance to Preston Brook Tunnel and I will never forget that day - the day the friendly pressure cooker that had provided me with tasty boatman stews turned nasty on us.

Dad always insisted on shin beef or skirt as the main ingredients for his stew. Along with some onion, carrot, potatoes and a stock cube. All the other ingredients went in first, the potatoes last. As the little top hissed and did it's dance puffing out a pleasant smell we would sit contentedly awaiting our tea.

That fateful day all went well with the first stage (the meat etc.) but too many potatoes were added to the pot for the second stage. Dad settled down with a brown Ale and a twiddle on his piano accordion and I was concentrating on assembling my latest Airfix model aircraft kit. Laddie the Dog was snoozing on the floor.

So on that cool September day with the comforting hiss of the pressure cooker we sat relaxed and contented.

Dad's playing masked the hissing sound that we had become accustomed to but, after he finished a tune I suddenly became aware of the silence. Just a low hiss of the gas jet under the pressure cooker could be heard. I looked at it and saw the little top was still. Not dancing and hissing as it should have been. It took a while to register. "Dad the top isn't spinning," I said in an urgent tone. Dad looked at me smiling then at the pressure cooker. His face dropped. "Bloody hell!" he blurted out and began to wrench the large accordion from his shoulders, but it was too late.... PHATT BANG BANG!! WHOOSH!!!!

The PHATT sound was the top flying off, the BANG BANG, it hitting the roof then ricocheting back down to hit the metal stove.... WHOOSH a jet of super-heated stew and steam then erupting like a volcano.

A SWAT team with CS gas & stun grenades would have been less of a shock.

As a 10 year old with lightning fast reactions, I scrambled away to my bed under the bow of the boat. Laddie started a loud high-pitched barking and leaping from the floor to the settee and back.

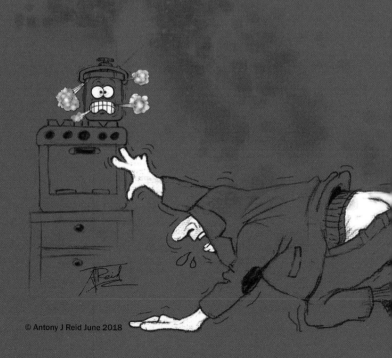

© Antony J Reid June 2018

For a few moments, my father sat like a statue...as if frozen in time...stunned and I suppose trying to comprehend what was happening. He looked at the pressure cooker and faced a scalding spewing menace like a demon from the very bowels of hell itself. When the skin on his forehead & face told his brain it was being scalded he sprang into action, flung himself backwards and joined me under the bow.

"Oh my God, Oh my God!" he kept repeating as the spray potato started to build up on the roof like a horrific creeping mould. "I've got to turn it off" he blurted. By now, Laddie was hysterical.

Pulling his sports jacket over his head dad crawled forward, down onto the floor on his hands and knees, and began to move forward. Laddie now started leaping from the settee to my father's back and then back again. As dad approached the cooker, he lifted his hand up to find the gas knob. The scalding spray landed on it and he started making yelping whimpering noises.

This was too much for Laddie to bear, determined to save his master he grabbed the right leg of my father's pants and started trying to pull him back away from danger. "STOP IT LADDIE" he cried in pain but that only made matters worse. His pants started to come down exposing the delicate skin of the lower back to the scorching potato droplets. He started to shriek, Laddie pulled harder and his buttocks became exposed.

In one last desperate effort moving in a jerking motion like some weird chameleon, he reached the cooker. Dad fumbled for the knob, screamed when he touched the hot metal then finally turned it off.

Scrambling back to the safety of the bow we all lay on the bunks and in a few minutes the spray stopped. It took a good while to clean up the mess, which was everywhere. What was left of the stew was ok, but he never overfilled the pressure cooker again.

Antony J Reid
June 2018

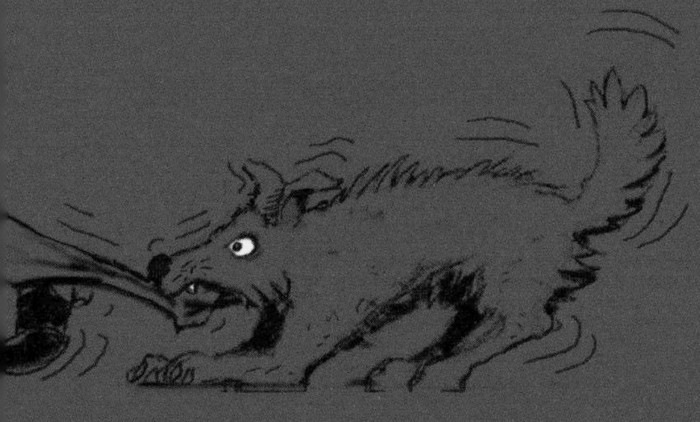

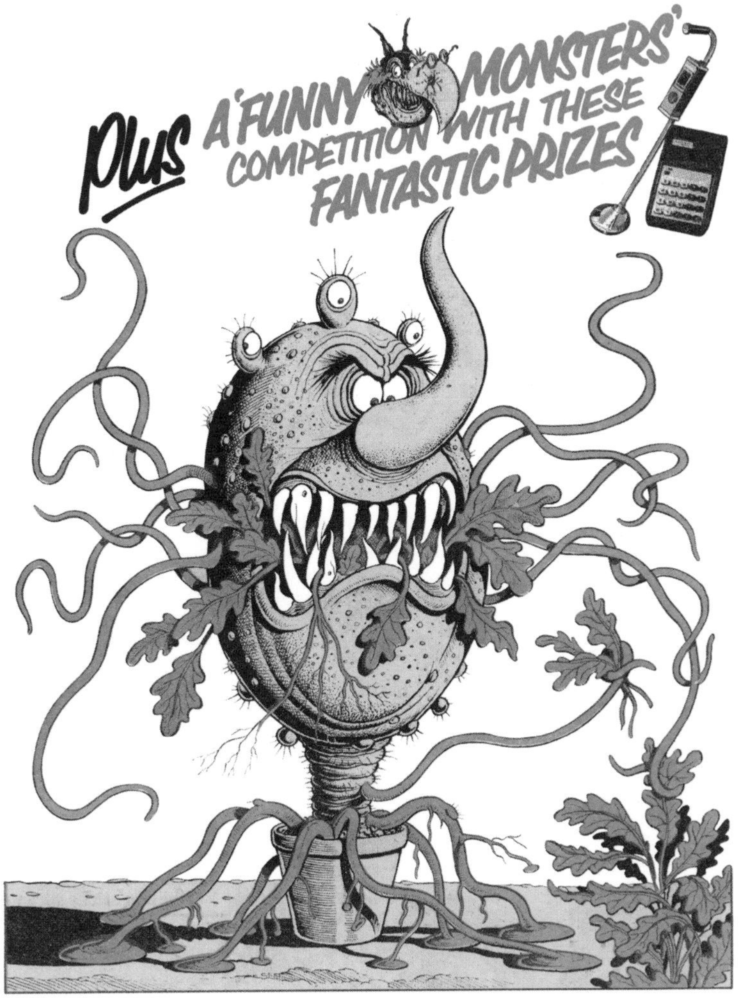
PLUS A 'FUNNY MONSTERS' COMPETITION WITH THESE FANTASTIC PRIZES

AS A LONG-TIME CONTRIBUTOR to British comics and newspapers, Ken Reid found the monotonous repetition of churning out the same characters week after week quite tiresome. Seeking something less tedious and with a greater scope for variety, he came up with an idea of a series featuring humorous fantastic creatures. Ken's first attempt to pitch the idea was in January 1967 when he approached Bob Bartholomew, senior member of the editorial team of **Power Comics**, with a feature called *Barmy Animal by Prof. Twot (Bristle-Backed Willinilly)*. The idea was rejected and Ken shelved it for a few years, until the demise of **Power Comics** in the late sixties left him with little regular work.

With his income sharply down, in January 1969 Ken offered his idea of a series featuring comical freaks of nature to several publishers, including William M. Gaines of EC Comics in New York, the publisher of **MAD**. The letter, sent in an envelope 'defaced' with drawings of *Jelly-Gilled Mollusc Hawk, Schnozzus Fascinatum* and a humorous self-portrait, accompanied by a finished sample of a Madimal that Ken called *Soarus Magnificus*, didn't go unnoticed. In his reply Jerry DeFuccio, Associate Editor of **MAD**, said they weren't much for fantasy material but suggested that Ken contacted Topps Chewing Gum Inc. – New York-based producers of chewing gum card series.

TREASURE
£1
TO BE WON
EVERY WEEK

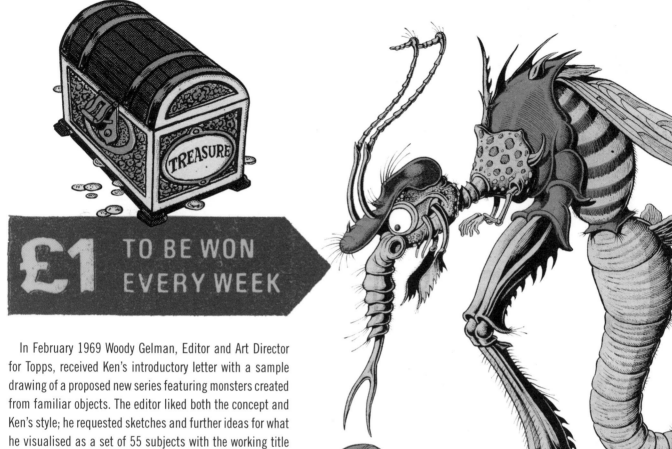

In February 1969 Woody Gelman, Editor and Art Director for Topps, received Ken's introductory letter with a sample drawing of a proposed new series featuring monsters created from familiar objects. The editor liked both the concept and Ken's style; he requested sketches and further ideas for what he visualised as a set of 55 subjects with the working title of *Weirdnicks*. Ken was taken by the prospect of being able to focus on monsters and getting published in America. He spent hours developing his approach to monsterizing familiar objects in a humorous way, and doodling monster-molasses, bubble bath flakes, freakish spin-driers, alarm clocks, one-armed bandits, mechanical grabs, etc. Letters and sketches travelled back and forth during the rest of 1969, Ken even received $200.00 as advance payment but Topps eventually put the project to rest.

The concept lurked at the back of Ken's mind until 1972 when IPC Magazines came up with a plan to launch **Shiver and Shake**. Bob Paynter, the Editor, remembered Ken's penchant for monsters and offered him a feature called *Creepy Creations*. The idea was to invite readers to send sketches of comical creatures for the 'not-so-tame' **Shiver and Shake** artist to finish. The drawings were to be used as pin-ups on the back cover, while the contributor of the sketch was to collect a prize of £1.

Ken took up the offer with enthusiasm. Bob Paynter requested a picture frame[1] and a finished *Creepy Creation* of Ken's own design for the 'dummy' of the proposed comic.

Ken mailed both drawings in the beginning of December 1972. The decision to proceed with **Shiver and Shake** was made in the first week of 1973 and *Creepy Creations* was approved as part of the package.

Production process took approximately two months in those days. This meant that the readers' sketches that were expected to start flowing in after the first issue came out could only be used from issue No. 8 at best. With that in mind, Ken was asked to draw a few *Creepy Creations* from his own ideas. By the time the debut issue of **Shiver and Shake** with Ken's *One-Eyed Wonk of Wigan* on the back cover arrived on the newsstands, Ken had supplied another five brilliant pin-ups – *The Hooter-Hiker of Harrogate, The Fanatical Fungus-Grower of Frogpool, The Manchester Aqua-Kwak, The Trumpington Trumpeter* and *The Boggle-Eyed Butty-Biter of Sandwich.* The *Long-Haired Luvvaduck* was the first one that Ken drew from a reader's suggestion, as were all the subsequent ones in the weeklies.

Young readers surely came up with some amazing characters, and Ken kept notes of contributors' names, addresses and age. Most of the crazy titles were also suggested by readers.

[1] A few weeks later Ken was asked to draw another picture frame so that the two could be rotated. The second version was first used with **Creepy Creation No. 15.**

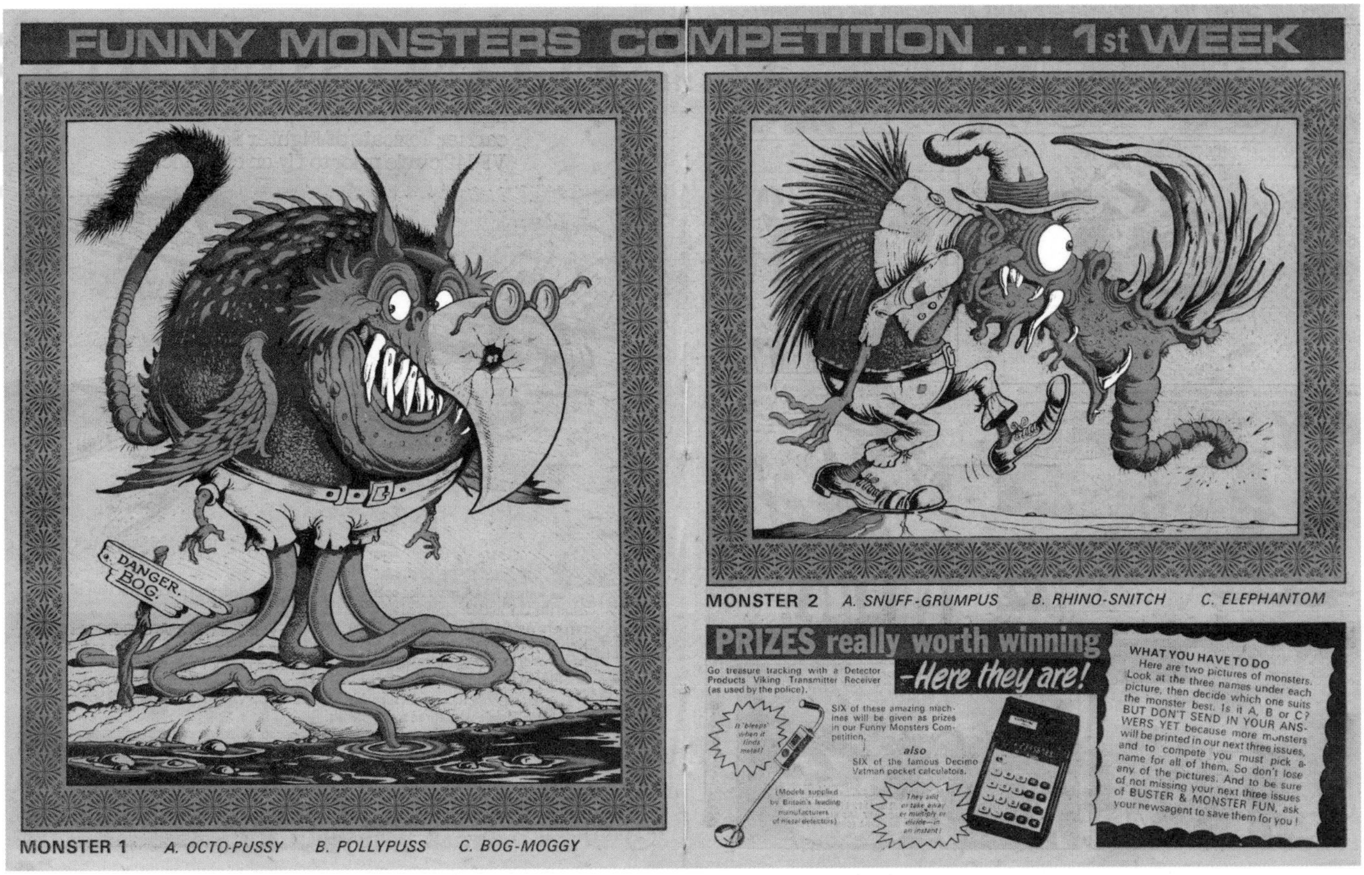
FUNNY MONSTERS COMPETITION ... 1st WEEK
DANGER BOG.
MONSTER 1 A. OCTO-PUSSY B. POLLYPUSS C. BOG-MOGGY
MONSTER 2 A. SNUFF-GRUMPUS B. RHINO-SNITCH C. ELEPHANTOM
PRIZES really worth winning
-Here they are!
Go treasure tracking with a Detector Products Viking Transmitter Receiver (as used by the police).
It 'bleeps' when it finds metal!
SIX of these amazing machines will be given as prizes in our Funny Monsters Competition.
(Models supplied by Britain's leading manufacturers of metal detectors)
also
SIX of the famous Decimo Vatman pocket calculators.
WHAT YOU HAVE TO DO
Here are two pictures of monsters. Look at the three names under each picture, then decide which one suits the monster best. Is it A, B or C? BUT DON'T SEND IN YOUR ANSWERS YET because more monsters will be printed in our next three issues, and to compete you must pick a name for all of them. So don't lose any of the pictures. And to be sure of not missing your next three issues of BUSTER & MONSTER FUN, ask your newsagent to save them for you!

A typical *Creepy Creation* page showed that week's monster in full height, sometimes suspended in mid-air, usually with few details or nothing but colour in the background. Ken's drawings were in black and white, unsigned and twice the size of their printed versions. Colour was applied in-house by IPC colourists.

The series consists of 79 numbered pin-ups in the weeklies, all but six by Ken[2]. One shouldn't forget the twelve *Zodiac signs* of *Your Horror Scope* in **Shiver and Shake** cover-dated March 23rd, 1974 – all conceived and drawn by Ken and possessing every characteristic of a typical *Creepy Creation.*

Ken also supplied some Creepies for **Shiver and Shake** annuals: two can be found in the 1974 Annual, while both endpapers of the 1975 edition were embellished with *The Creepy Creations* 1975 Calendar – a fine assortment of delightful monsters, one for each month.

Poor health and worries over family problems put Ken out of work a few times during the early and mid-seventies. Deadlines had to be kept so the editor found a substitute in Robert Nixon – another first-rate artist who worked on a few horror comedy strips in IPC children's comics at that time. Robert Nixon supplied four *Creepy Creations* for the weeklies, two *Mini-Monsters* printed in the issue cover-dated March 9th, 1974 and four *Christmas Creations* in **Shiver and Shake** Christmas Holiday Special in 1973.

[2] **Creepy Creations No. 2** (***The Chip Chomping Tater Terror***) and **No. 9** (***The Cowley Cowdog***) were borrowed from the **Hire A Horror** strip in *COR!!* comic drawn by Reg Parlett, while **No. 14** (***The Sunningdale Golf Ball Bat***), **No. 56** (***The Huge Humbug-Hugging Honey Sucker***), **No. 60** (***The Feathered Flop***) and **No. 64** (***Lamplight Larry***) were by Robert Nixon.

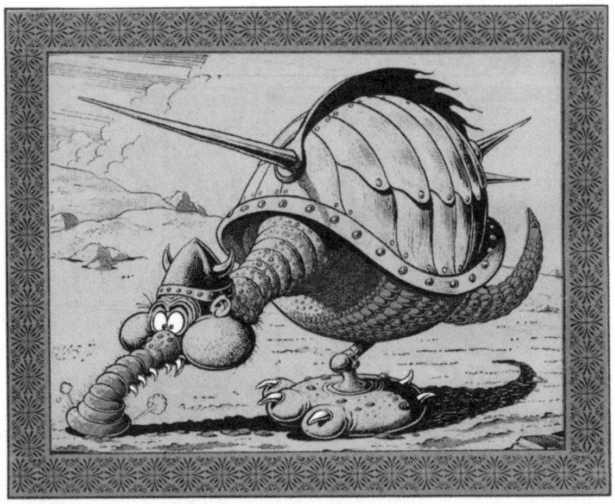

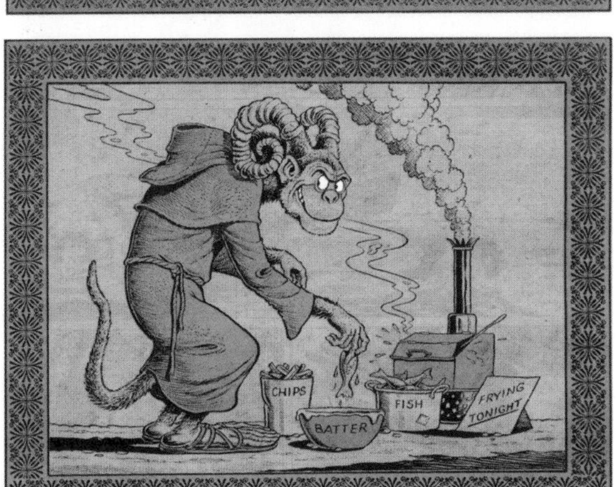
CHIPS
BATTER
FISH
FRYING TONIGHT

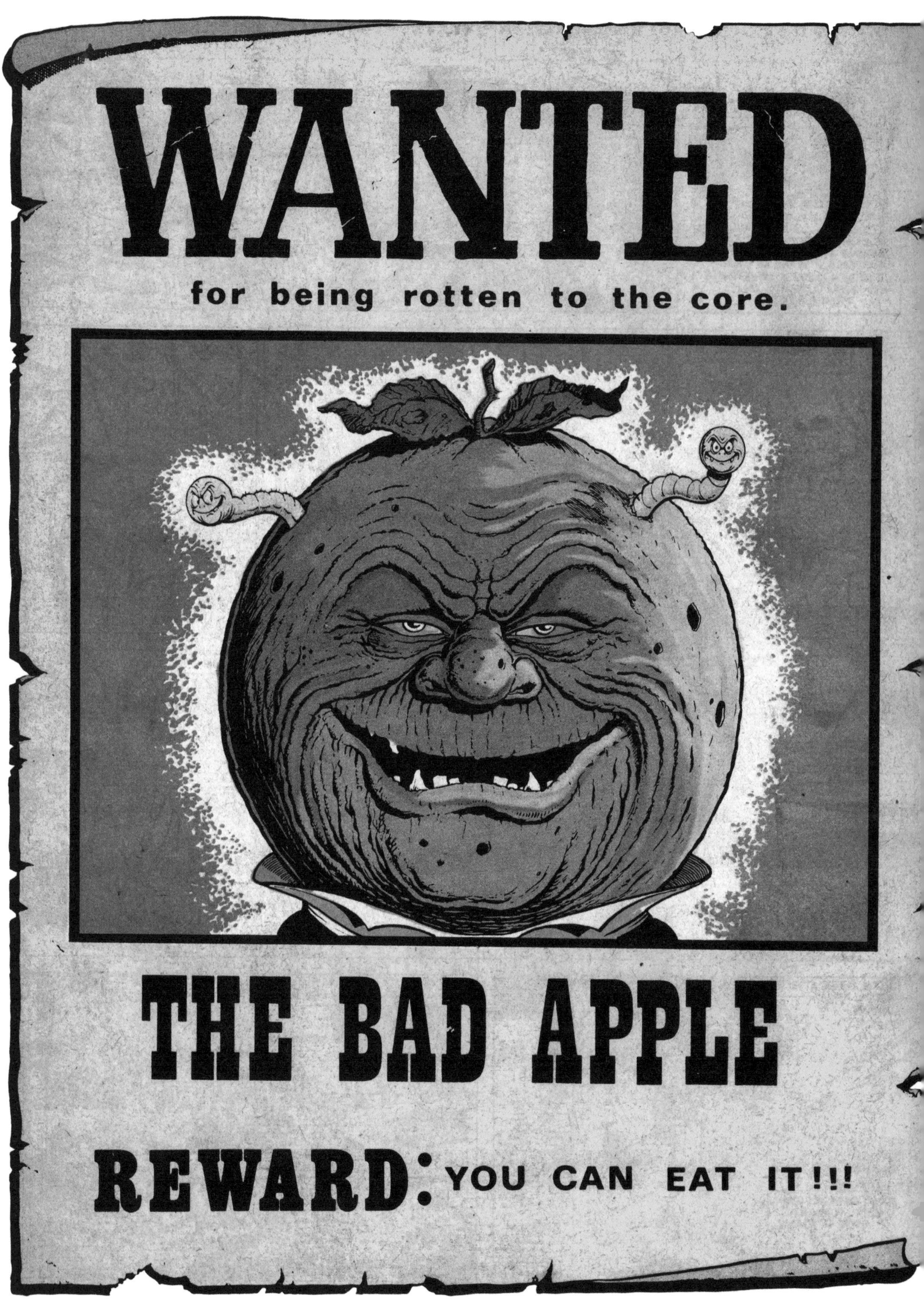
WANTED
for being rotten to the core.
THE BAD APPLE
REWARD: YOU CAN EAT IT!!!

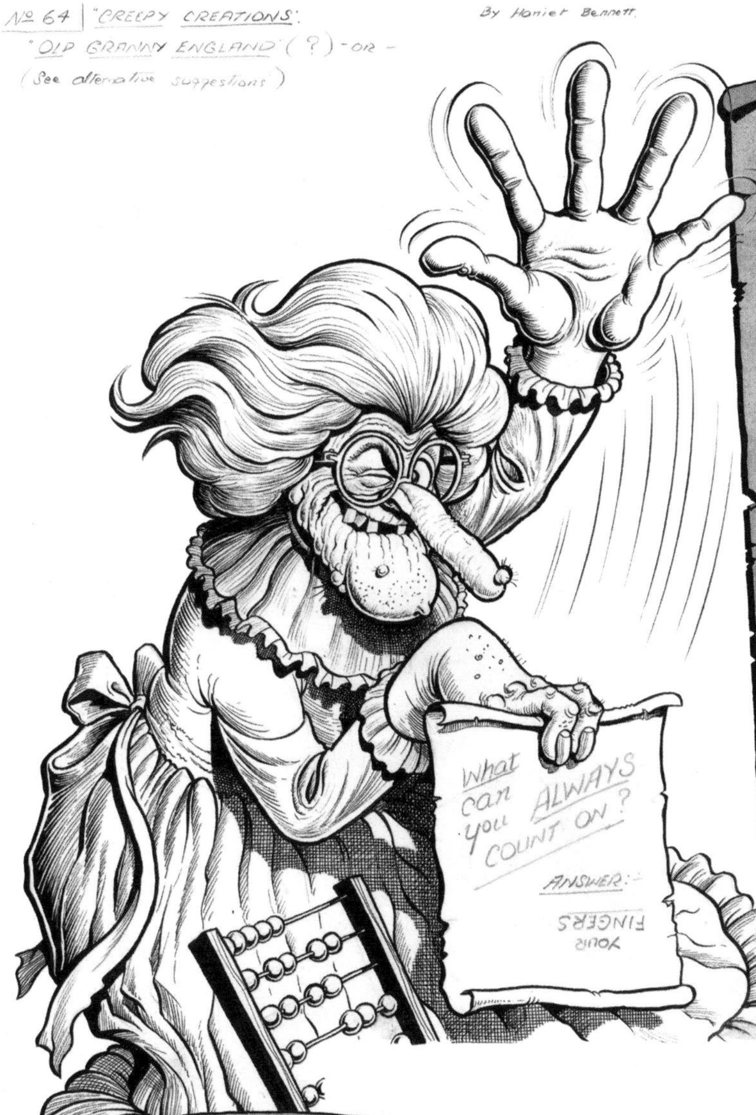

No 64 | "Creepy Creations"
"Old Granny England" (?) - or -
(See alternative suggestions)
By Harriet Bennett
What can you ALWAYS COUNT ON?
ANSWER:-
YOUR FINGERS

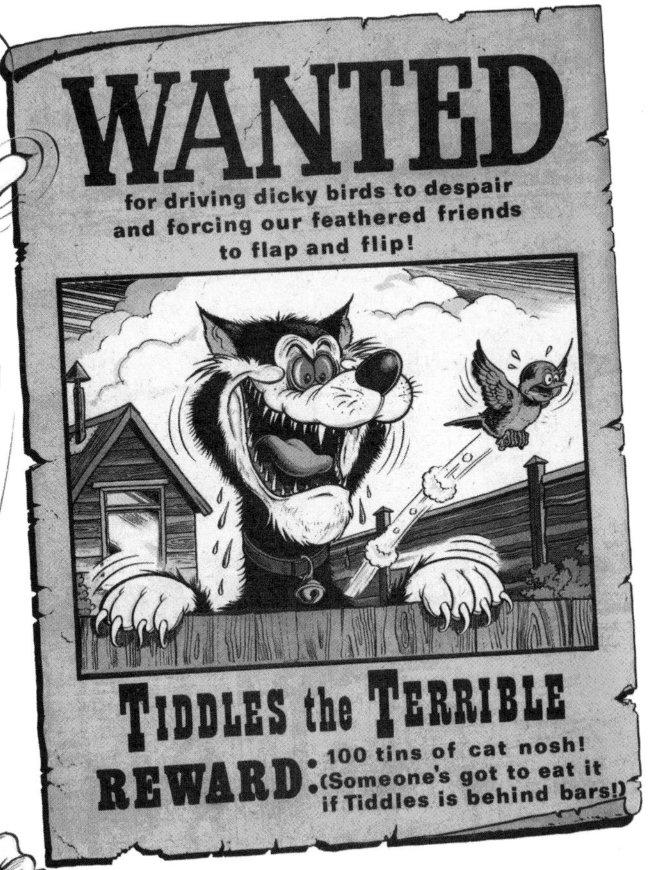

WANTED
for driving dicky birds to despair and forcing our feathered friends to flap and flip!
TIDDLES the TERRIBLE
REWARD: 100 tins of cat nosh! (Someone's got to eat it if Tiddles is behind bars!)

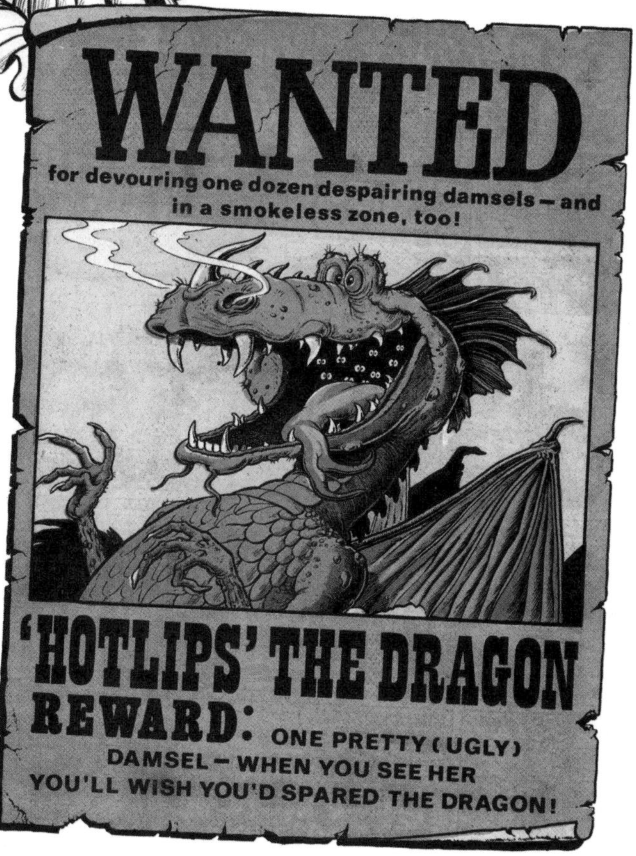

WANTED
for devouring one dozen despairing damsels – and in a smokeless zone, too!
'HOTLIPS' THE DRAGON
REWARD: ONE PRETTY (UGLY) DAMSEL – WHEN YOU SEE HER YOU'LL WISH YOU'D SPARED THE DRAGON!

Two of Ken's *Creepy Creations* weren't published: *Old Granny England* was rejected without compensation, while *Number Nibbler from Northampton* either went astray in the mail or was lost in the hectic process of **Shiver and Shake** and **Whoopee!** merger.

Ken worked on the feature until 9th July, 1974 when he was informed that it was to be cancelled due the decision to merge **Shiver and Shake** into **Whoopee!** in October 1974. His final two *Creepy Creations* – *Snailmobile* and *Sherlock Foot (Detective)*, were used as *Mini-Monsters* in the second combined issue of **Whoopee! and Shiver & Shake**.

The last thing that deserves to be mentioned in this context is the surprise one-off *Funny Monsters Competition* in the first four issues of **Buster** and **Monster Fun** in 1976, for which Ken provided eight brilliant drawings of exotic creatures of his own design that were classic *Creepy Creations* in everything but title.

Creepy Creations captured the imaginations of thousands of **Shiver and Shake** readers in 1973 and 1974. For Ken it was the fulfilment of a long-term craving to escape the monotony of drawing the same characters week after week. Alongside the *Wanted Posters* that Ken Reid drew concurrently for **Whoopee!** comic, *Creepy Creations* was a perfect warm-up exercise for his *World-Wide Weirdies* that was to follow soon after.

Irmantas Povilaika 2017

A CRAZY "MONSTER PIECE" FOR YOU TO CUT OUT AND COLLECT!

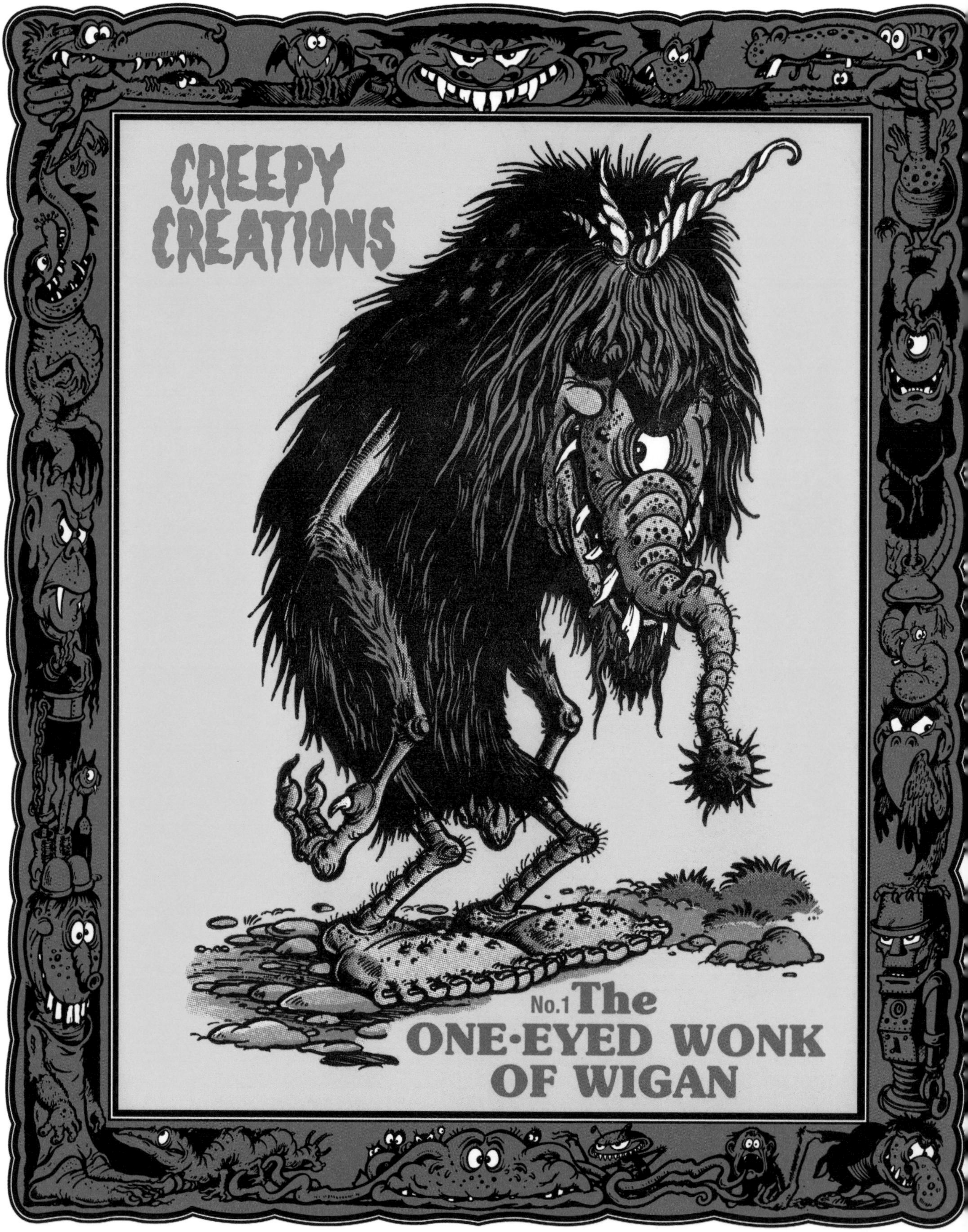
CREEPY CREATIONS
No.1 The
ONE-EYED WONK
OF WIGAN

A CRAZY "MONSTER PIECE" FOR YOU TO CUT OUT AND COLLECT!

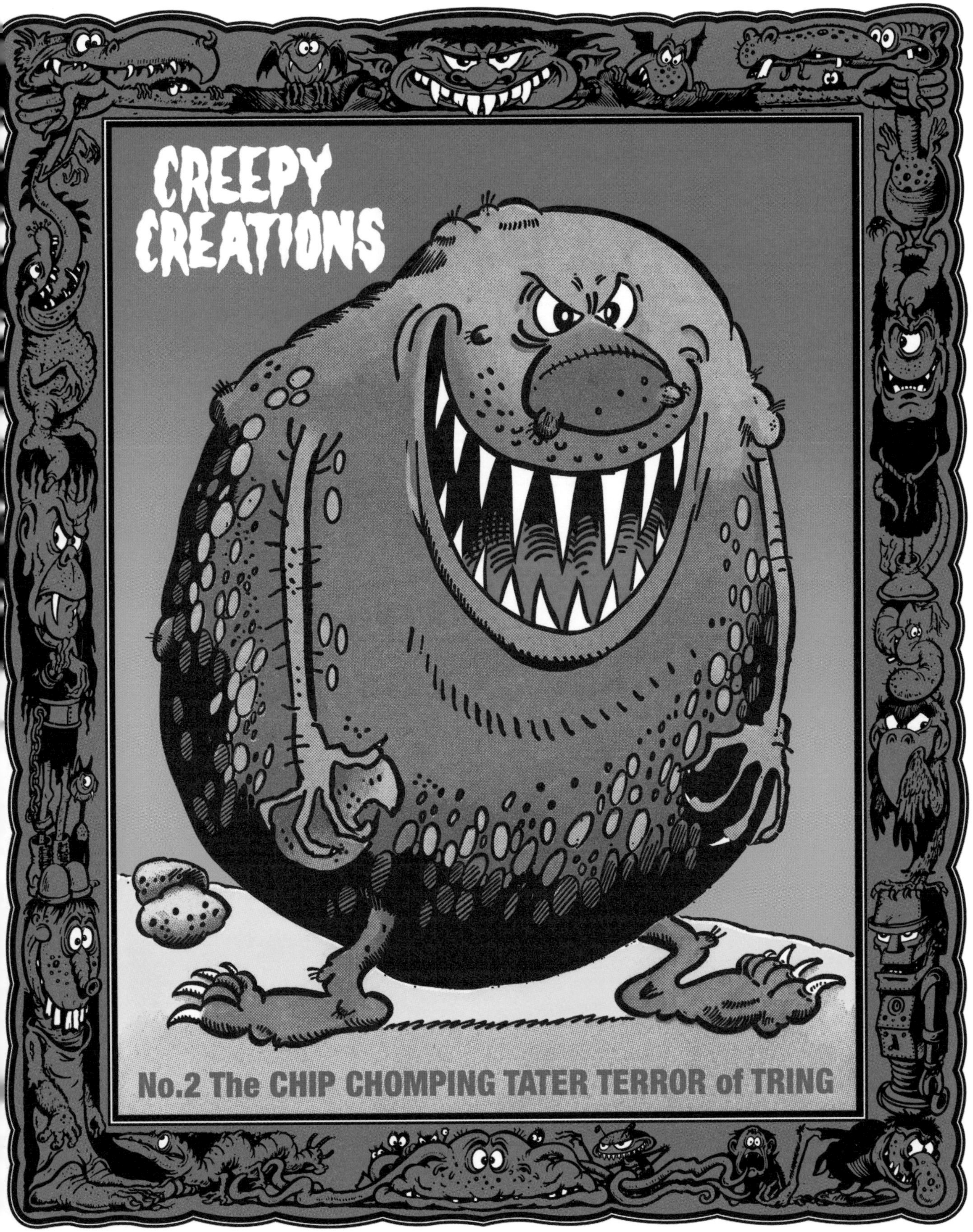
CREEPY CREATIONS
No.2 The CHIP CHOMPING TATER TERROR of TRING

A CRAZY "MONSTER PIECE" FOR YOU TO CUT OUT AND COLLECT!

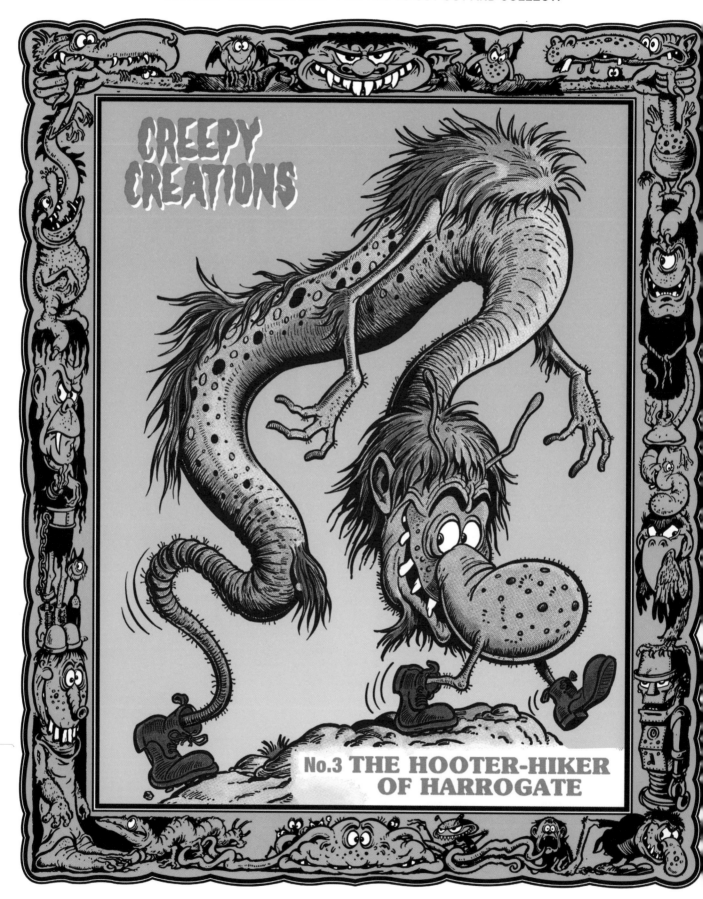

CREEPY CREATIONS
No.3 THE HOOTER-HIKER OF HARROGATE

A CRAZY "MONSTER PIECE" FOR YOU TO CUT OUT AND COLLECT!

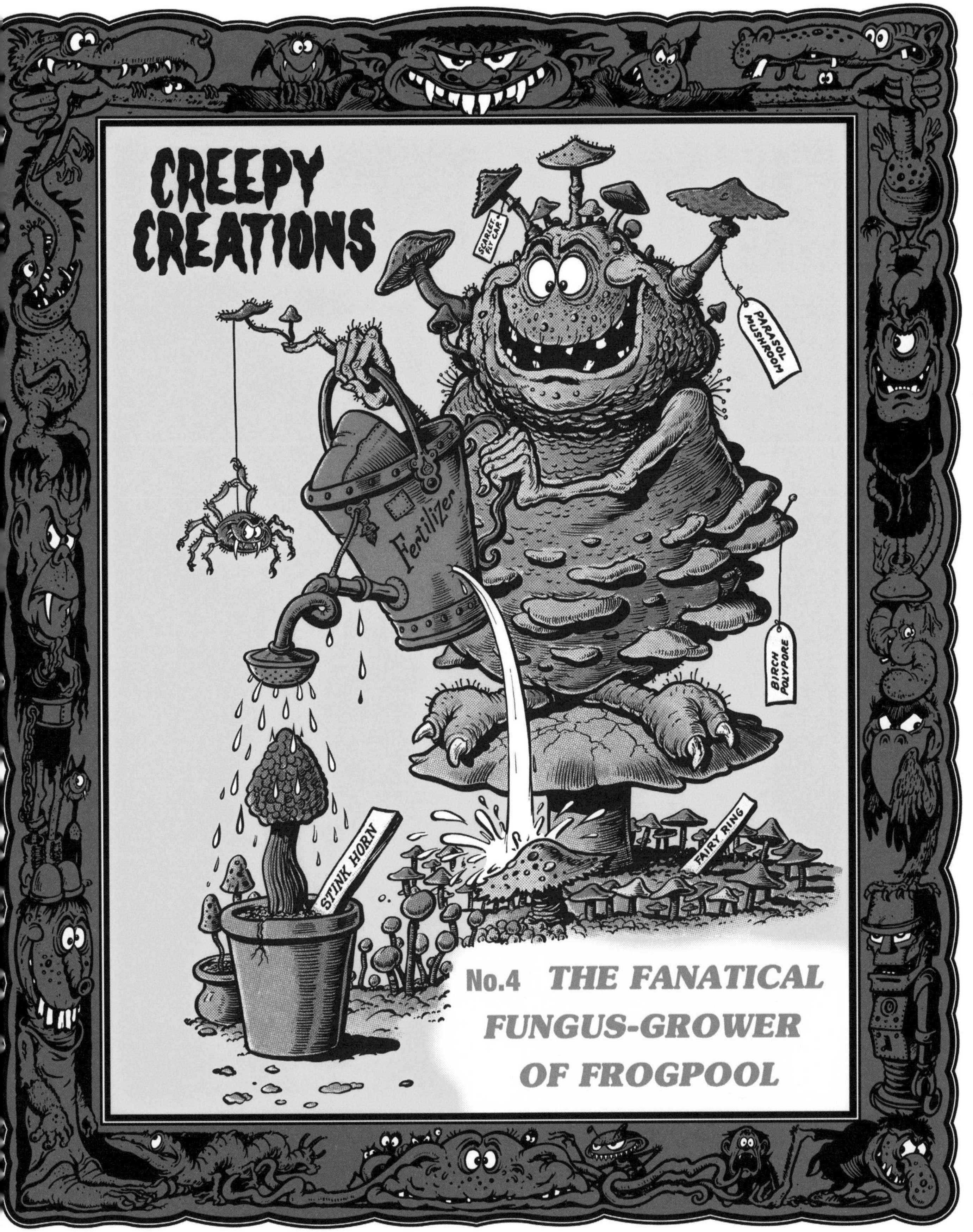
CREEPY CREATIONS
SCARLET FLY CAP
PARASOL MUSHROOM
Fertilizer
BIRCH POLYPORE
STINK HORN
FAIRY RING
No.4 THE FANATICAL FUNGUS-GROWER OF FROGPOOL

A CRAZY "MONSTER PIECE" FOR YOU TO CUT OUT AND COLLECT!

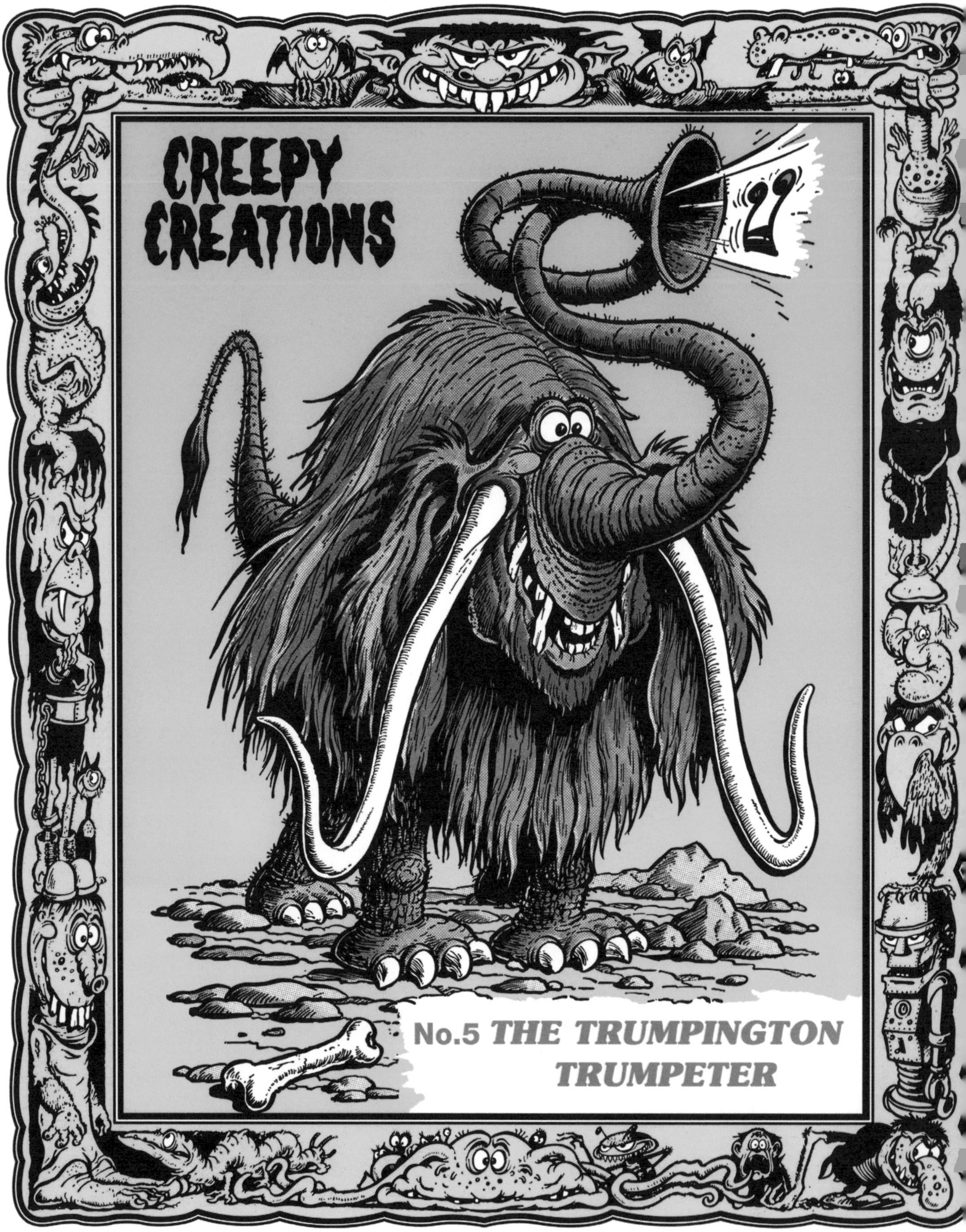

CREEPY CREATIONS
No.5 THE TRUMPINGTON TRUMPETER

A CRAZY "MONSTER PIECE" FOR YOU TO CUT OUT AND COLLECT!

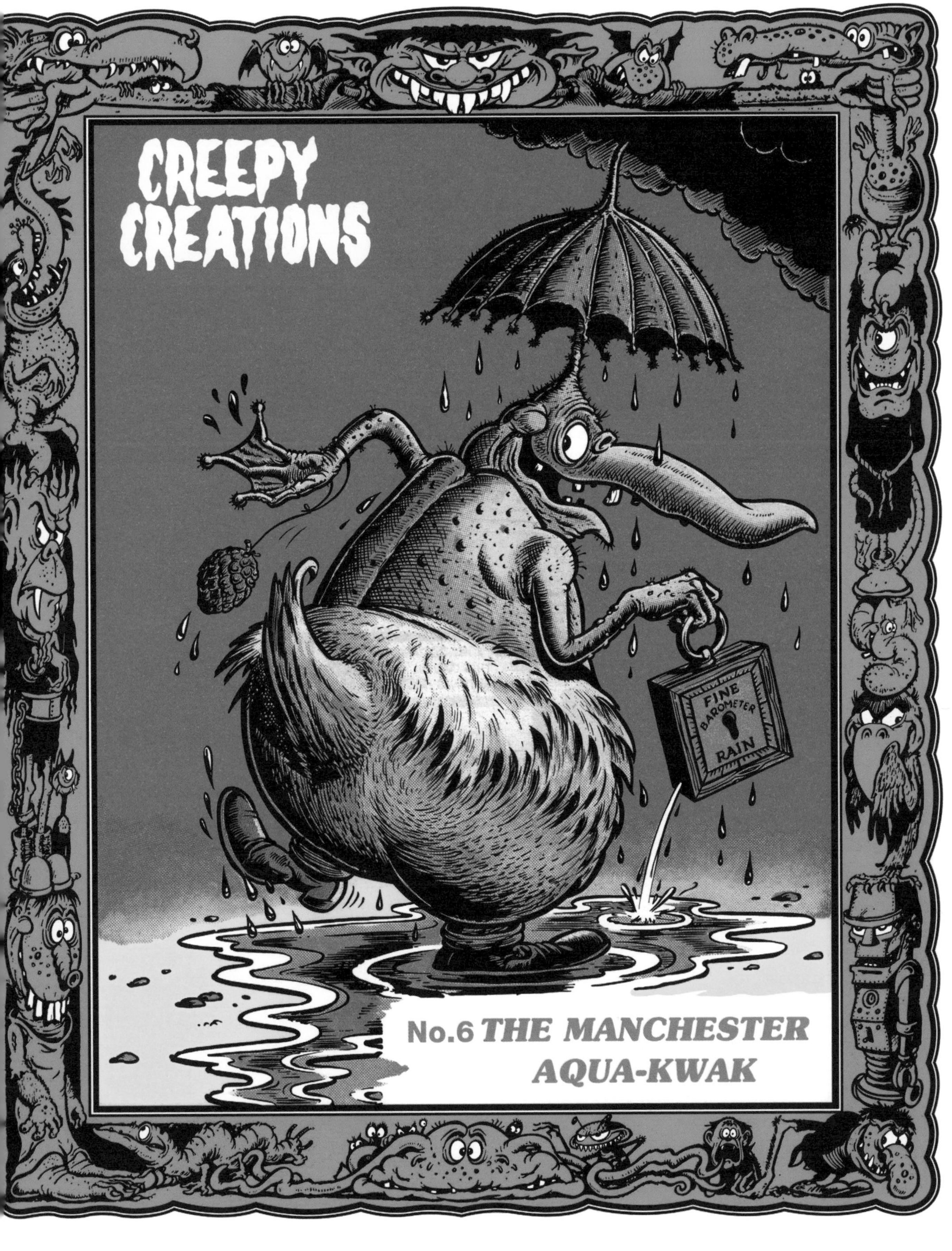
CREEPY CREATIONS
FINE
BAROMETER
RAIN
No.6 THE MANCHESTER AQUA-KWAK

A CRAZY "MONSTER PIECE" FOR YOU TO CUT OUT AND COLLECT!

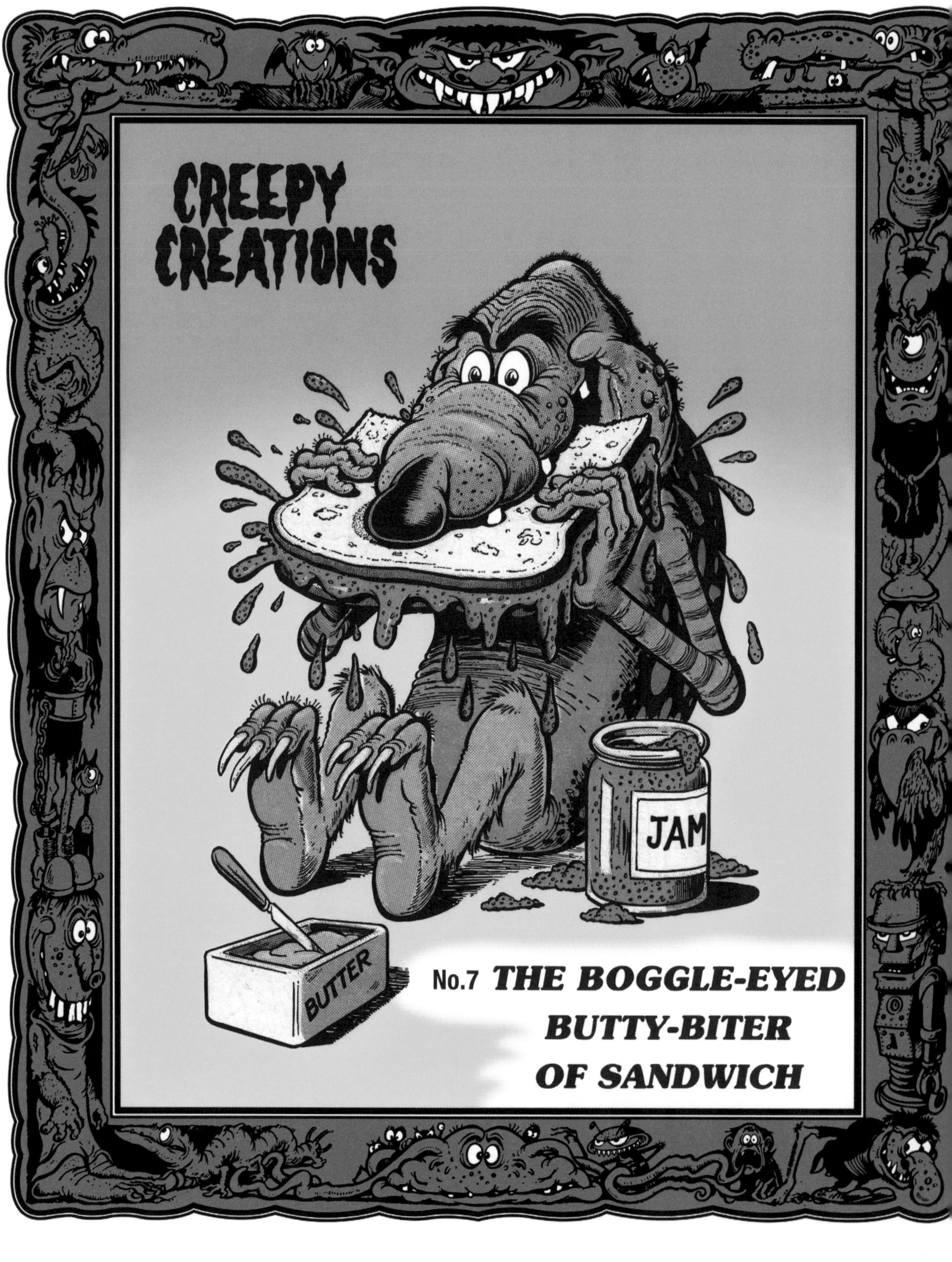
CREEPY CREATIONS
JAM
BUTTER
No.7 THE BOGGLE-EYED BUTTY-BITER OF SANDWICH

This crazy "monster piece" wins £1 for W. STAMFORD of BRIDLINGTON

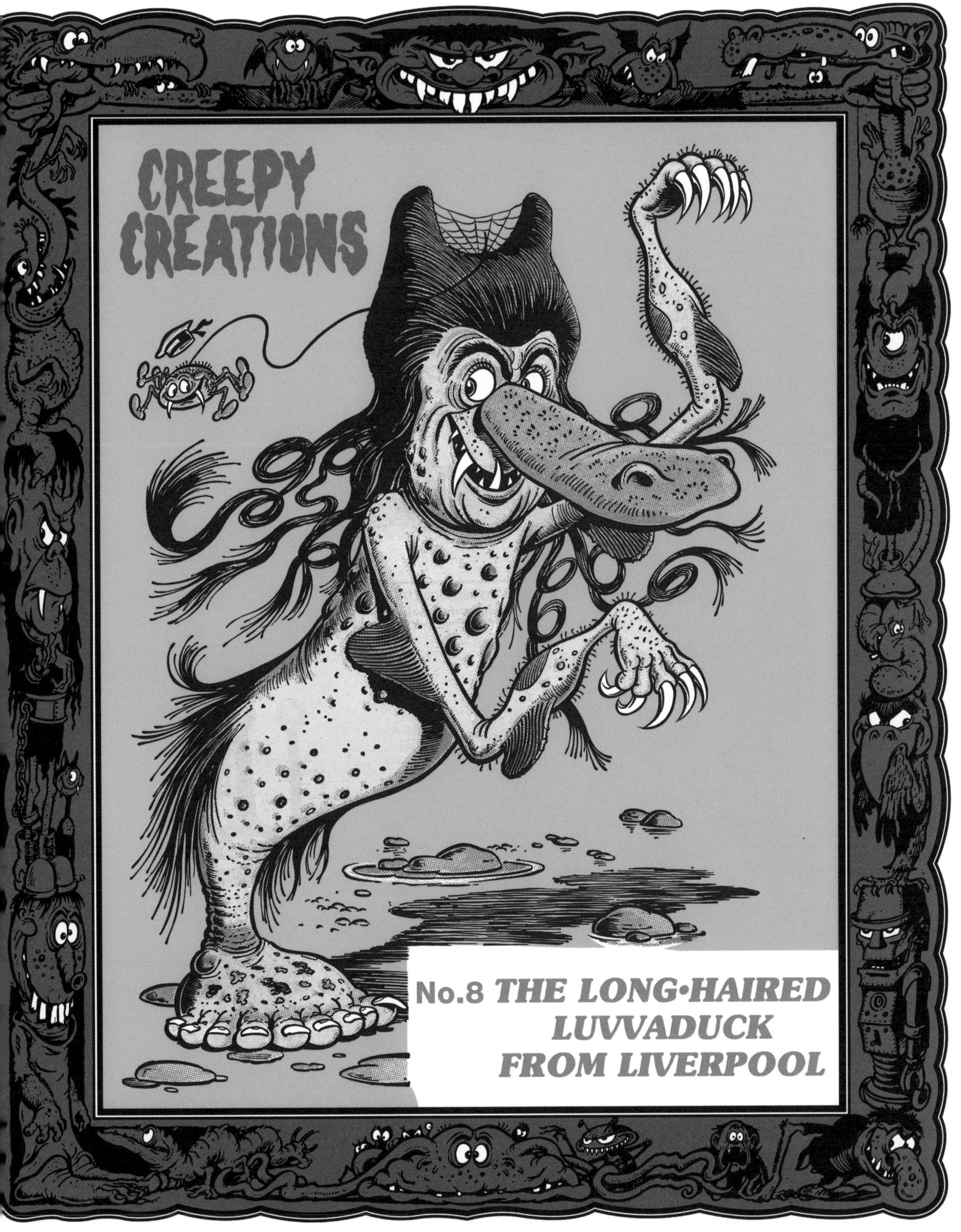
CREEPY CREATIONS
No.8 THE LONG•HAIRED LUVVADUCK FROM LIVERPOOL

This crazy "monster piece" wins £1 for Matthew Ralph of NORTHOLT

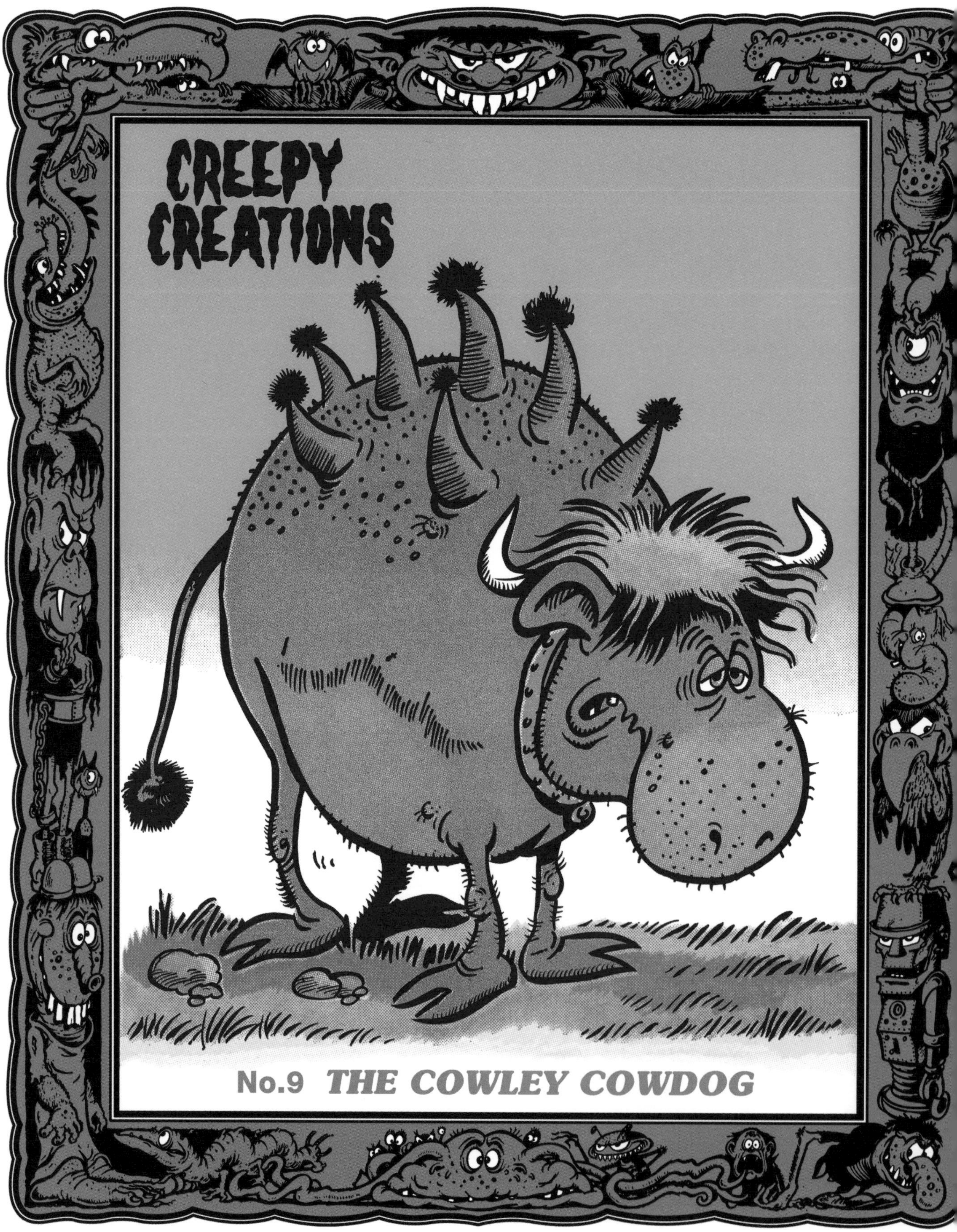
CREEPY CREATIONS
No.9 THE COWLEY COWDOG

This crazy "monster piece" wins £1 for MICHAEL ENTICOTT of HARROW

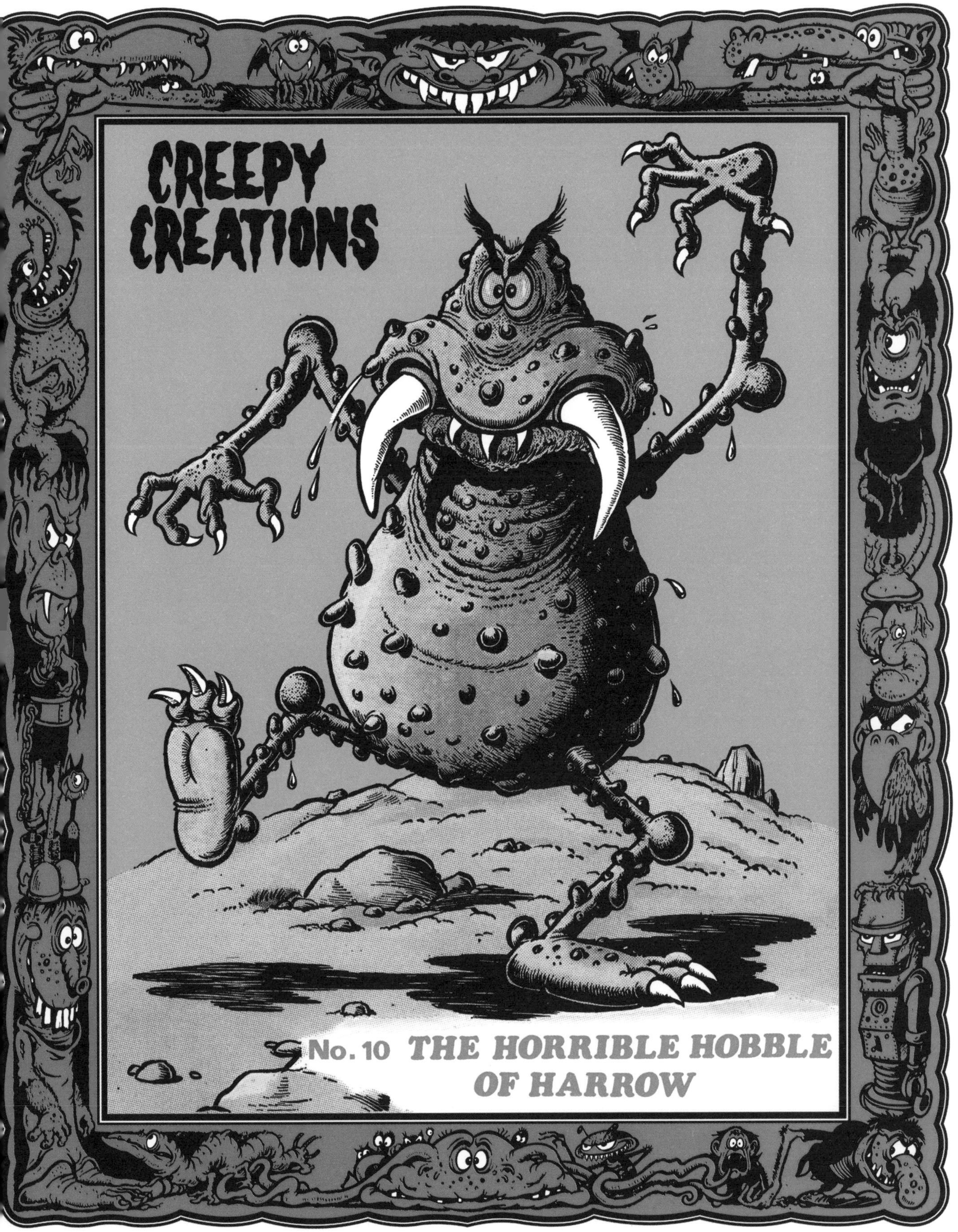
CREEPY CREATIONS
No. 10 THE HORRIBLE HOBBLE OF HARROW

This crazy "monster piece" wins £1 for COLIN DENCH of RAYLEIGH

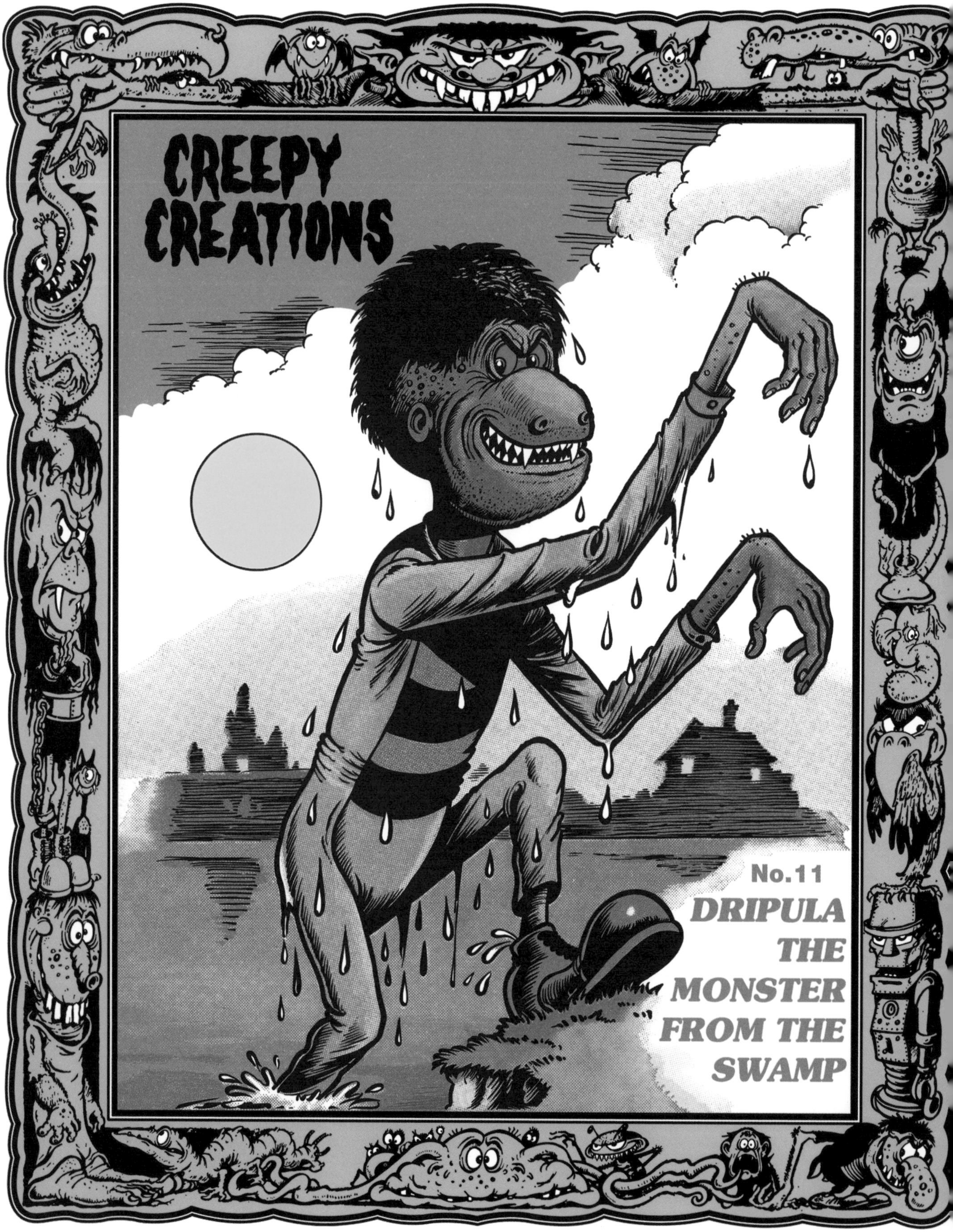
CREEPY CREATIONS
No.11
DRIPULA THE MONSTER FROM THE SWAMP

This crazy "monster piece" wins £1 for IAN ROSS of SHEFFIELD

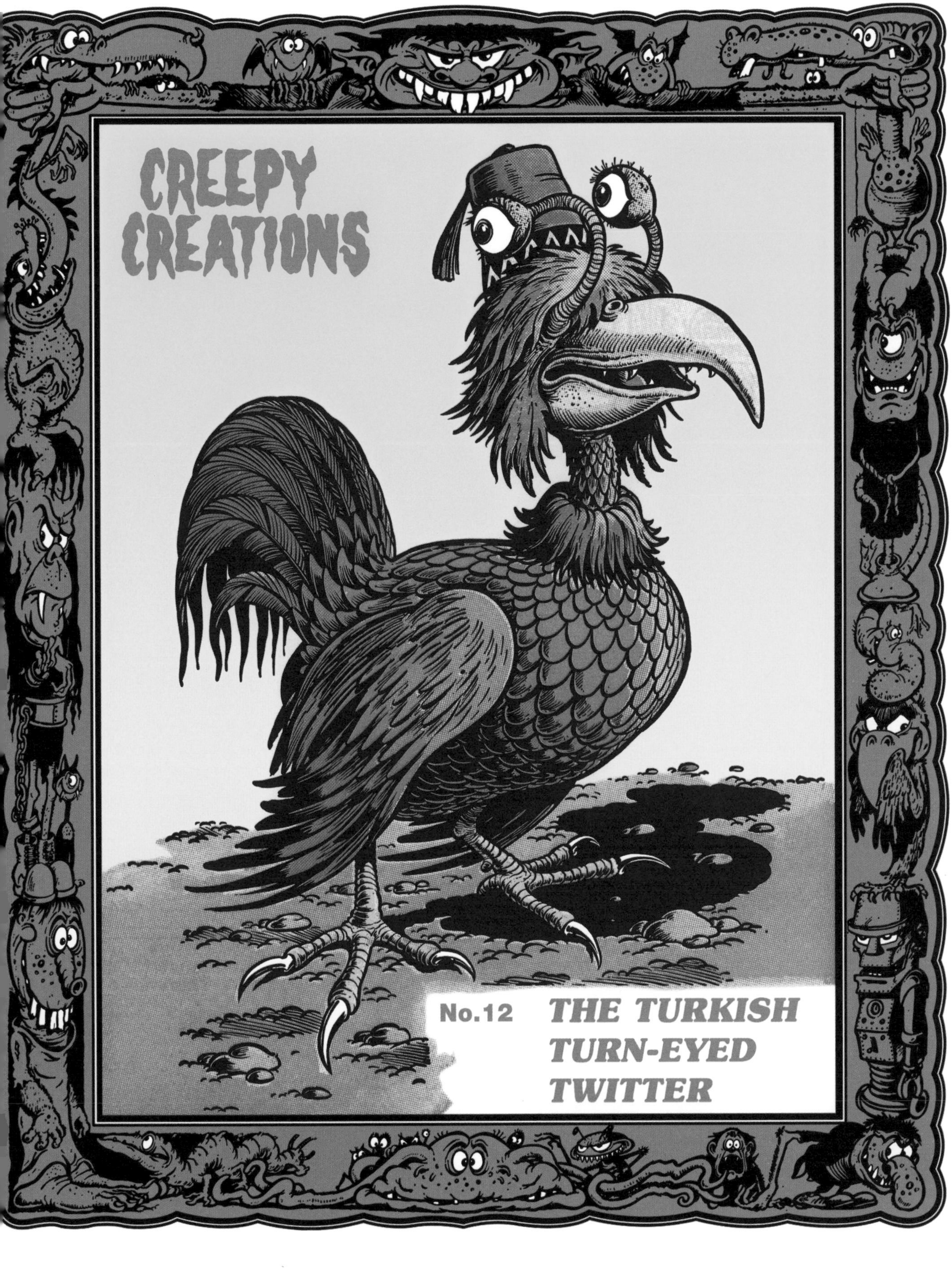
CREEPY CREATIONS
No.12 THE TURKISH TURN-EYED TWITTER

This crazy “monster piece” wins £1 for D. GRAHAM of FLEET

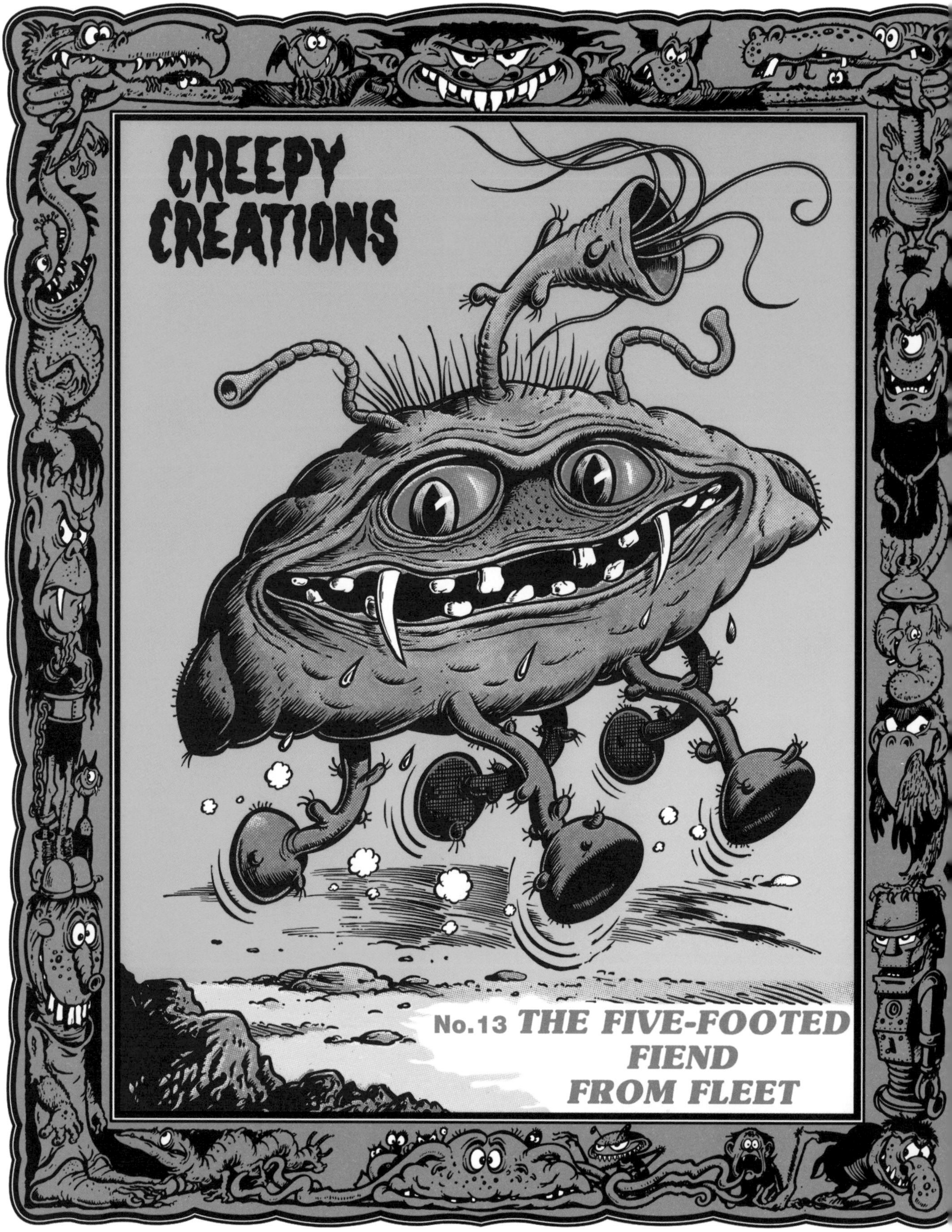
CREEPY CREATIONS
No.13 THE FIVE-FOOTED FIEND FROM FLEET

This crazy "monster piece" wins £1 for JONATHAN BALAM of SUNNINGDALE

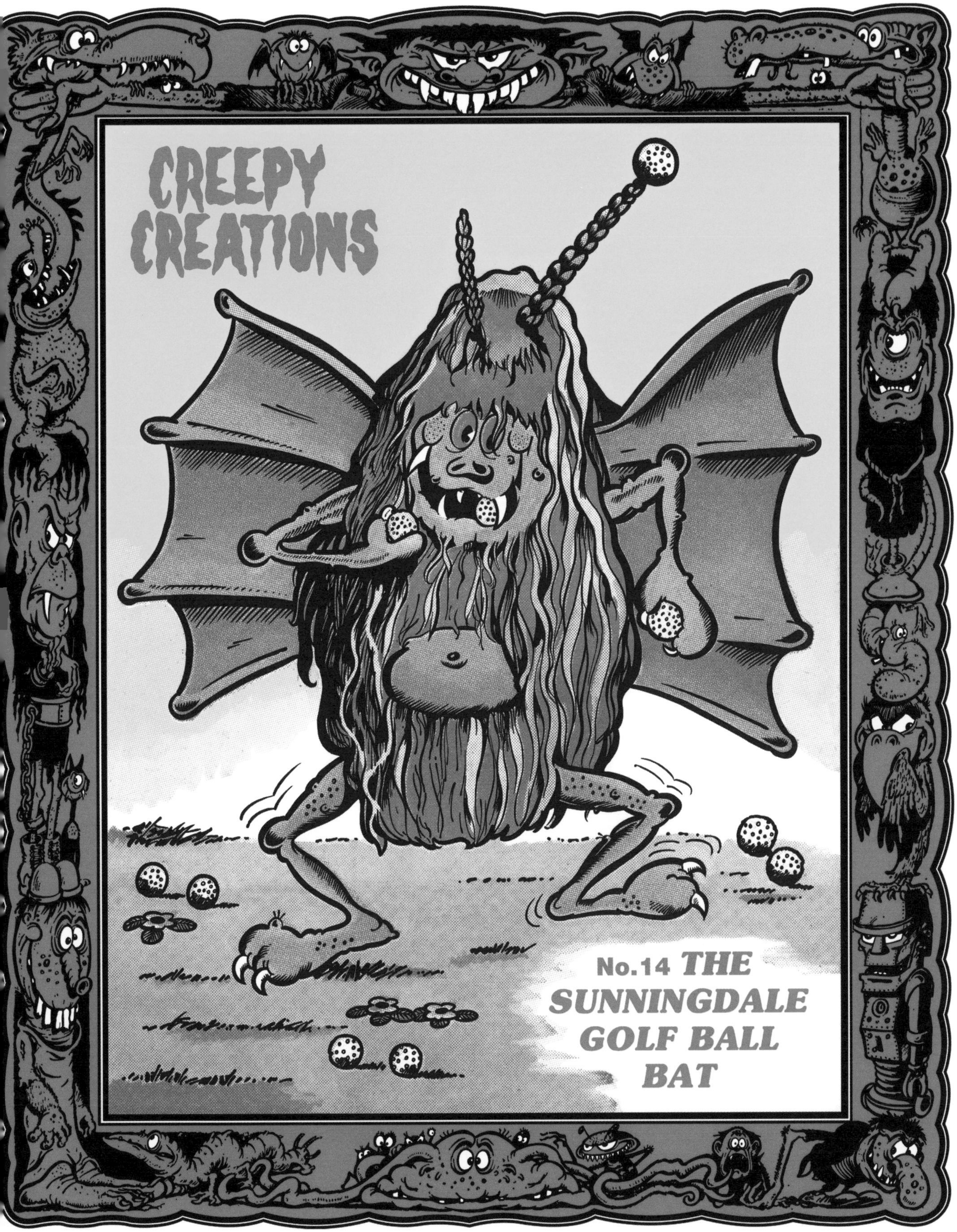
CREEPY CREATIONS
No.14 THE SUNNINGDALE GOLF BALL BAT

This crazy "monster piece" wins £1 for JEFFREY SUTTON of WALWORTH

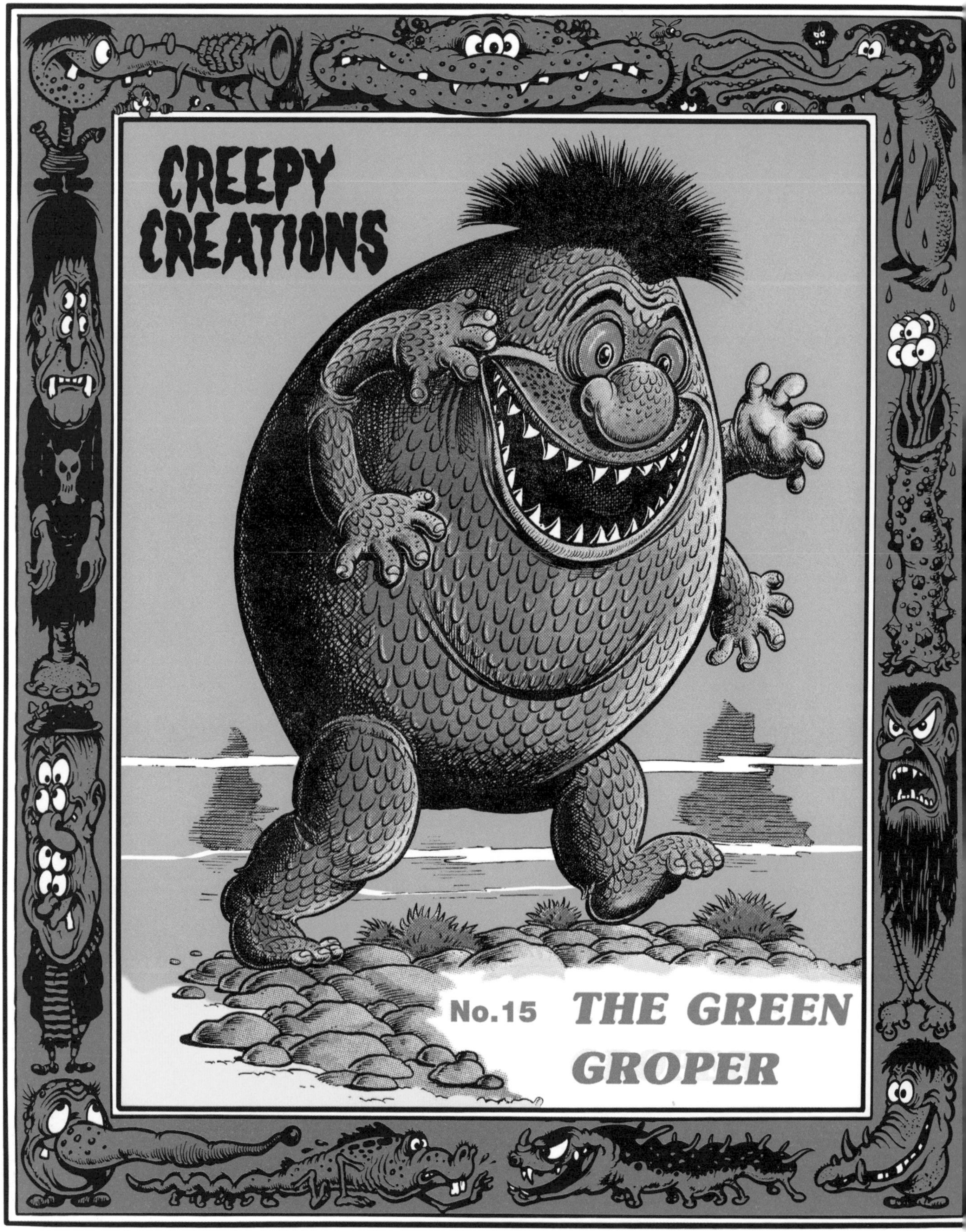
CREEPY CREATIONS
No.15 THE GREEN GROPER

This crazy "monster piece" wins £1 for ROMAN SZABLOWSKI of DOLLIS HILL

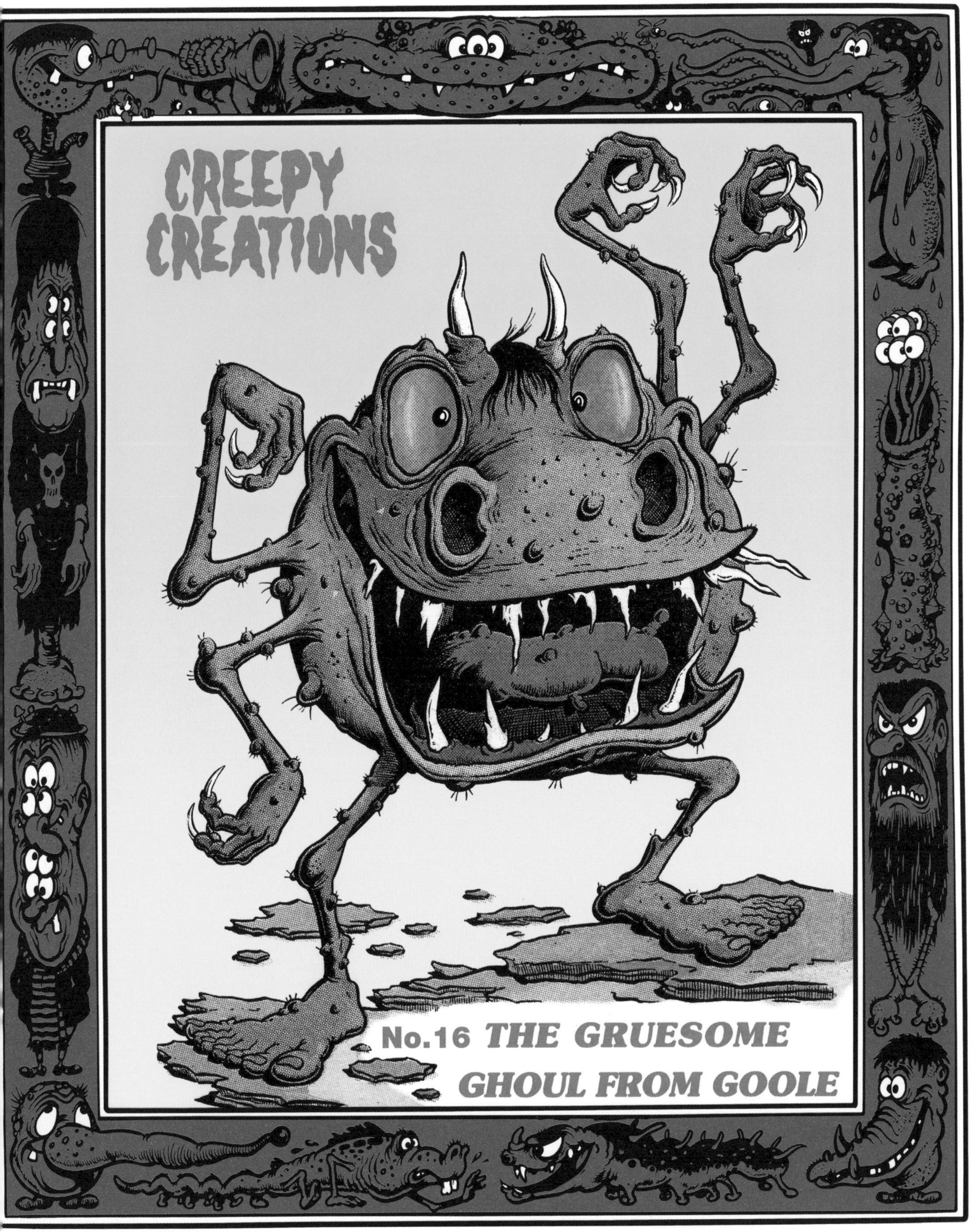
CREEPY CREATIONS
No.16 THE GRUESOME GHOUL FROM GOOLE

This crazy "monster piece" wins £1 for STUART BRAY of HOCKLEY

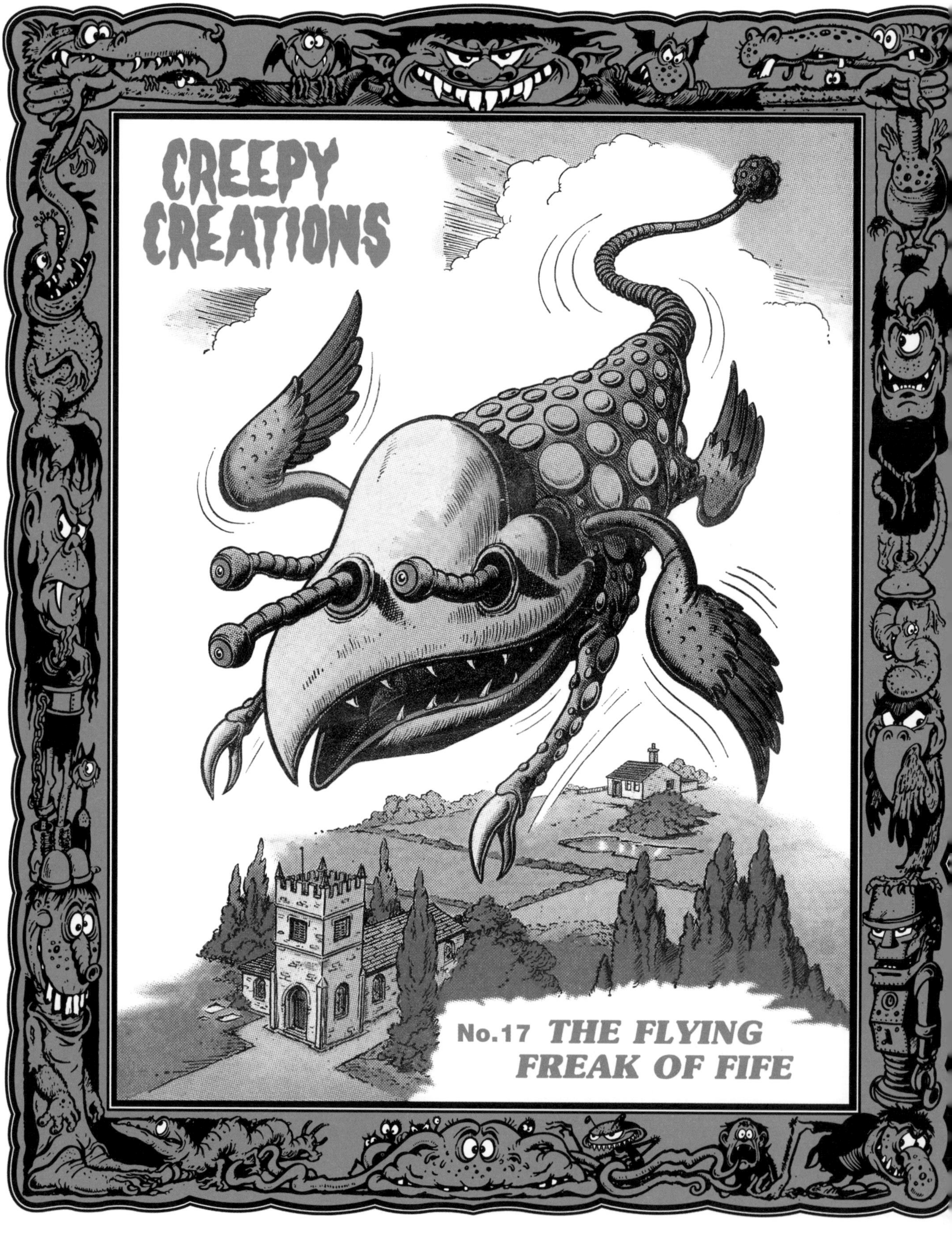
CREEPY CREATIONS
No.17 THE FLYING FREAK OF FIFE

This crazy "monster piece" wins £1 for M. THOMAS of HULL

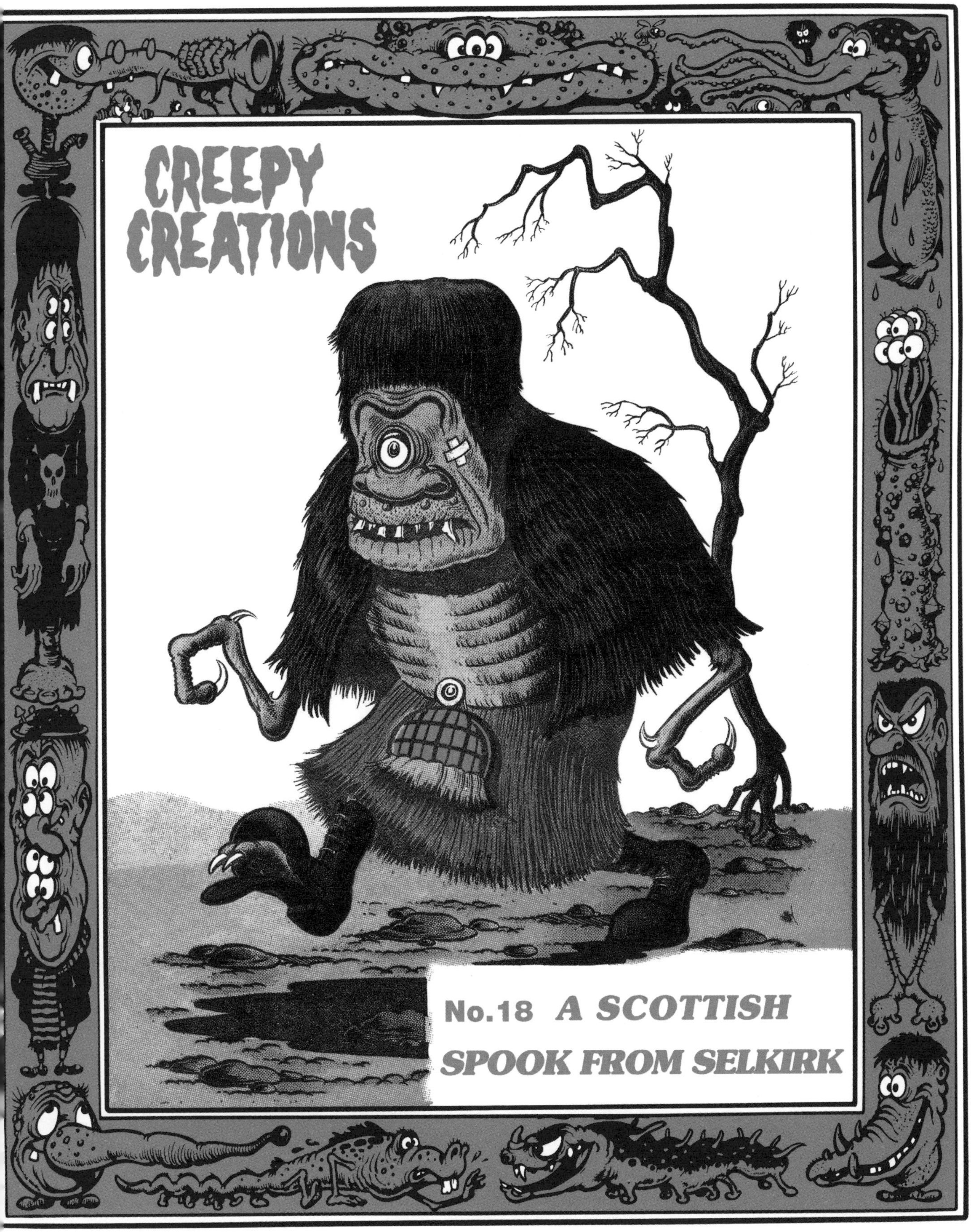
CREEPY CREATIONS
No.18 A SCOTTISH SPOOK FROM SELKIRK

This crazy "monster piece" wins £1 for DAVID CHILTON of SOUTHPORT

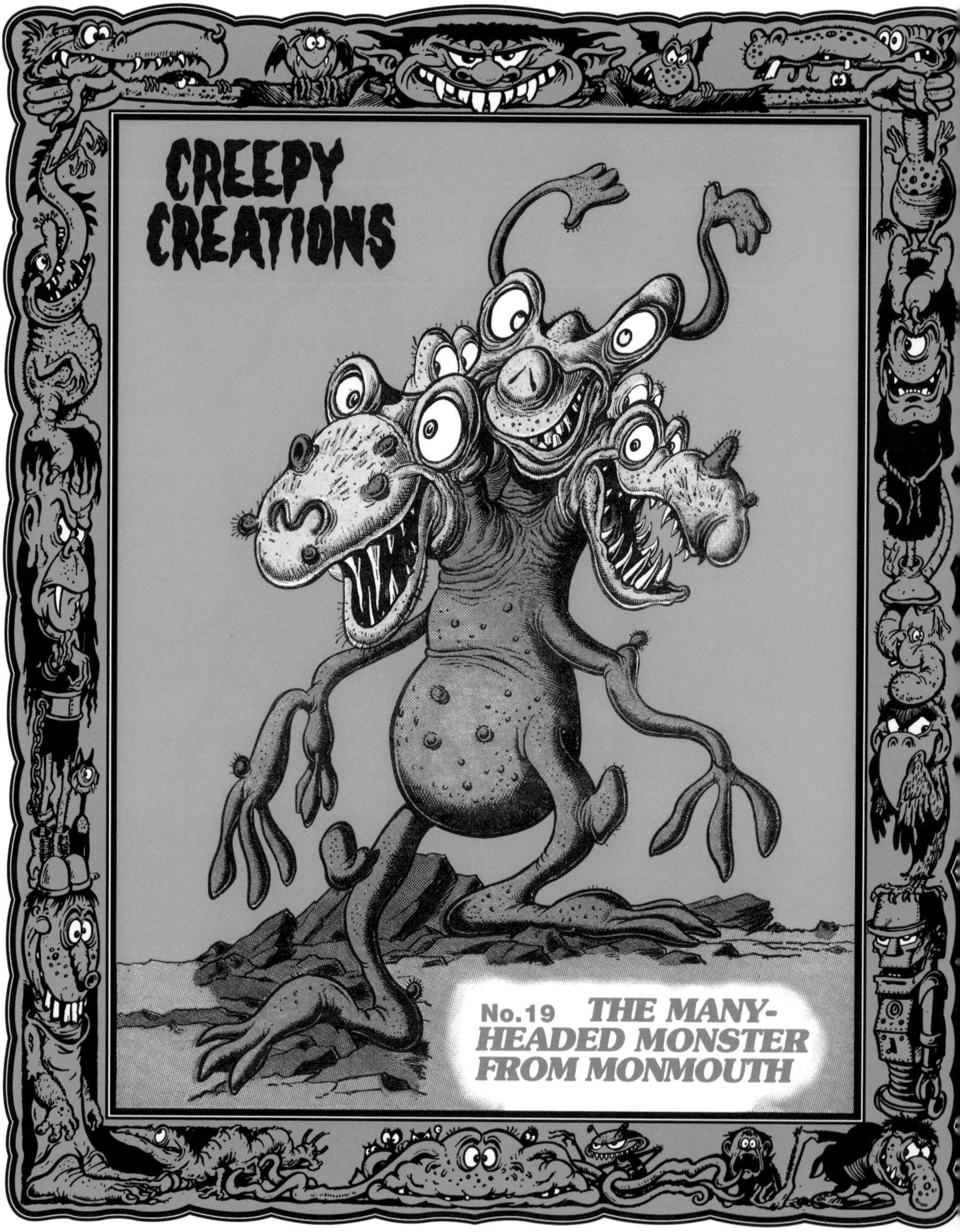
CREEPY CREATIONS
No.19 THE MANY-HEADED MONSTER FROM MONMOUTH

This crazy "monster piece" wins £1 for STEPHEN TURNER of RUSTINGTON

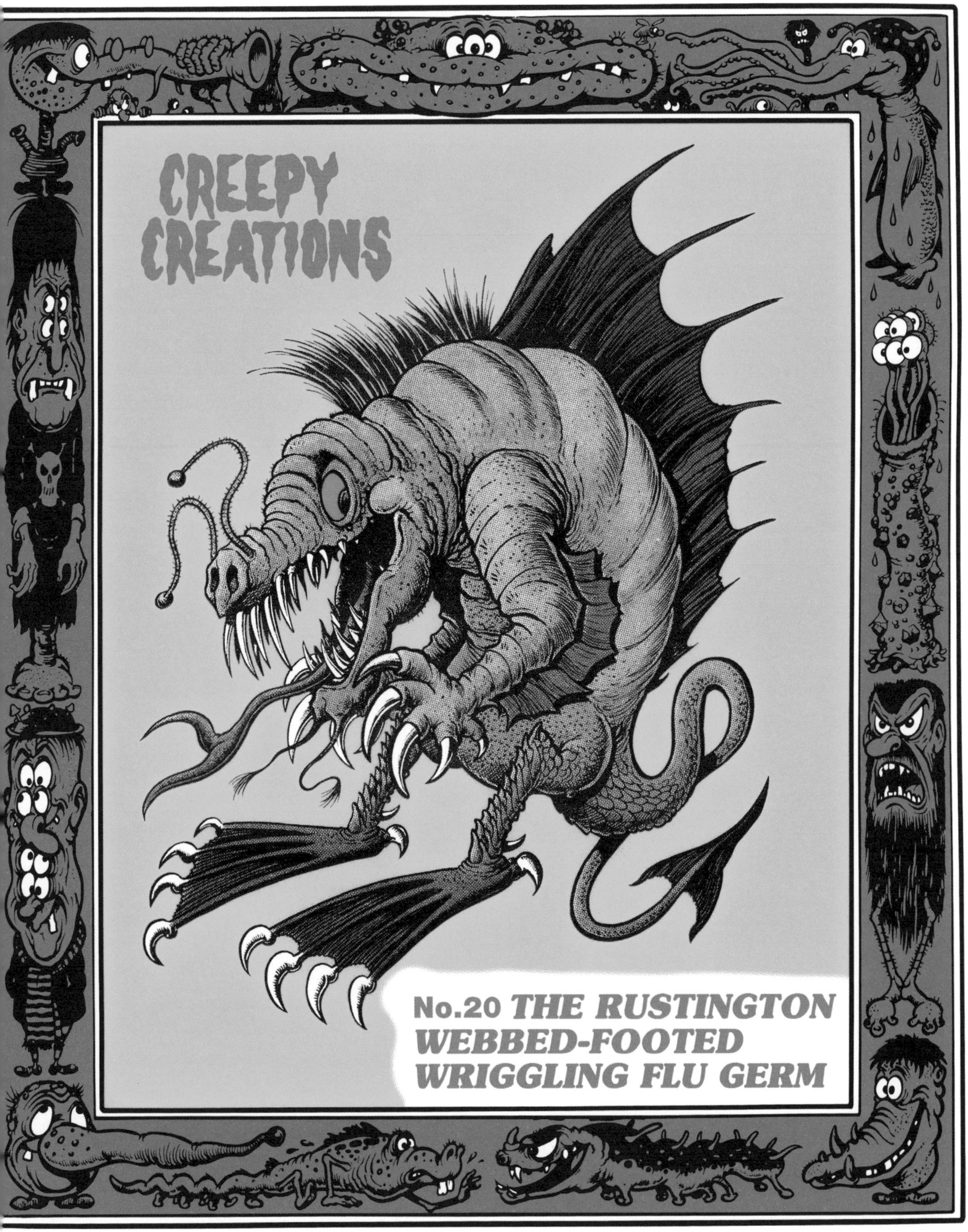
CREEPY CREATIONS
No.20 THE RUSTINGTON WEBBED-FOOTED WRIGGLING FLU GERM

This crazy “monster piece” wins £1 for GORDON ROBSON of GLASGOW

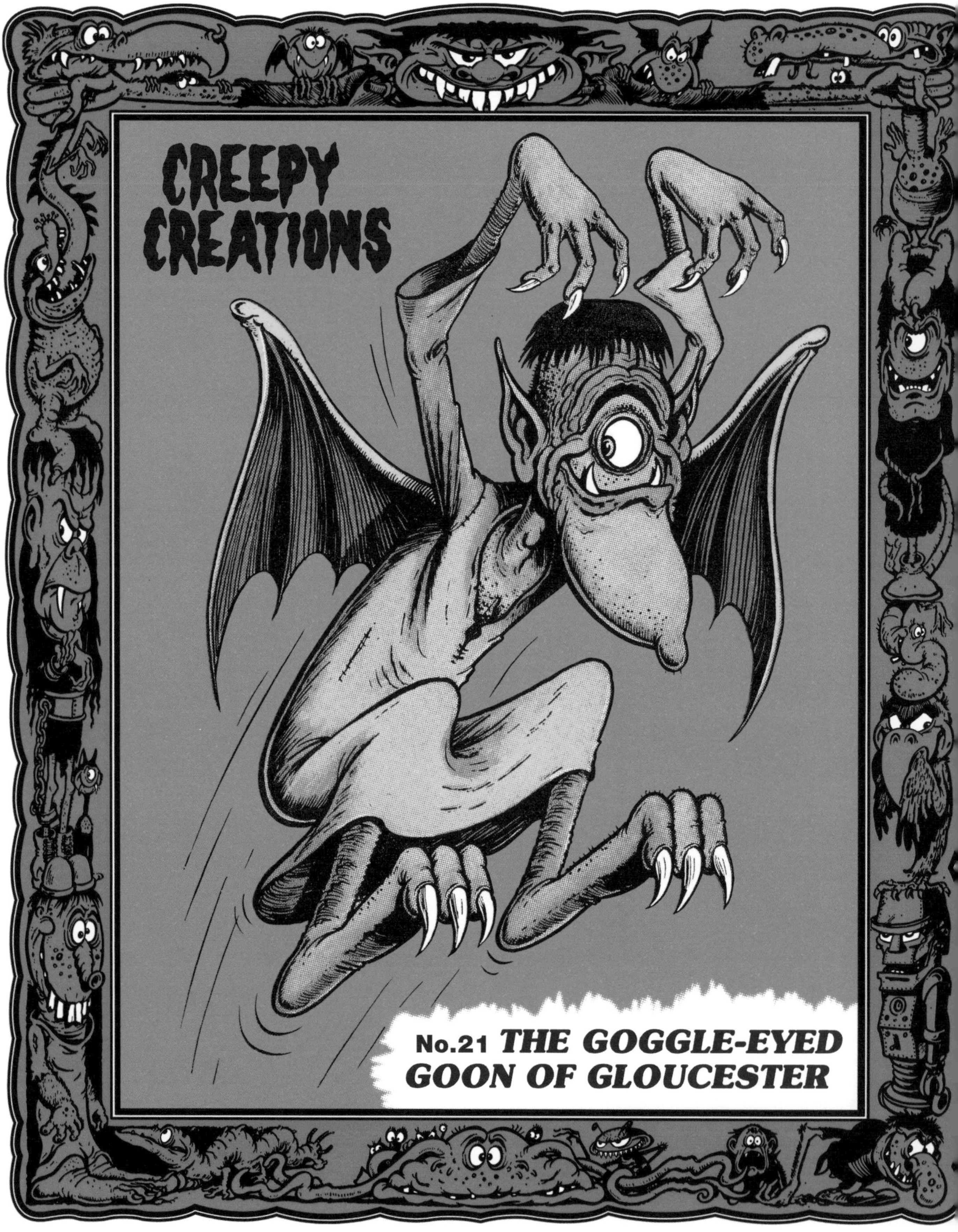
CREEPY CREATIONS
No.21 THE GOGGLE-EYED GOON OF GLOUCESTER

This crazy "monster piece" wins £1 for JOHN MEAN of HACKNEY

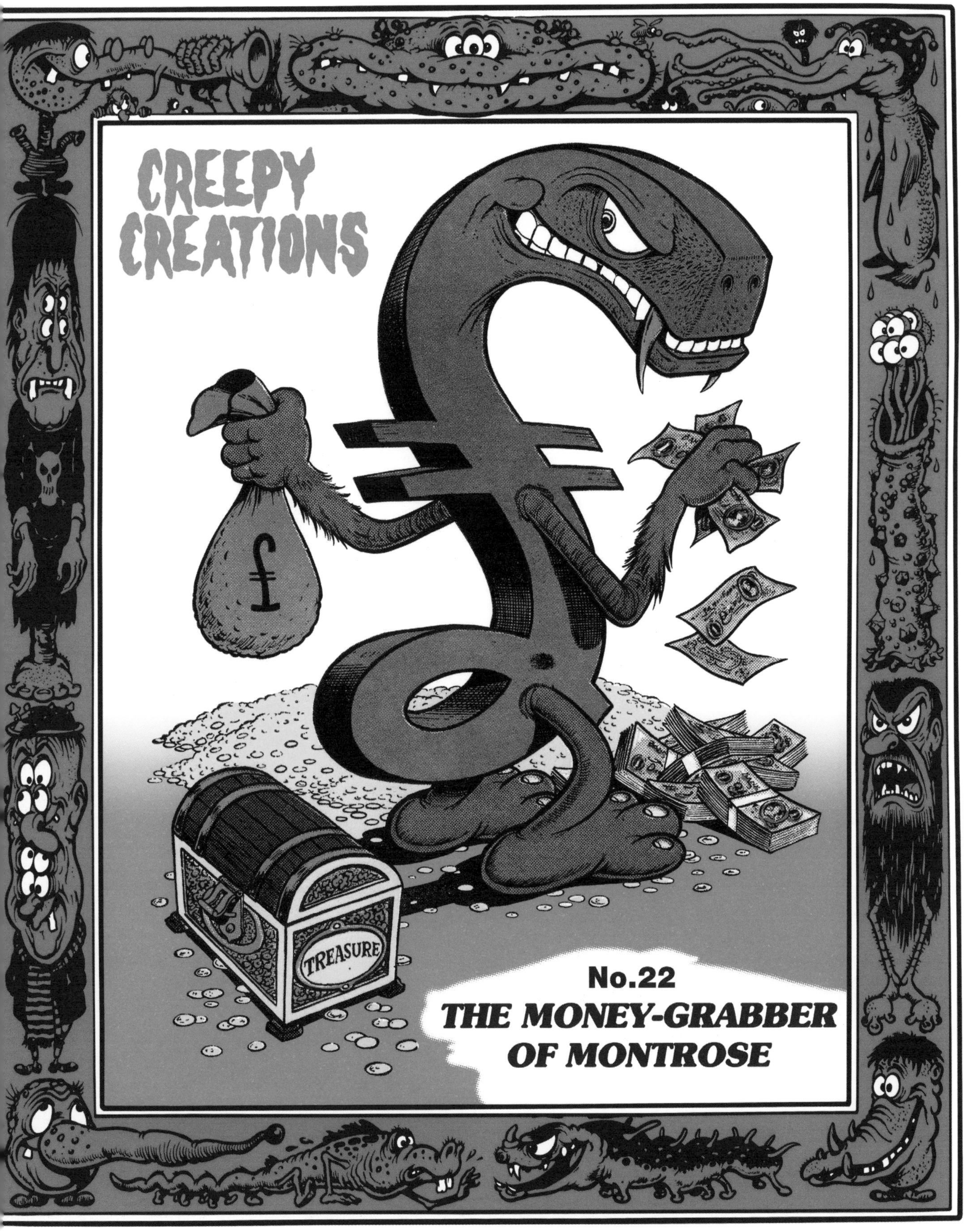
CREEPY CREATIONS
£
TREASURE
No.22
THE MONEY-GRABBER OF MONTROSE

This crazy "monster piece" wins £1 for DOMINIC MANSELL of ORLINGBURY

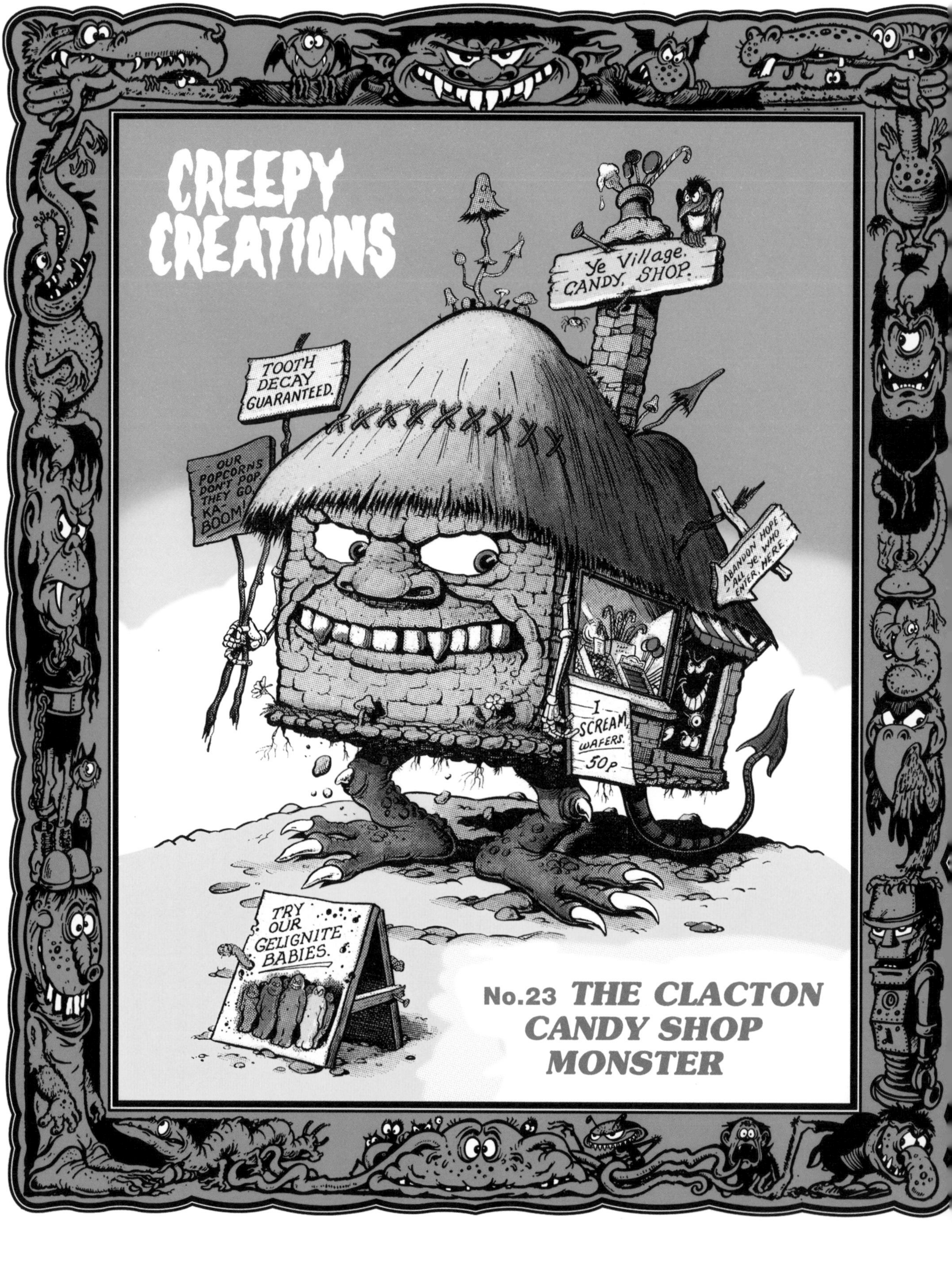
CREEPY CREATIONS
Ye Village. CANDY SHOP.
TOOTH DECAY GUARANTEED.
OUR POPCORNS DON'T POP, THEY GO KA-BOOM!
ABANDON HOPE ALL YE WHO ENTER HERE.
I SCREAM WAFERS. 50p
TRY OUR GELIGNITE BABIES.
No.23 THE CLACTON CANDY SHOP MONSTER

This crazy "monster piece" wins £1 for DAVID KINGSFORD of STOCKPORT

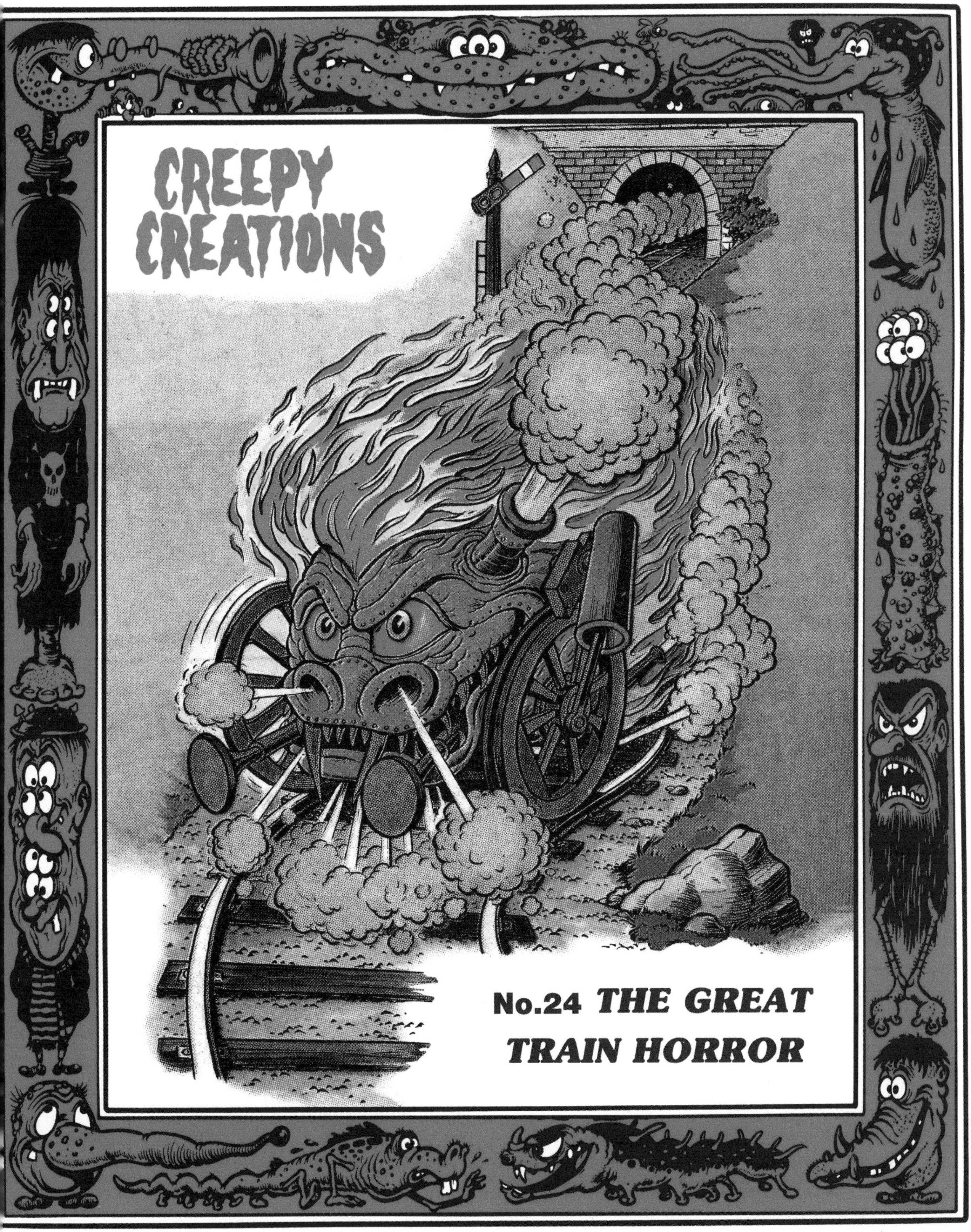
CREEPY CREATIONS
No.24 THE GREAT TRAIN HORROR

This crazy "monster piece" wins £1 for FIONA SMITH of WORTHING

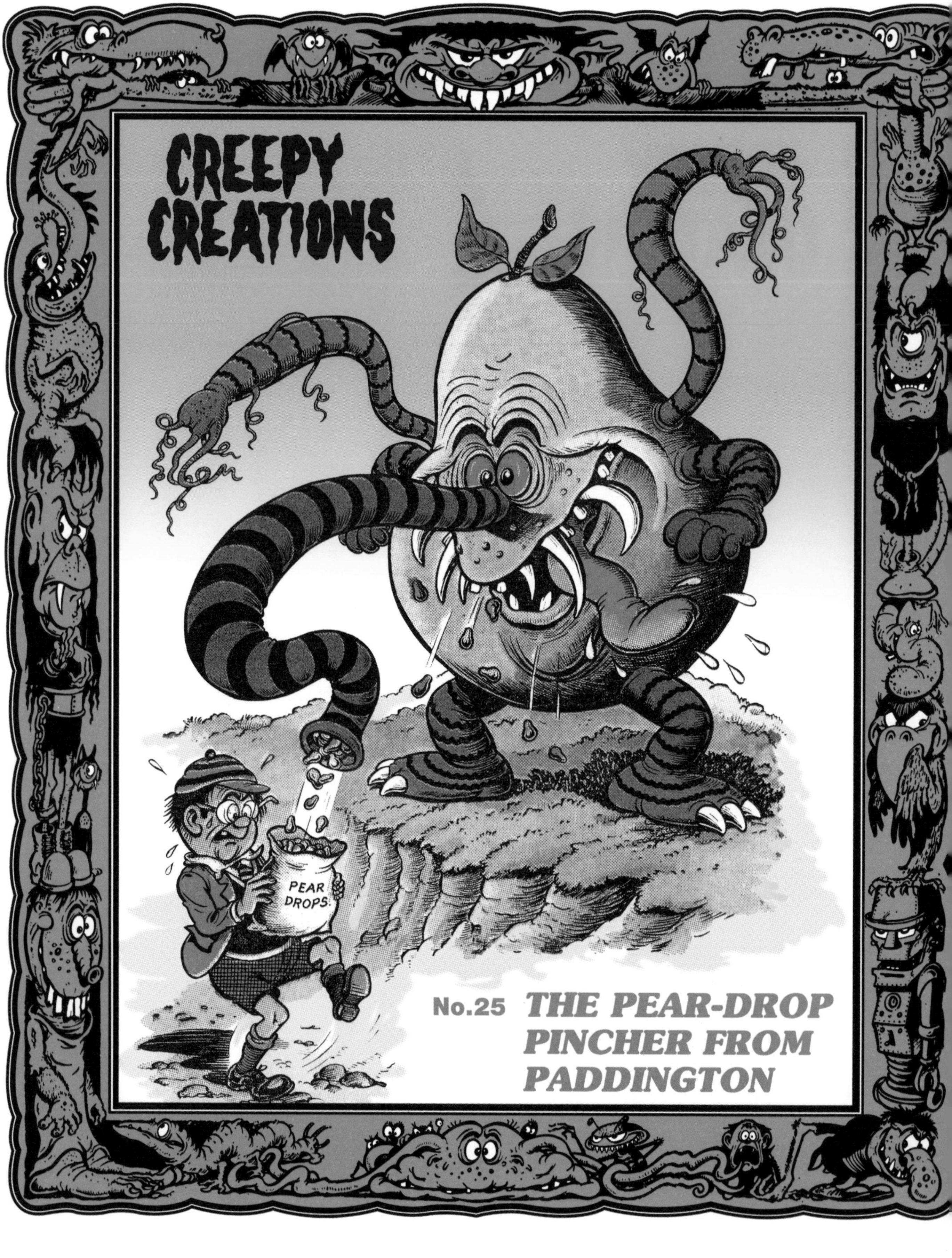

CREEPY CREATIONS
PEAR DROPS
No.25 THE PEAR-DROP PINCHER FROM PADDINGTON

This crazy "monster piece" wins £1 for KEVIN JONES of LYDNEY

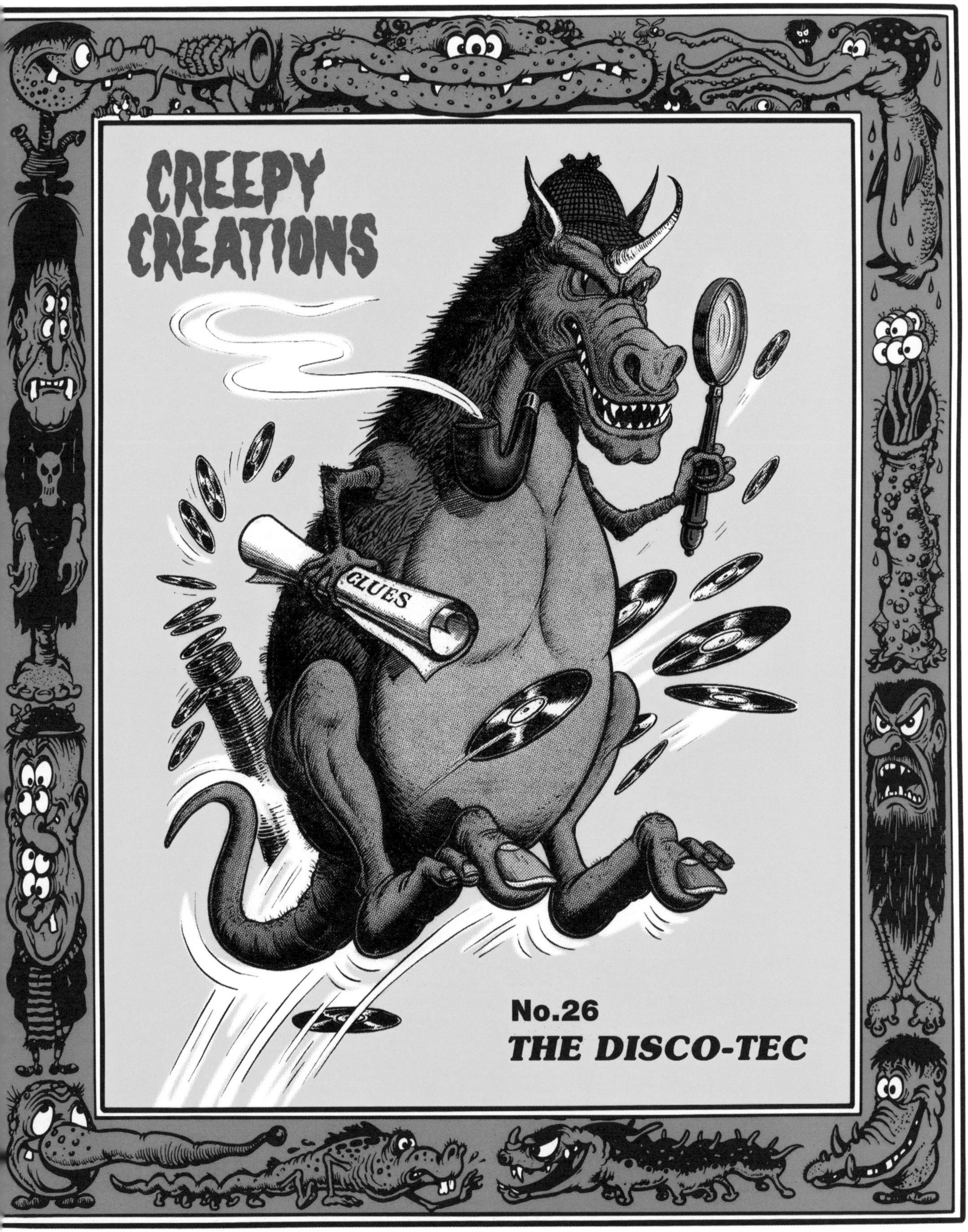
CREEPY CREATIONS
CLUES
No.26
THE DISCO-TEC

This crazy "monster piece" wins £1 for REBECCA BUCKTON of BEXHILL-ON-SEA

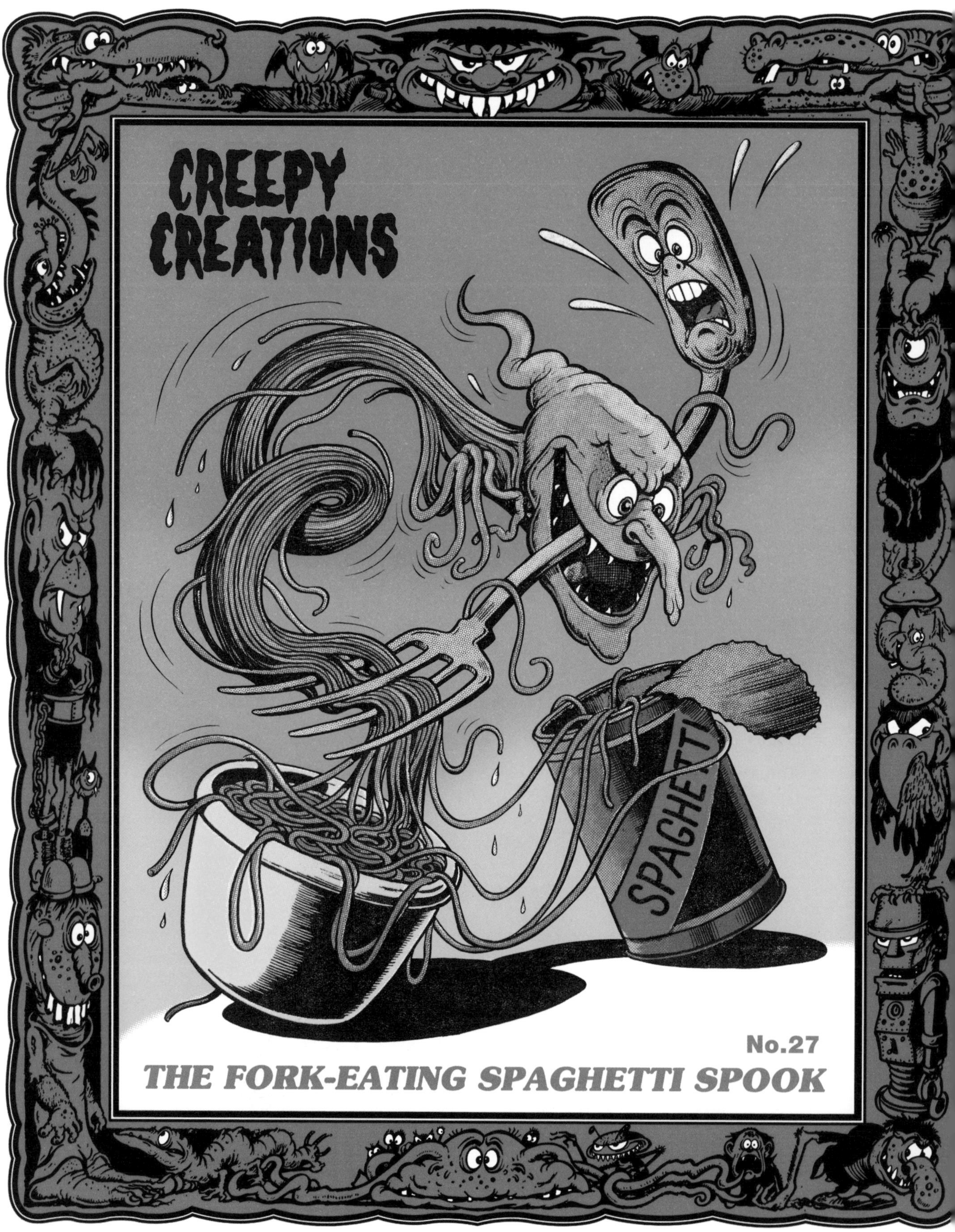
CREEPY CREATIONS
SPAGHETTI
No.27
THE FORK-EATING SPAGHETTI SPOOK

This crazy "monster piece" wins £1 for LORETTA EDE of POOLE

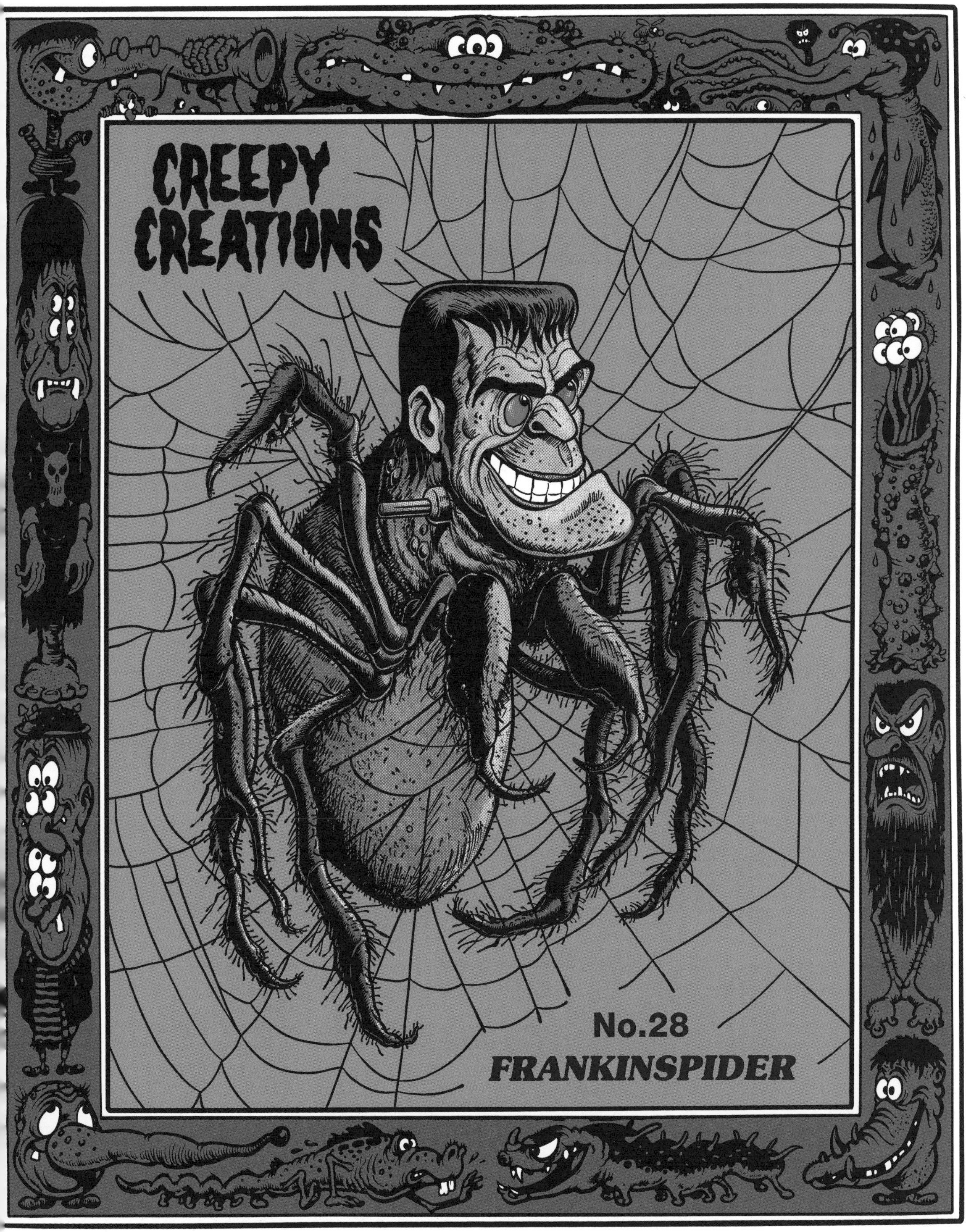

CREEPY CREATIONS
No.28
FRANKINSPIDER

This crazy “monster piece” wins £1 for DAVID CARR of BROMLEY

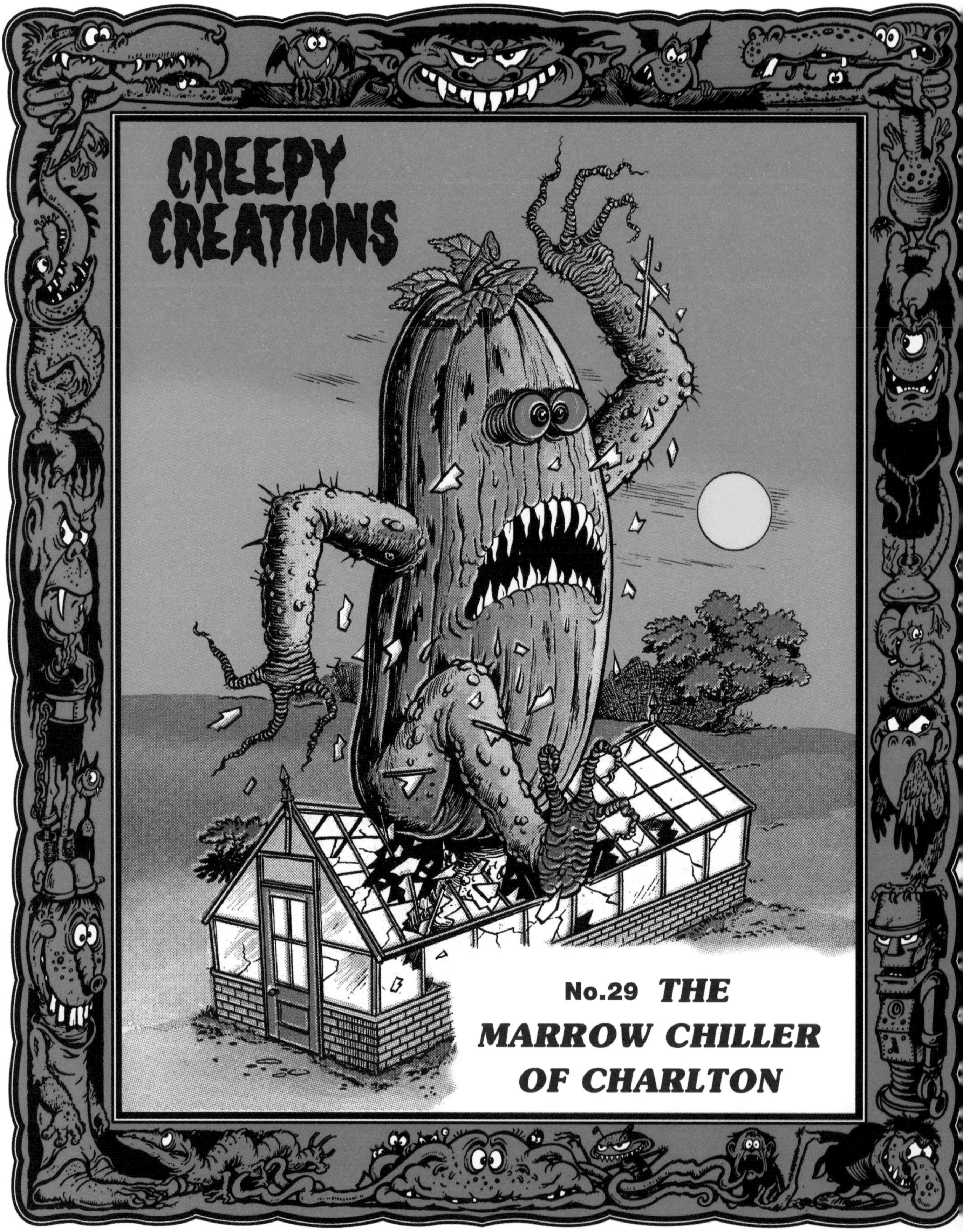
CREEPY CREATIONS
No.29 THE MARROW CHILLER OF CHARLTON

This crazy "monster piece" wins £1 for CHRISTOPHER WHITEHEAD of SHEFFIELD

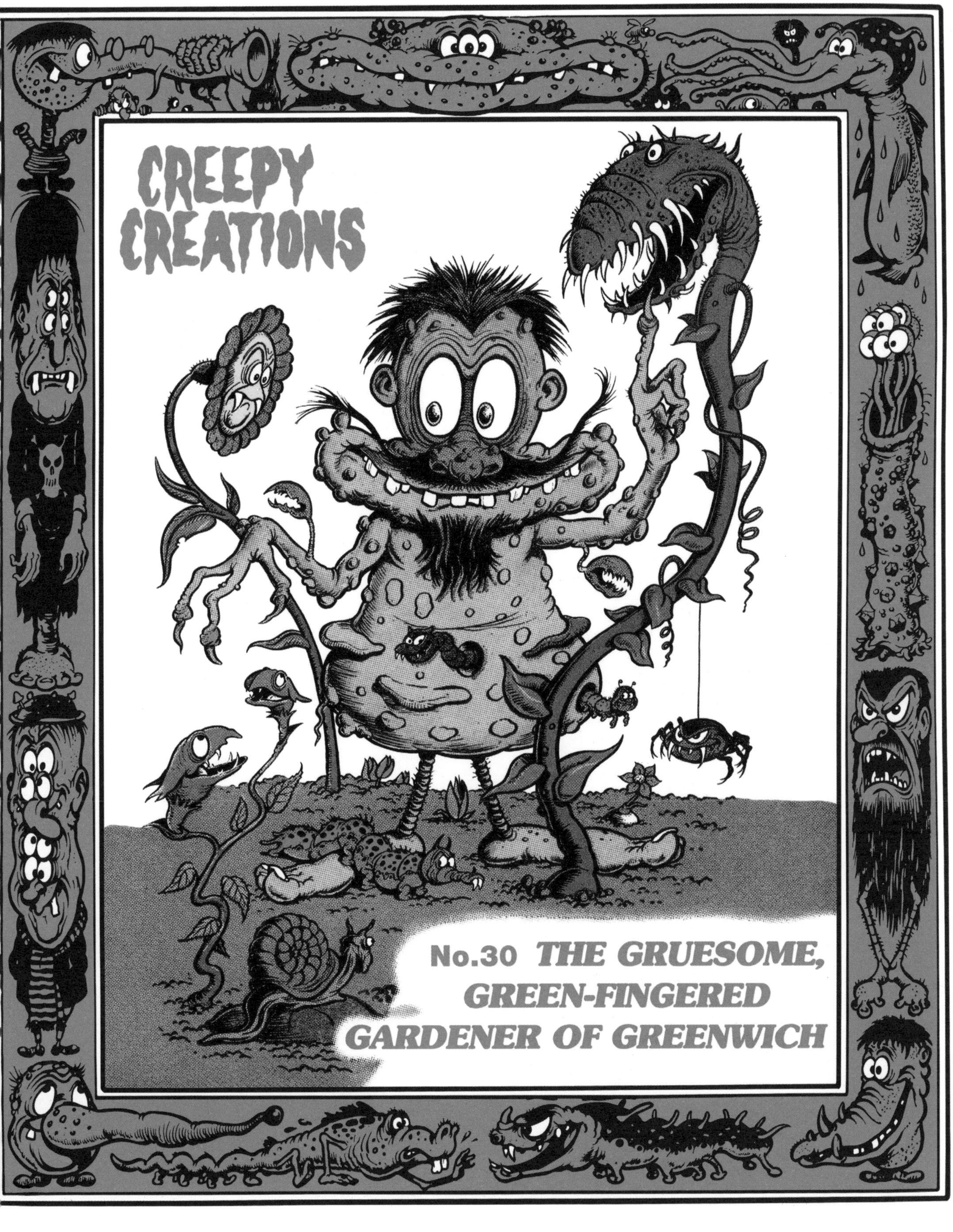
CREEPY CREATIONS
No.30 THE GRUESOME, GREEN-FINGERED GARDENER OF GREENWICH

This crazy "monster piece" wins £1 for SUSAN SZKUDLAPSKI of KIRBY

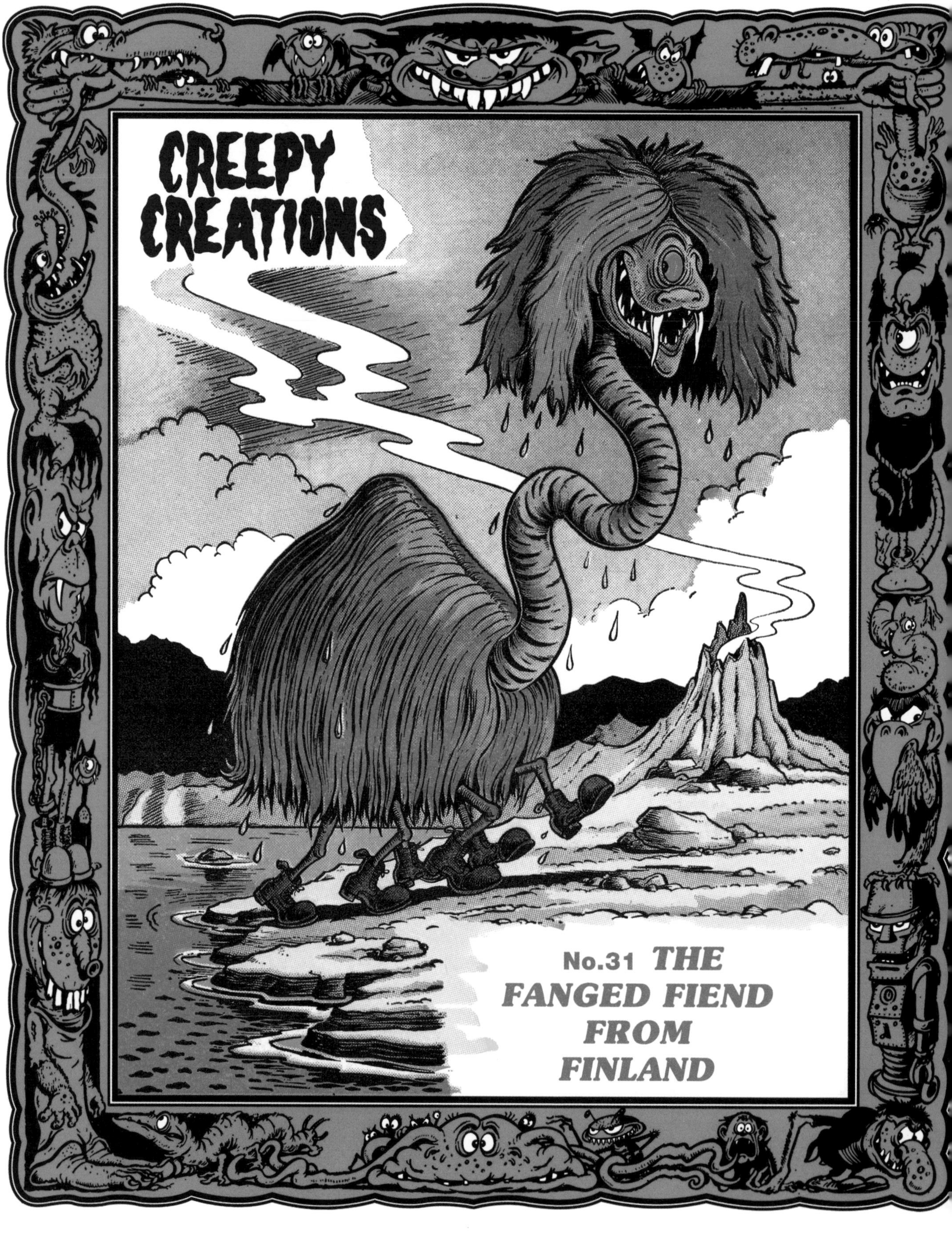
CREEPY CREATIONS
No.31 THE FANGED FIEND FROM FINLAND

This crazy "monster piece" wins £1 for STEPHEN WACKETT of BROMLEY

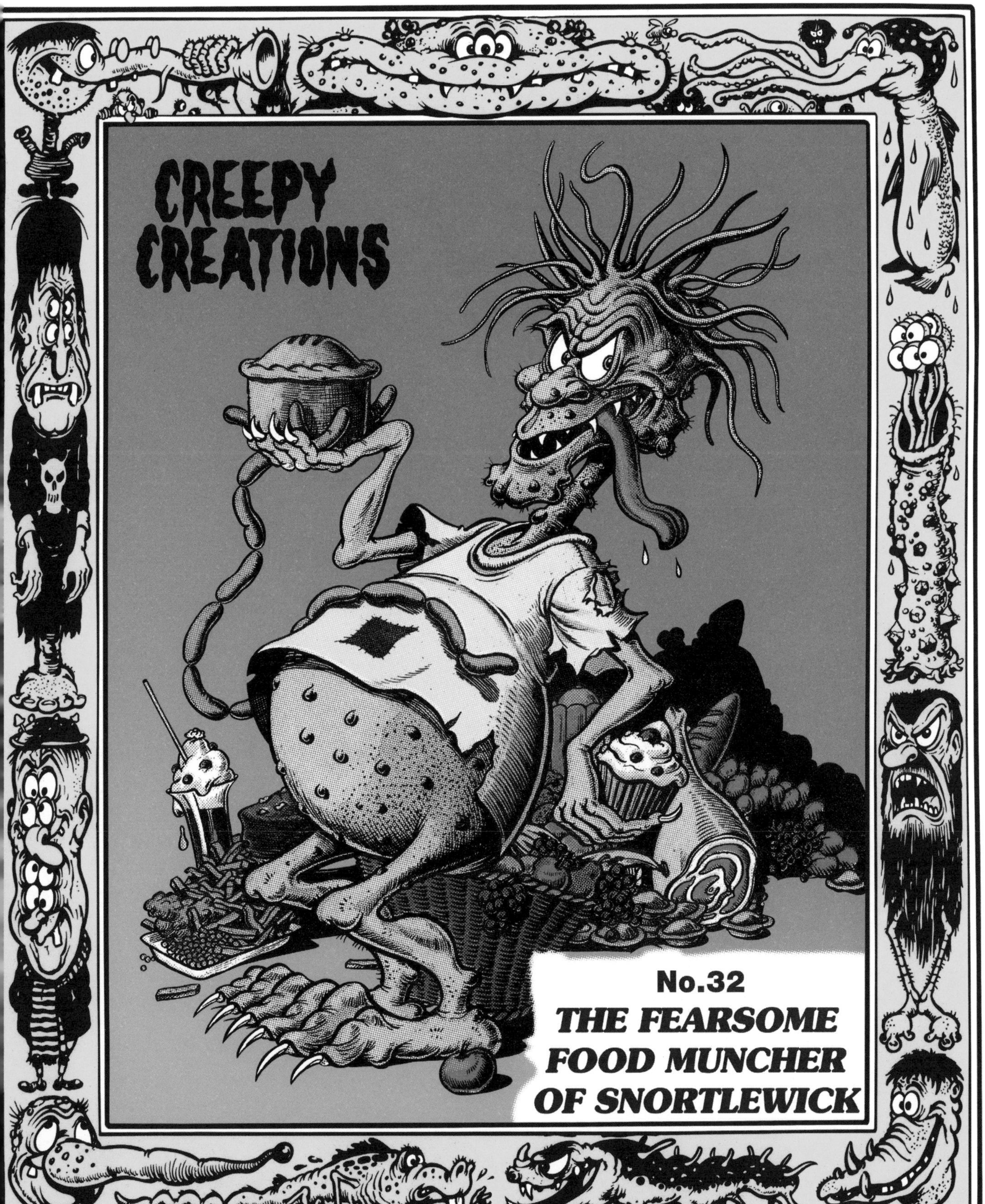
CREEPY CREATIONS
No.32
THE FEARSOME FOOD MUNCHER OF SNORTLEWICK

This crazy "monster piece" wins £1 for PAUL CHESWICK of CONISBROUGH

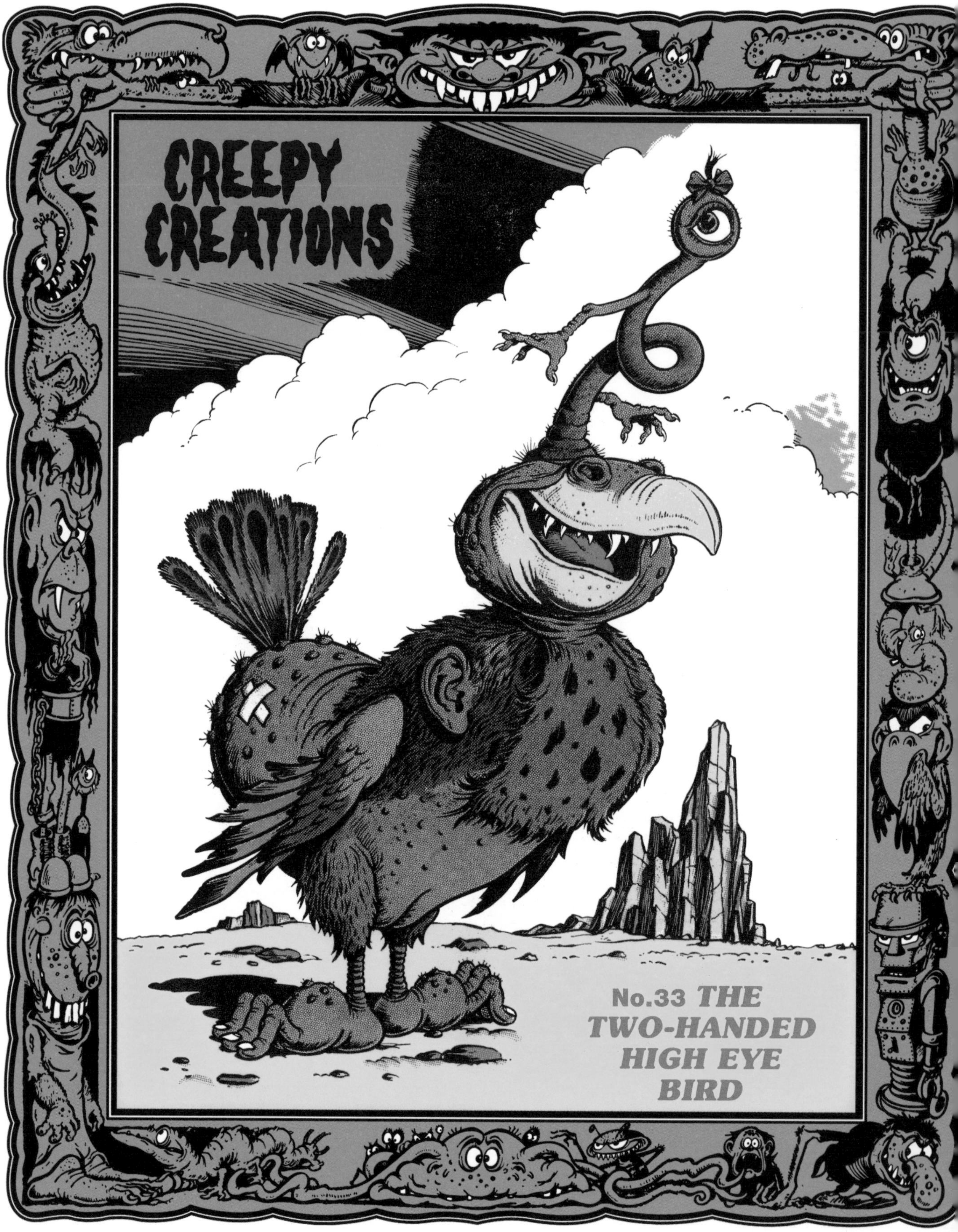
CREEPY CREATIONS
No.33 THE TWO-HANDED HIGH EYE BIRD

This crazy "monster piece" wins £1 for DENNIS KEMPSON of BIRMINGHAM

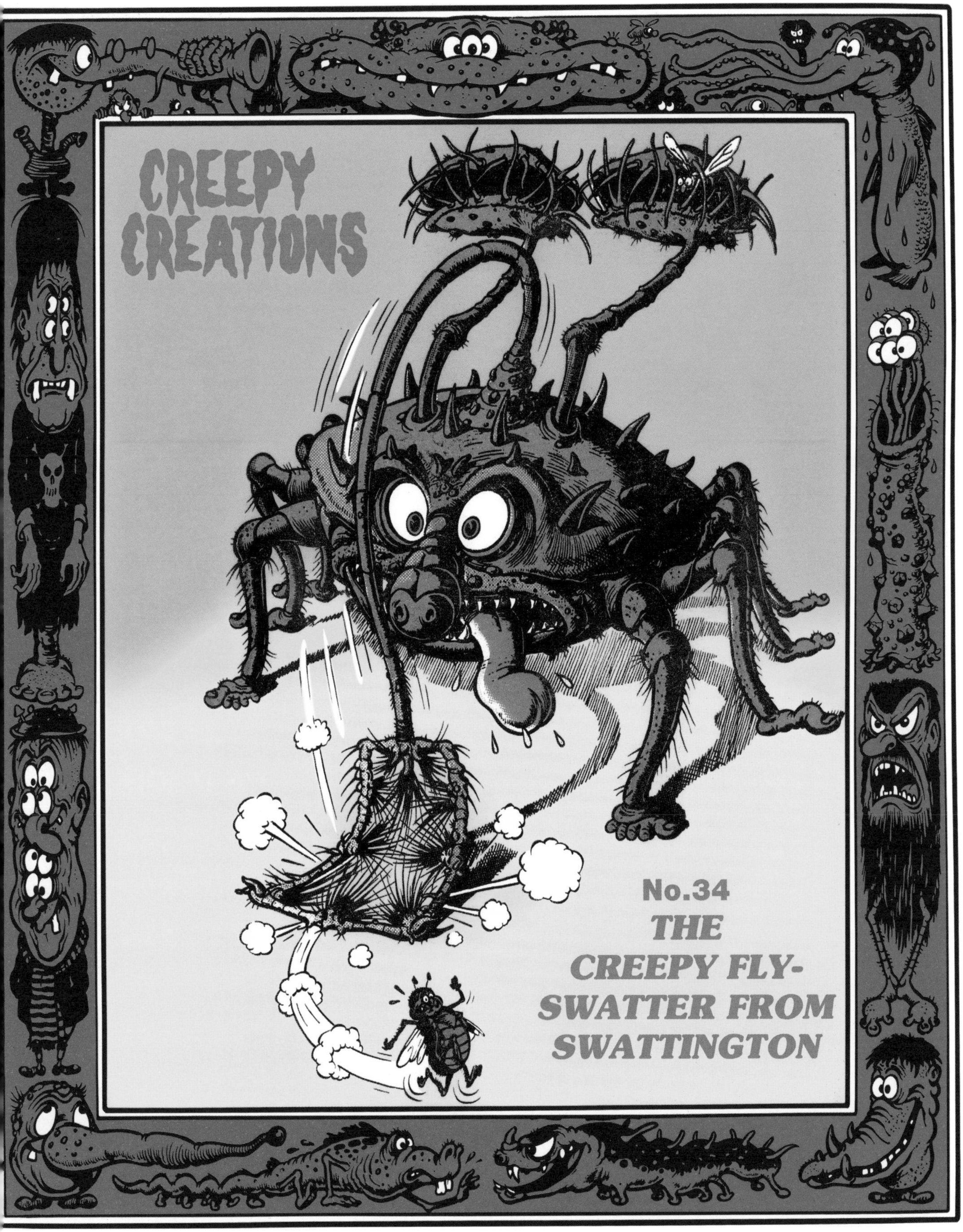

CREEPY CREATIONS
No.34
THE CREEPY FLY-SWATTER FROM SWATTINGTON

This crazy "monster piece" wins £1 for GERALDINE GODDEN of PERIVALE

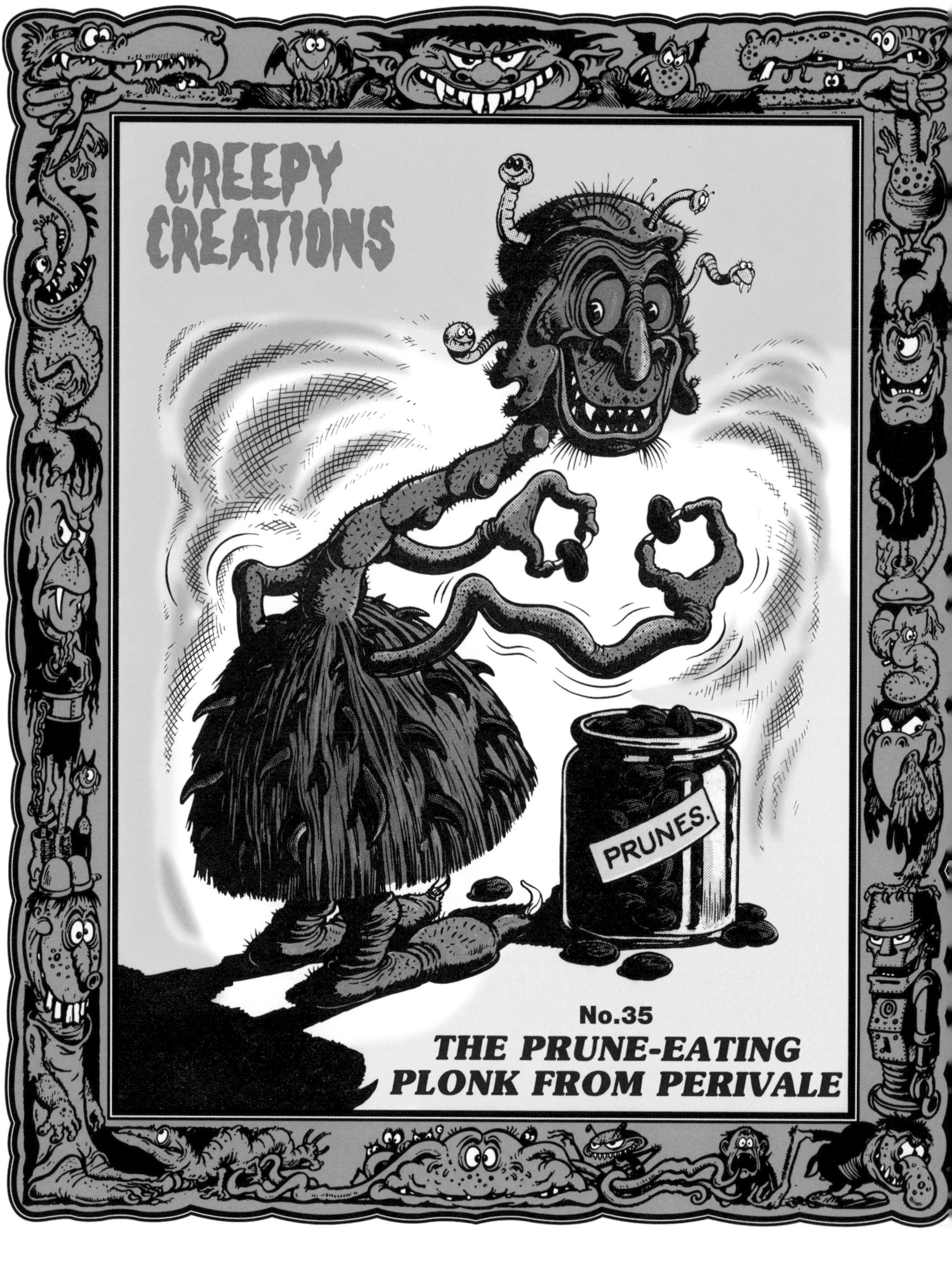
CREEPY CREATIONS
PRUNES.
No.35
THE PRUNE-EATING PLONK FROM PERIVALE

This crazy "monster piece" wins £1 for JOHN BICKERTON of BARTON

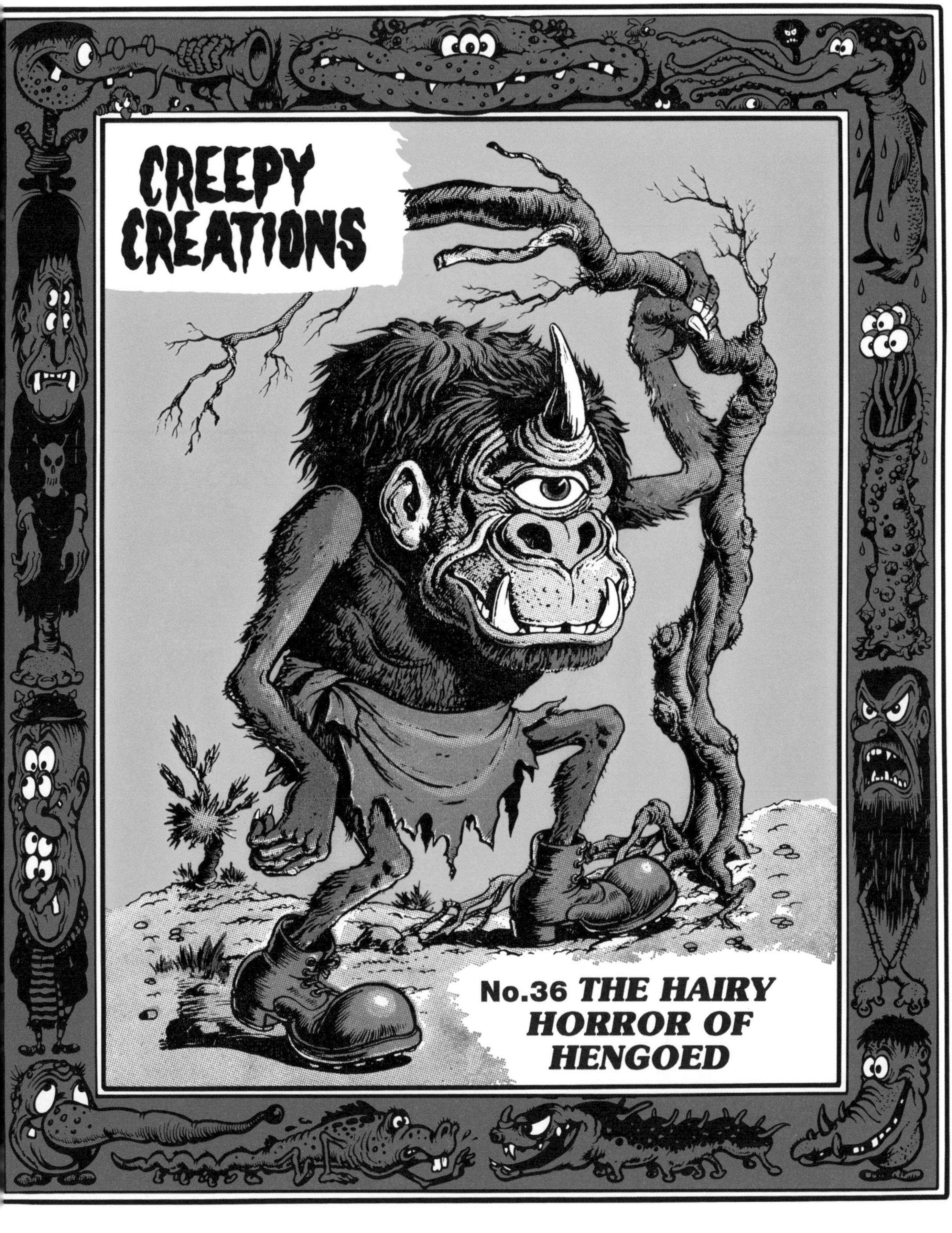
CREEPY CREATIONS
No.36 THE HAIRY HORROR OF HENGOED

This crazy "monster piece" wins £1 for RUSSELL FISHER of KENWORTH

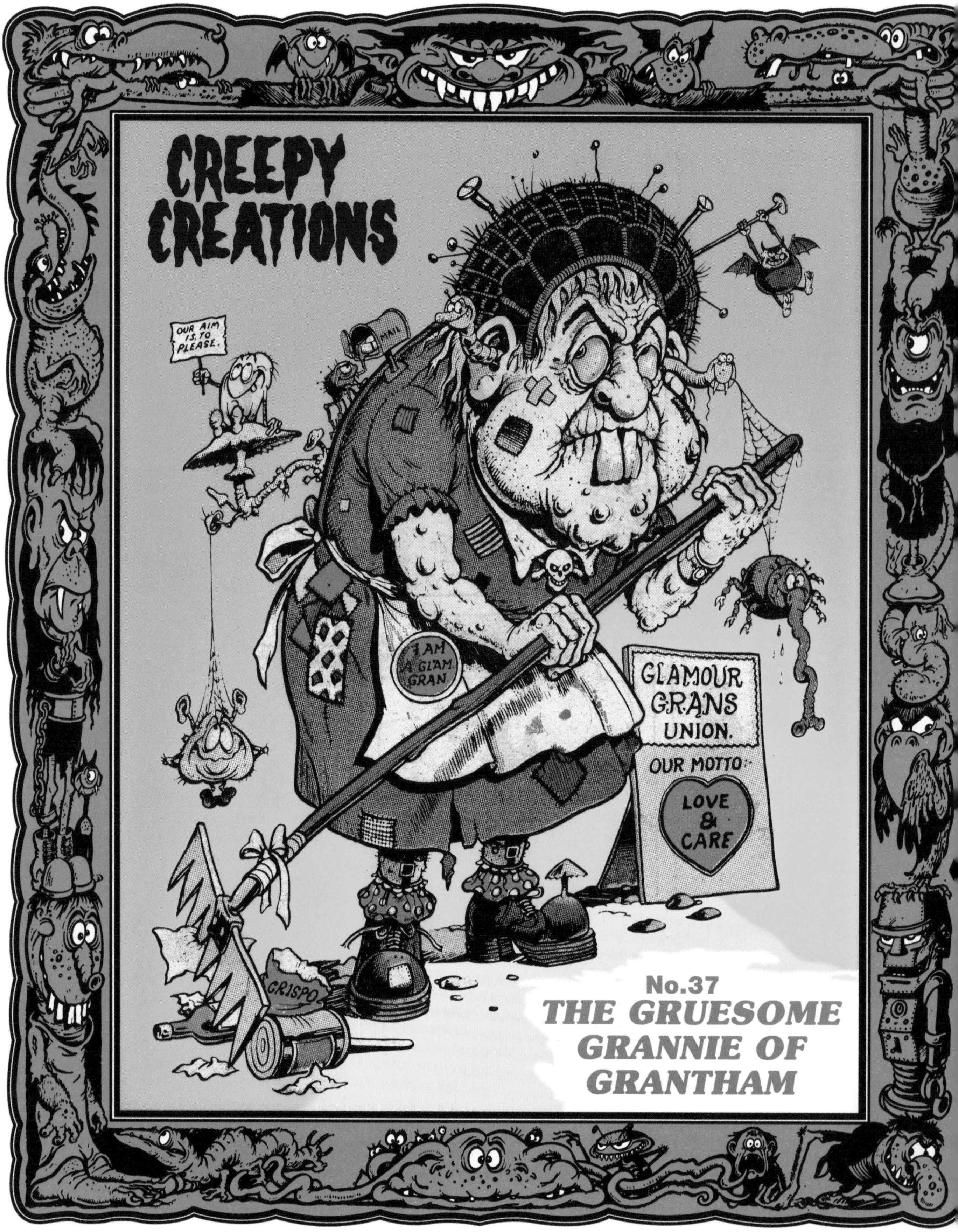
CREEPY CREATIONS
OUR AIM IS TO PLEASE.
MAIL
I AM A GLAM. GRAN
GLAMOUR GRANS UNION.
OUR MOTTO
LOVE & CARE
CRISPO
No.37
THE GRUESOME GRANNIE OF GRANTHAM

This crazy "monster piece" wins £1 for JEANETTE ATHERTON of WALLASEY

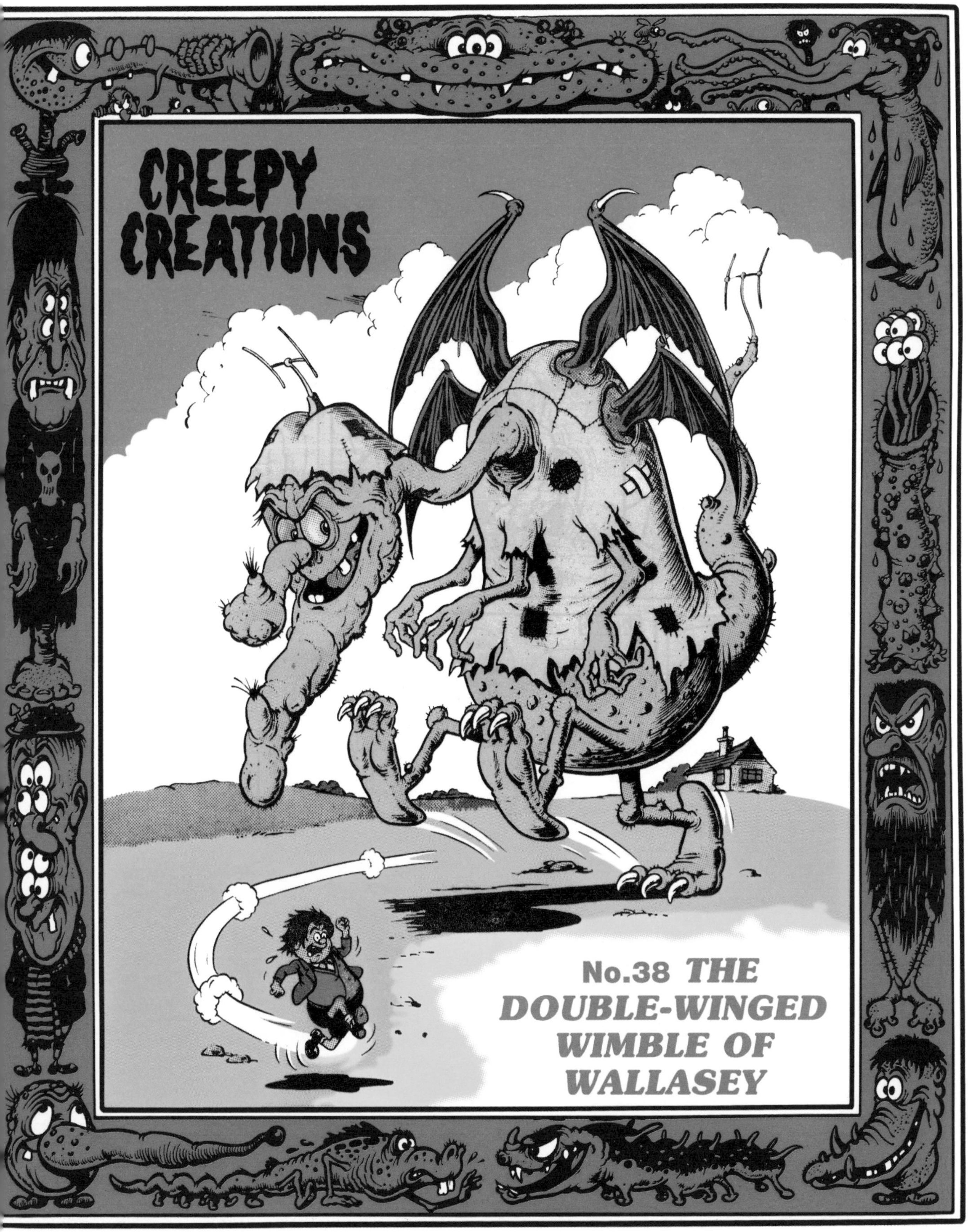
CREEPY CREATIONS
No.38 THE DOUBLE-WINGED WIMBLE OF WALLASEY

This crazy "monster piece" wins £1 for IAIN CROSBIE of HAMILTON

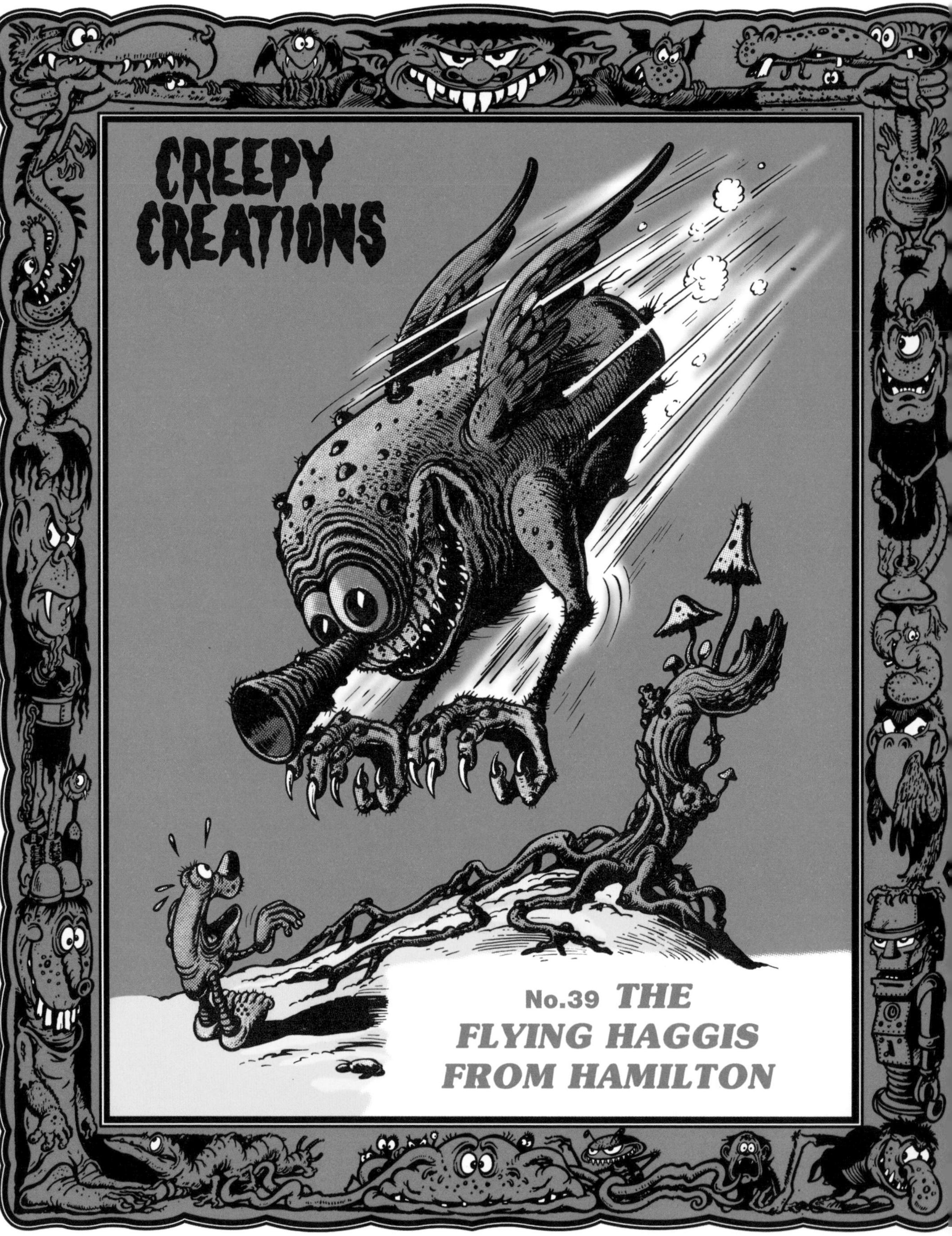
CREEPY CREATIONS
No.39 THE FLYING HAGGIS FROM HAMILTON

This crazy "monster piece" wins £1 for GARY STINTON of TUPSLEY

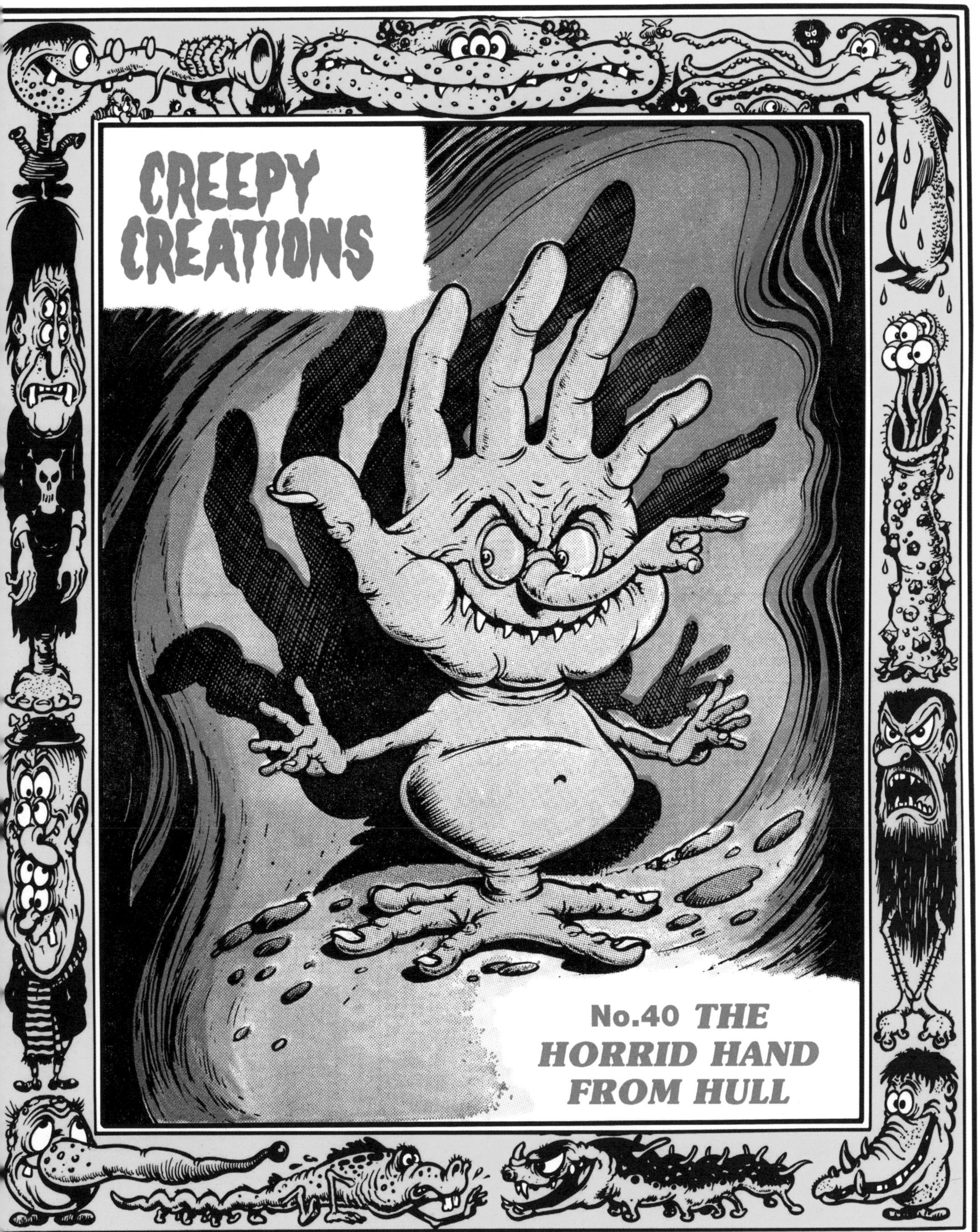
CREEPY CREATIONS
No.40 THE HORRID HAND FROM HULL

This crazy "monster piece" wins £1 for KARL KEELING of CONISBROUGH

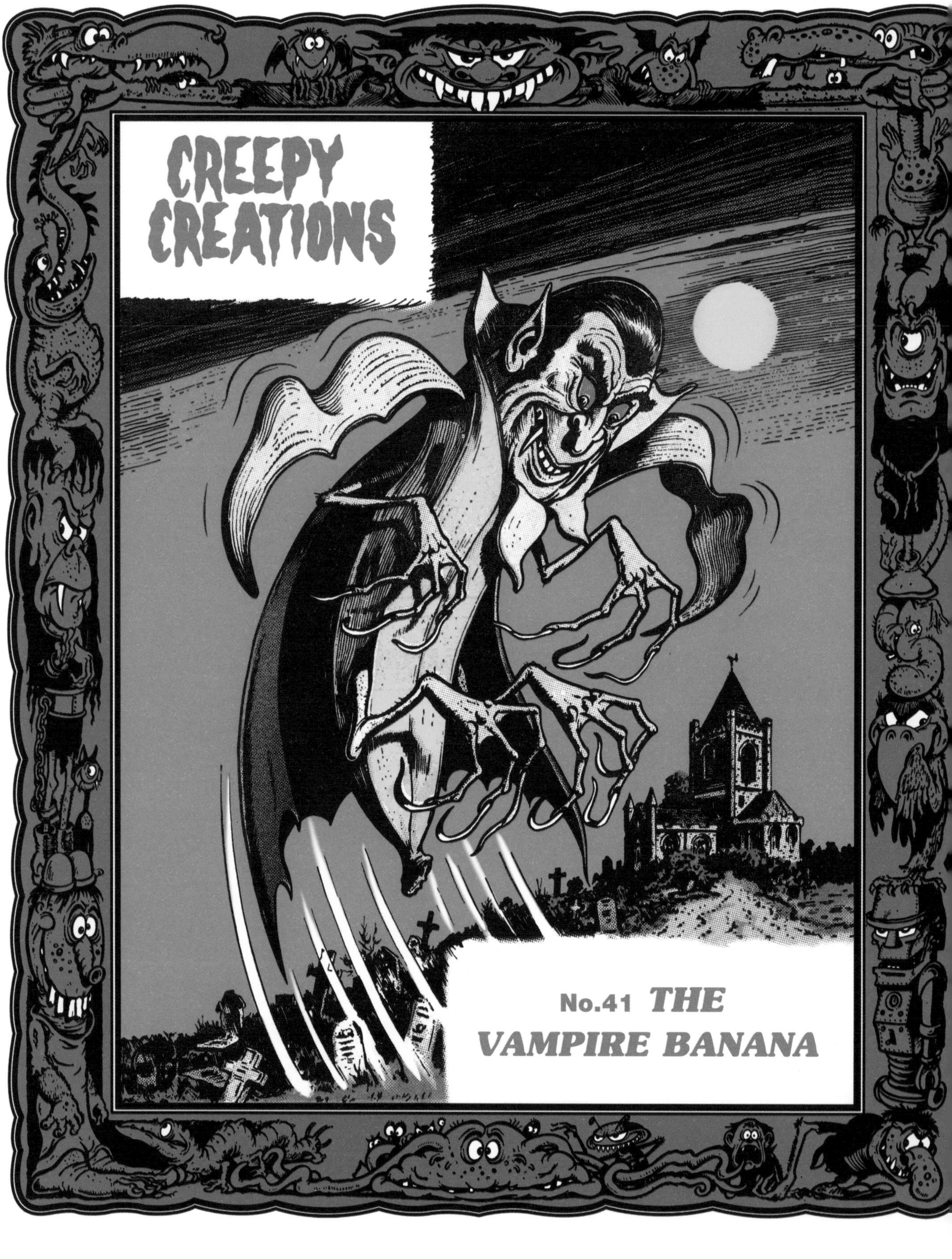
CREEPY CREATIONS
No.41 THE VAMPIRE BANANA

This crazy "monster piece" wins £1 for PAUL LISHMAN of PUDSEY

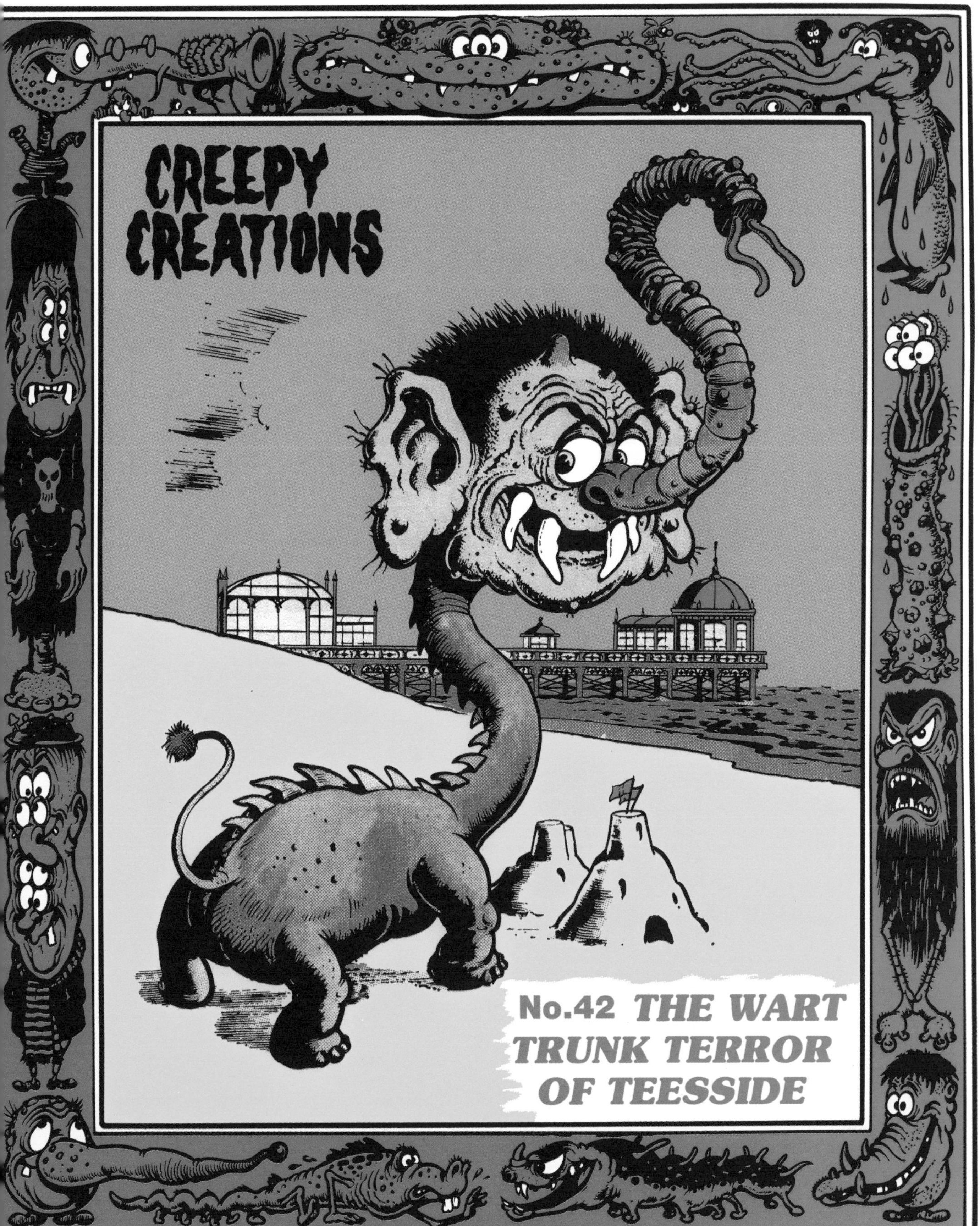
CREEPY CREATIONS
No.42 THE WART TRUNK TERROR OF TEESSIDE

This crazy "monster piece" wins £1 for JONATHAN LEE of CHARLESWORTH

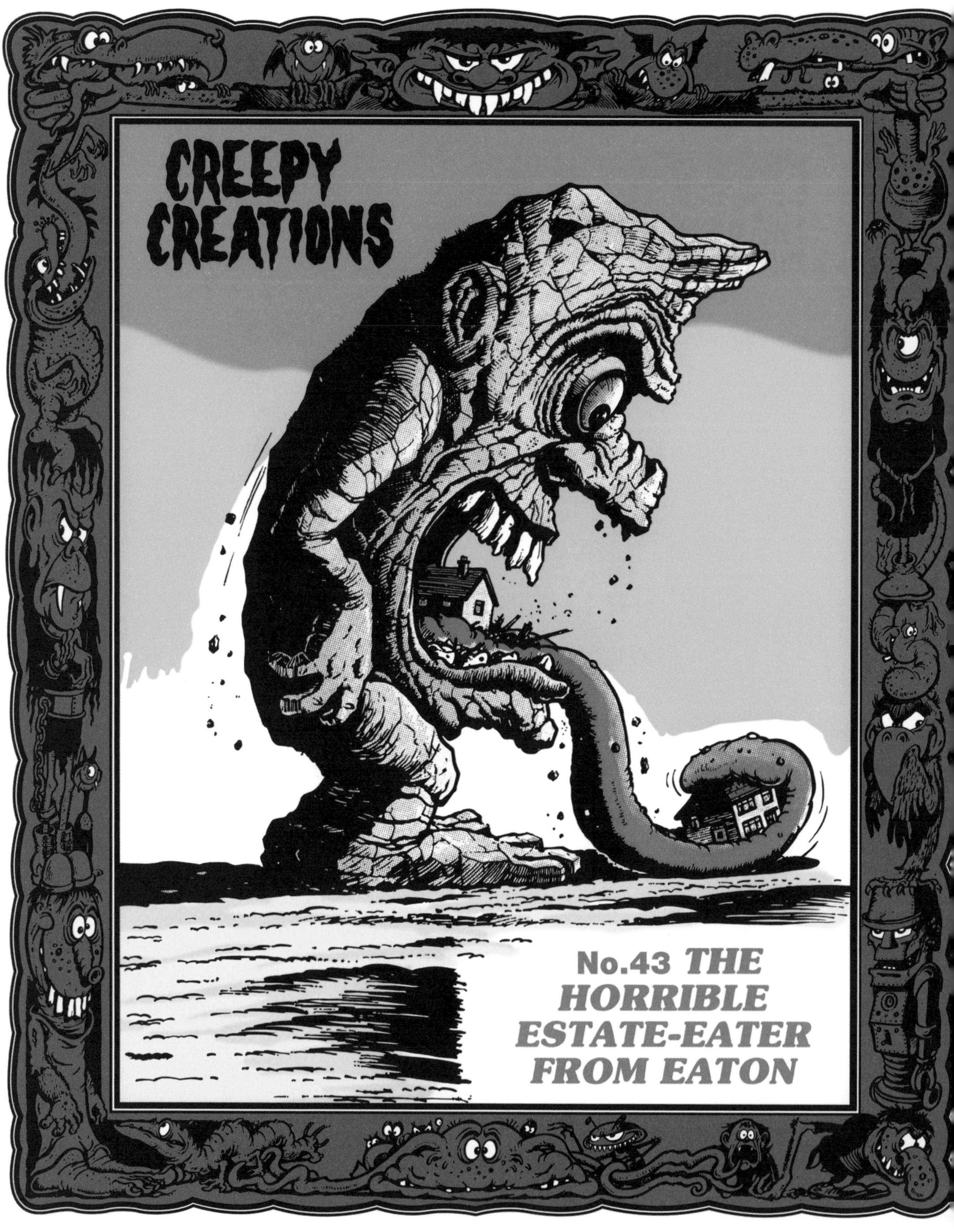
CREEPY CREATIONS
No.43 THE HORRIBLE ESTATE-EATER FROM EATON

This crazy "monster piece" wins £1 for AUSTIN BURROWS of CHORLEY

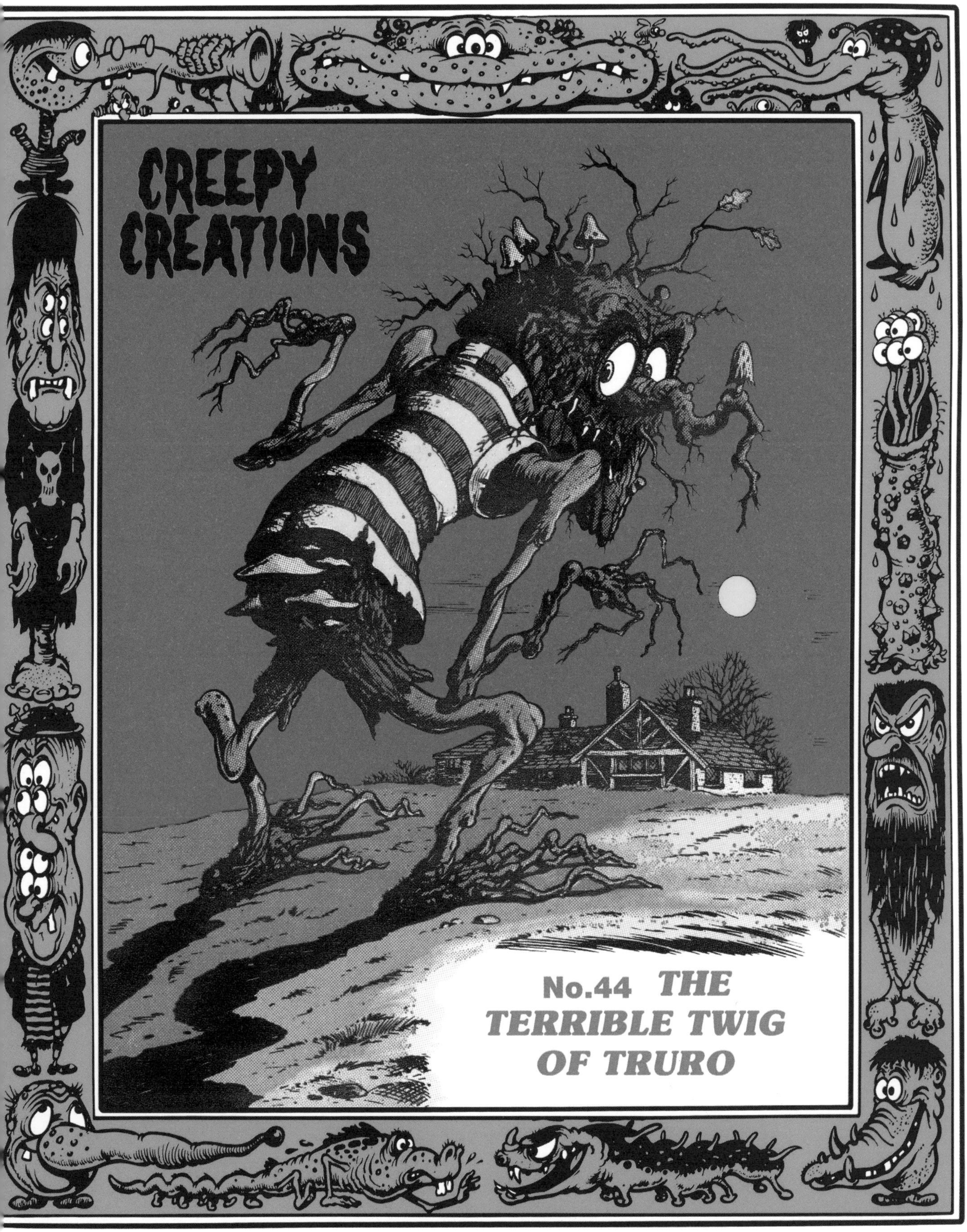
CREEPY CREATIONS
No.44 THE TERRIBLE TWIG OF TRURO

This crazy "monster piece" wins £1 for ANDREW CRINSON of BALSHAM

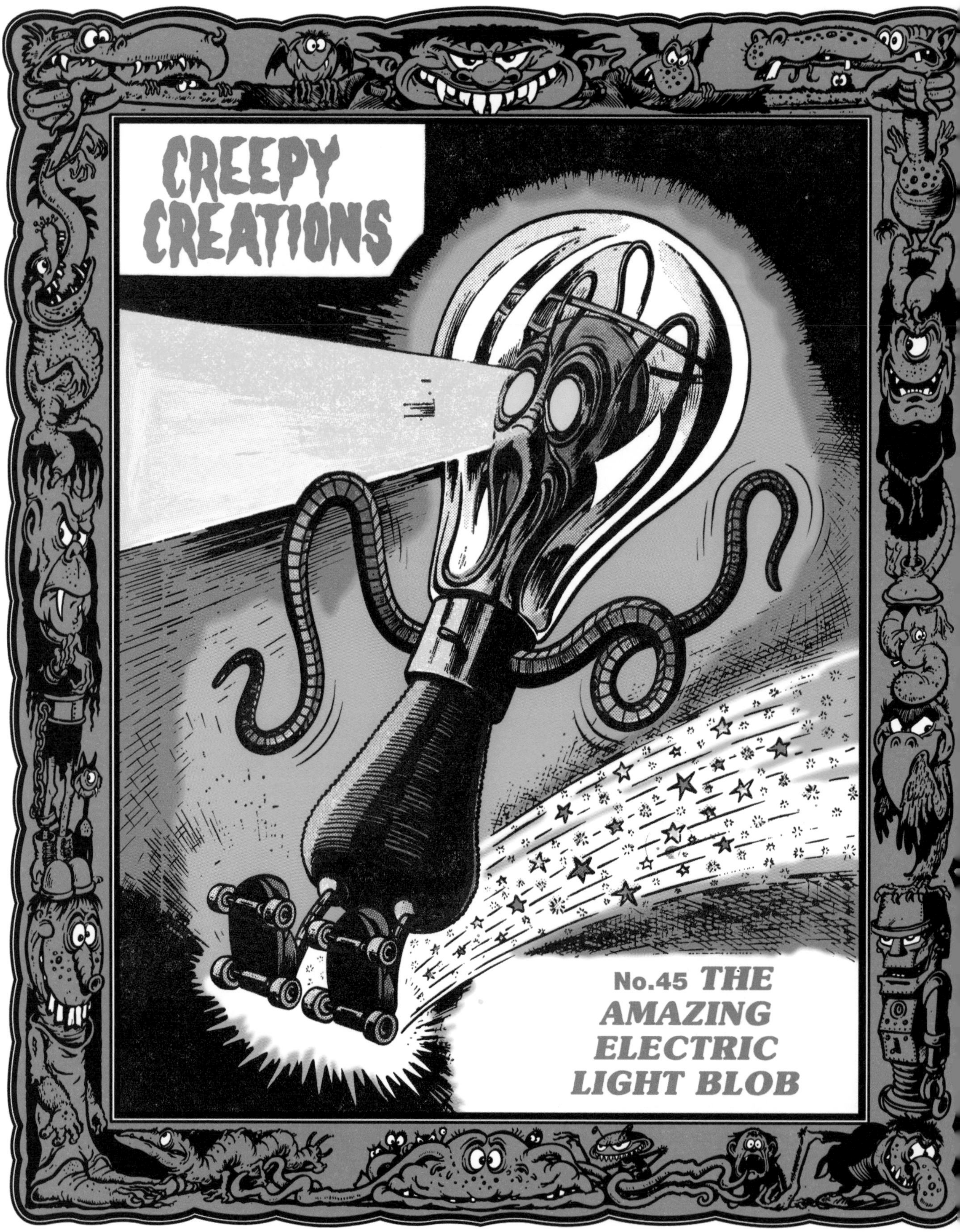
CREEPY CREATIONS
No.45 THE AMAZING ELECTRIC LIGHT BLOB

This crazy "monster piece" wins £1 for DEREK WAUGH of CHELMSFORD

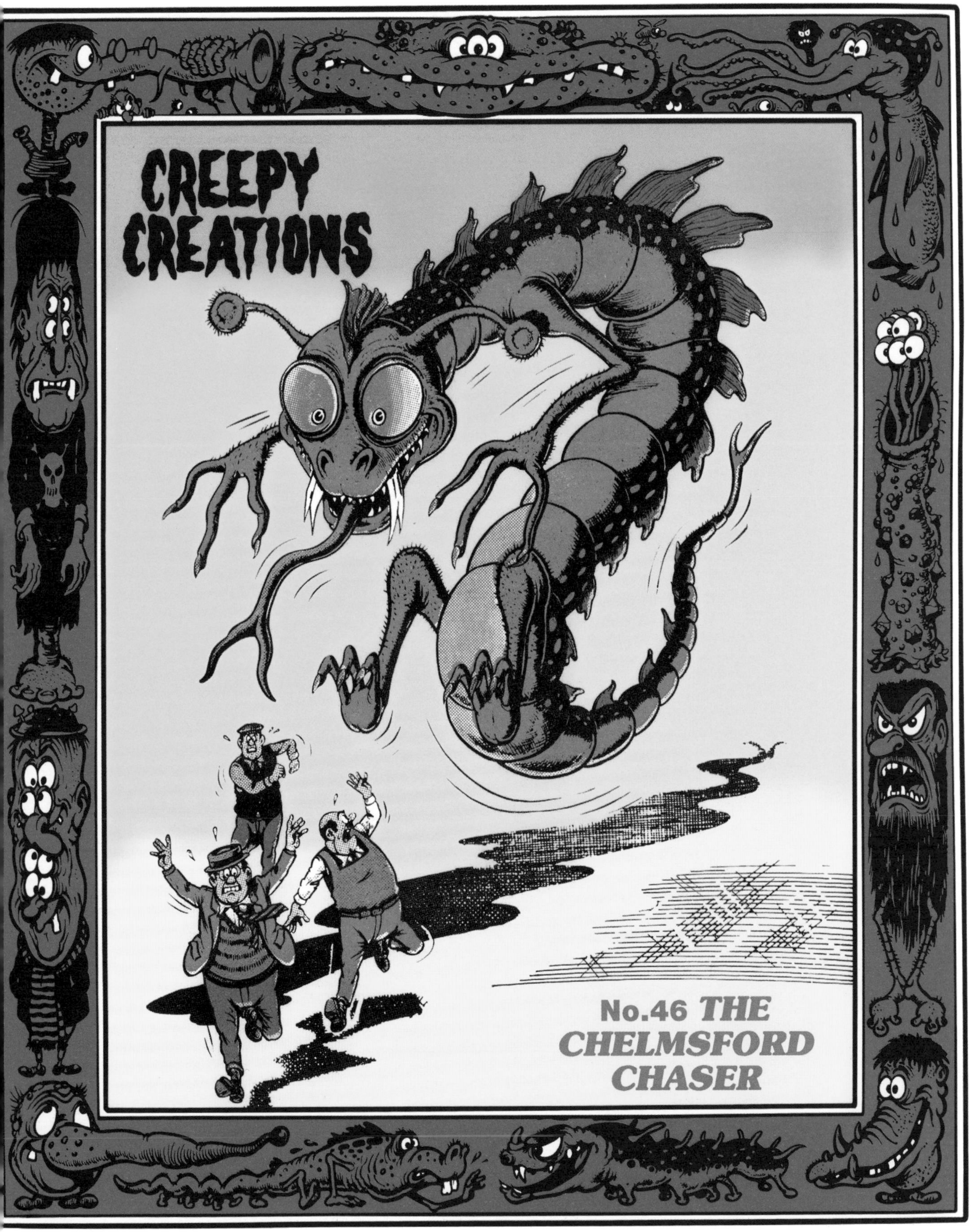
CREEPY CREATIONS
No.46 THE CHELMSFORD CHASER

This crazy "monster piece" wins £1 for GARY PATON of PRESTON

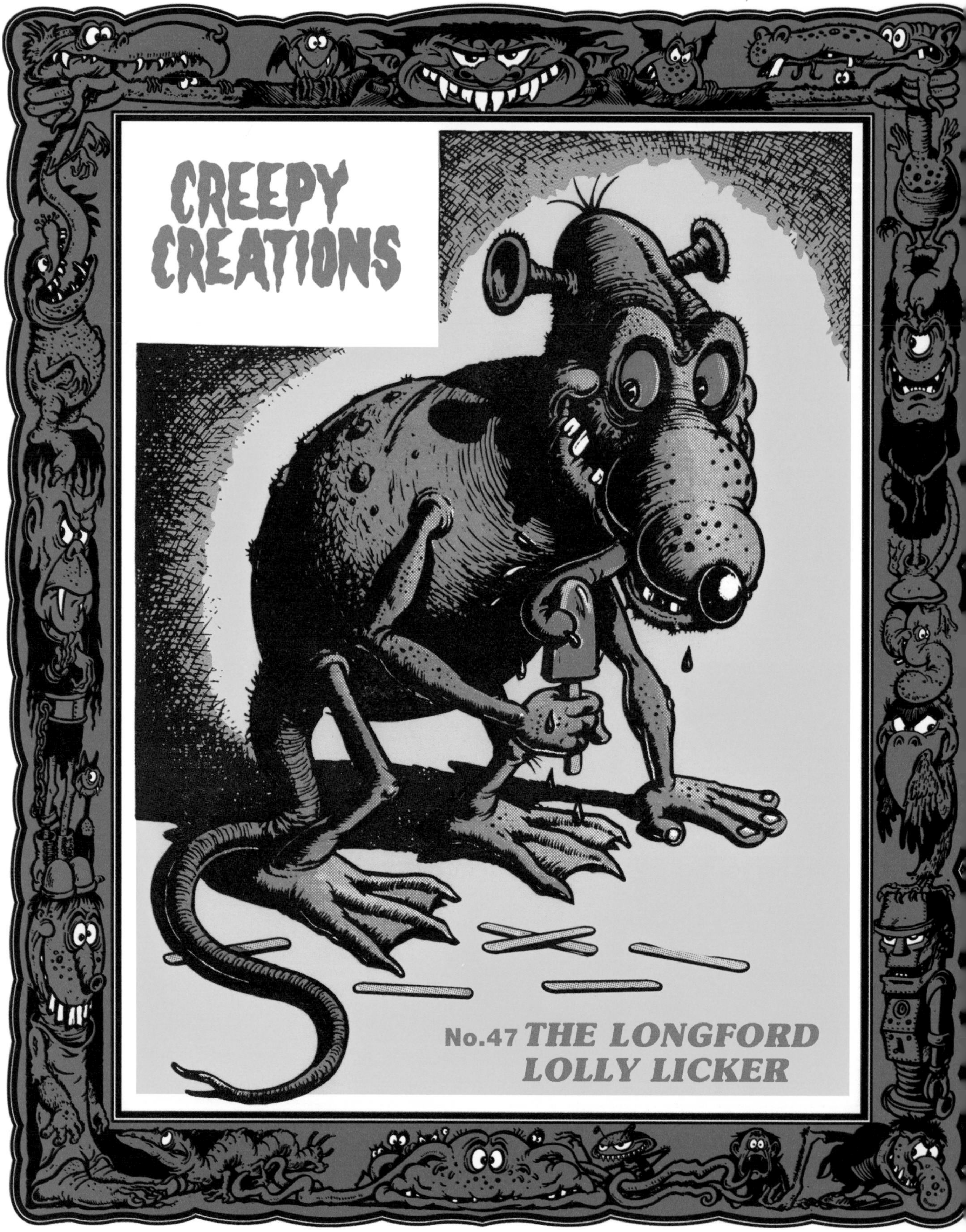
CREEPY CREATIONS
No.47 THE LONGFORD LOLLY LICKER

This crazy "monster piece" wins £1 for JOHN CHESHIRE of PORTSMOUTH

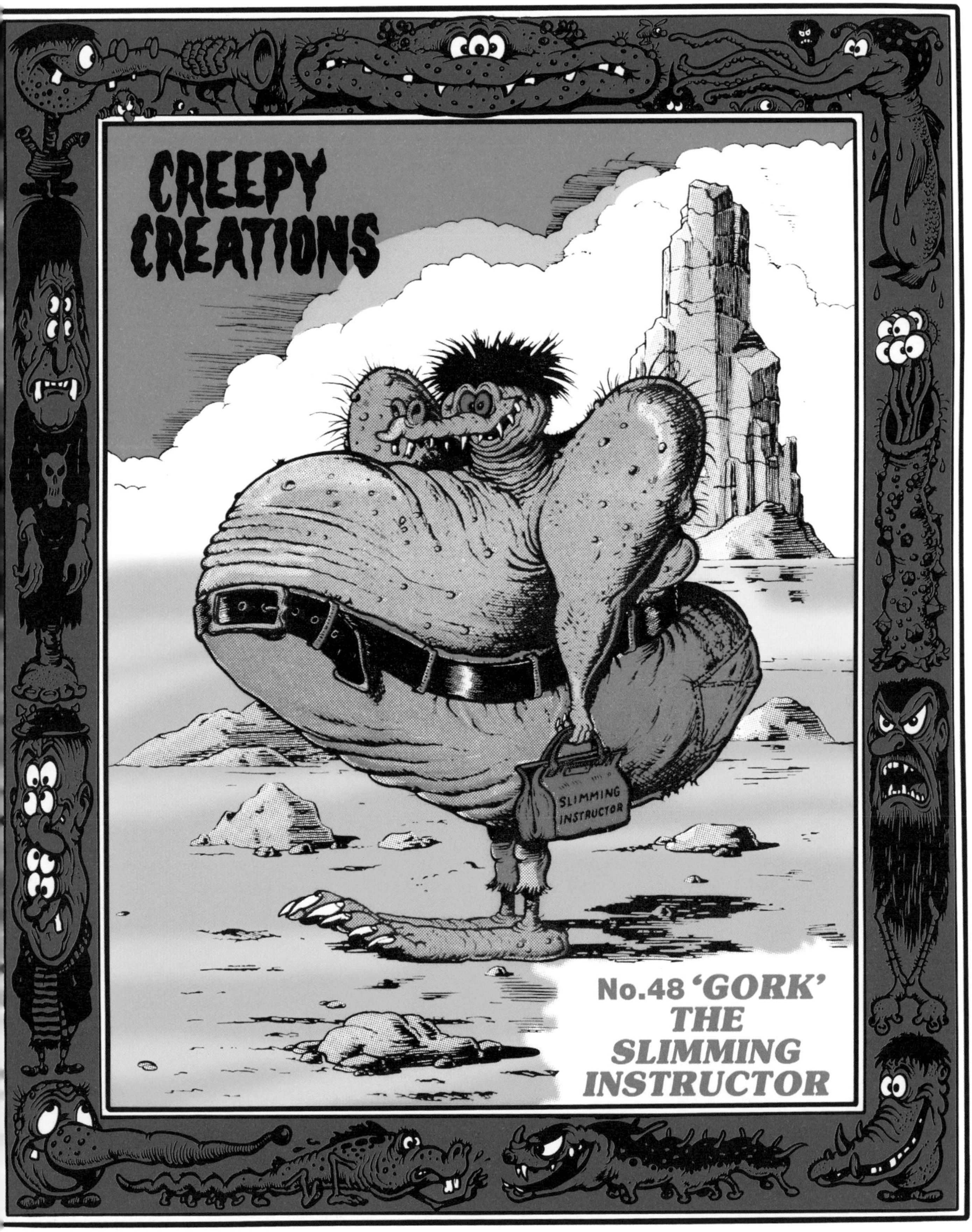
CREEPY CREATIONS
SLIMMING INSTRUCTOR
No.48 'GORK' THE SLIMMING INSTRUCTOR

This crazy "monster piece" wins £1 for ELIZABETH SHALLCROSS of NEWCASTLE

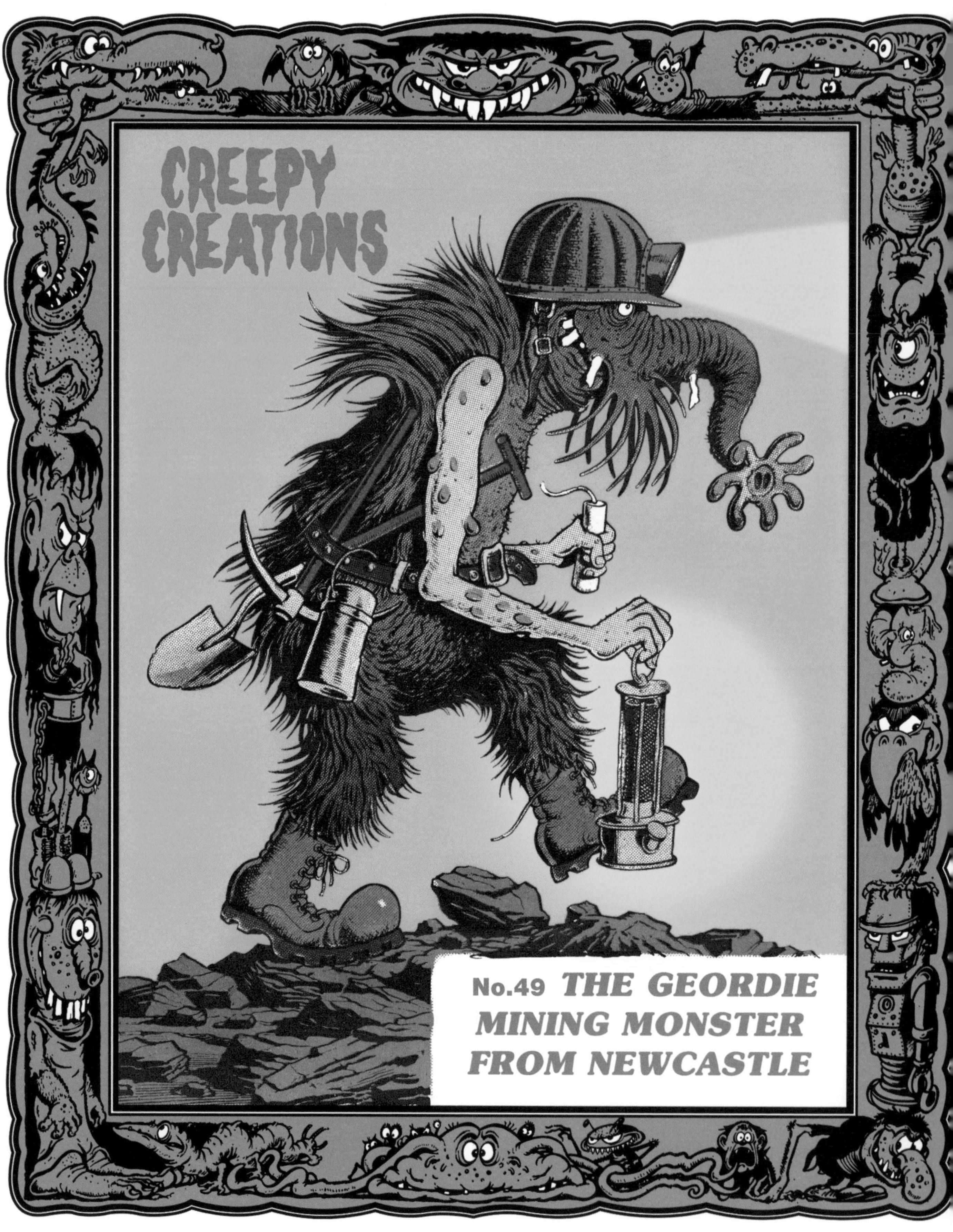
CREEPY CREATIONS
No.49 THE GEORDIE MINING MONSTER FROM NEWCASTLE

This crazy “monster piece” wins £1 for DUNCAN KOHN of TAUNTON

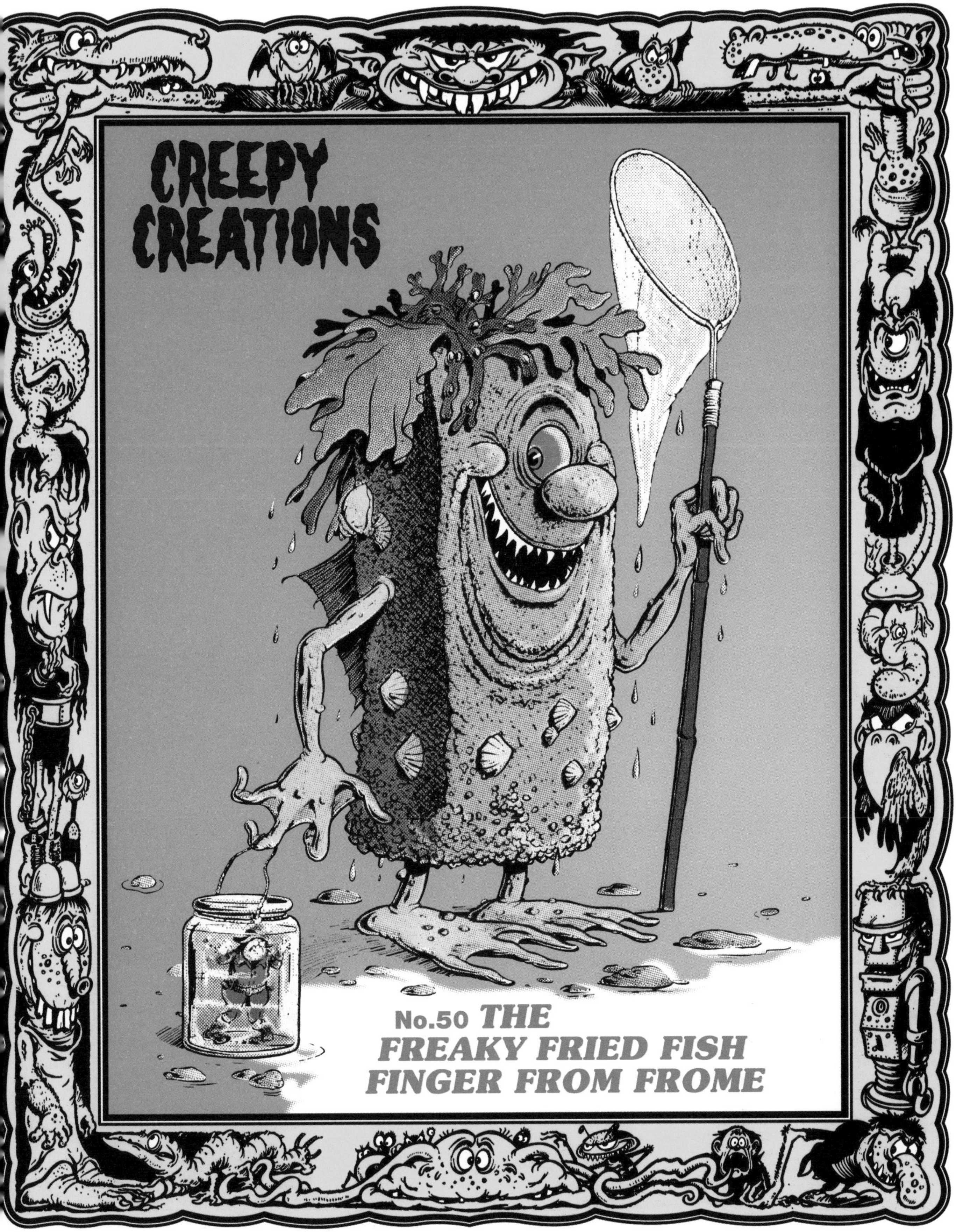
CREEPY CREATIONS
No.50 THE FREAKY FRIED FISH FINGER FROM FROME

This crazy "monster piece" wins £1 for JEREMY STEENE of EDGWARE

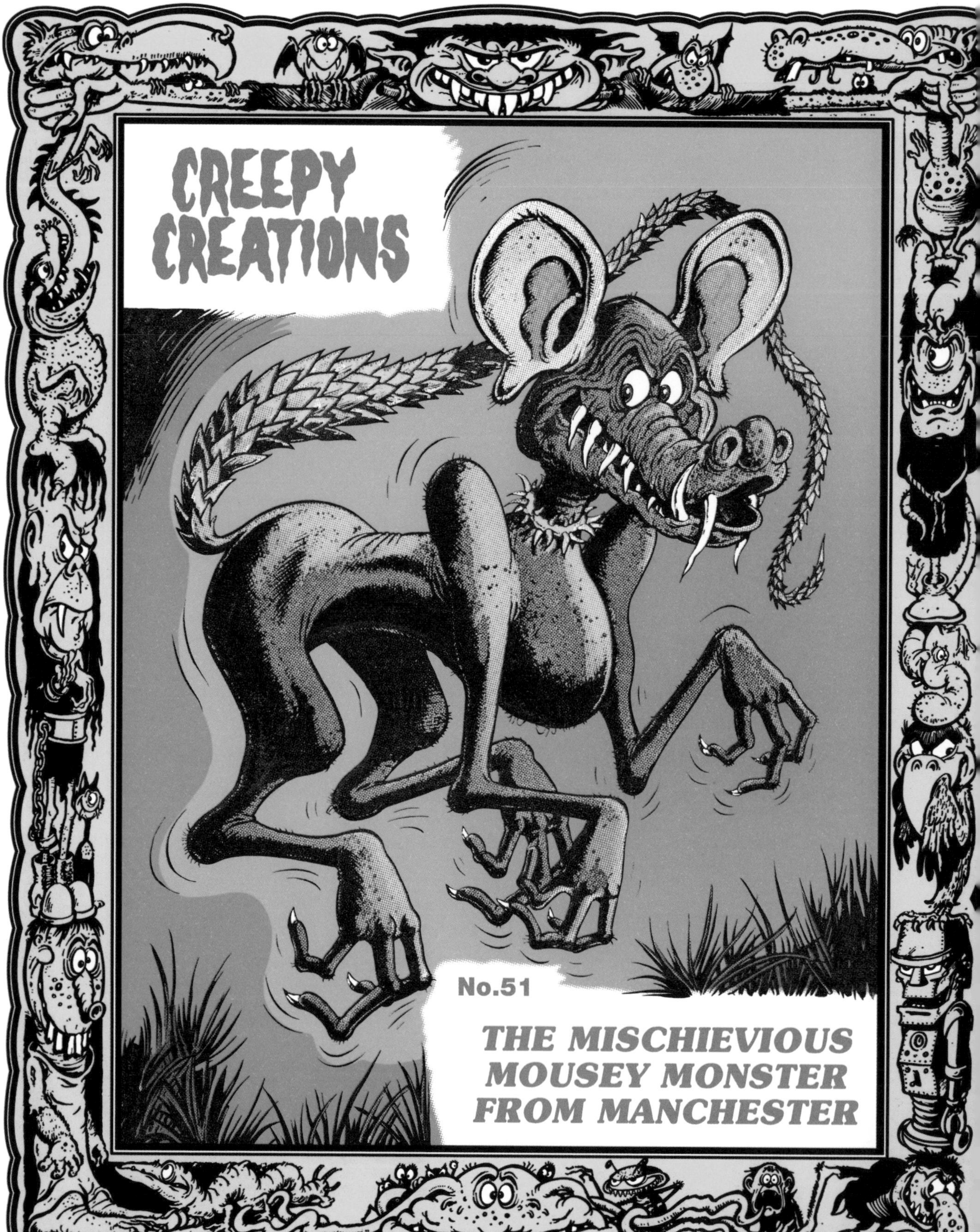
CREEPY CREATIONS
No.51
THE MISCHIEVIOUS MOUSEY MONSTER FROM MANCHESTER

This crazy "monster piece" wins £1 for JOSEPH UNSWORTH of WIGAN

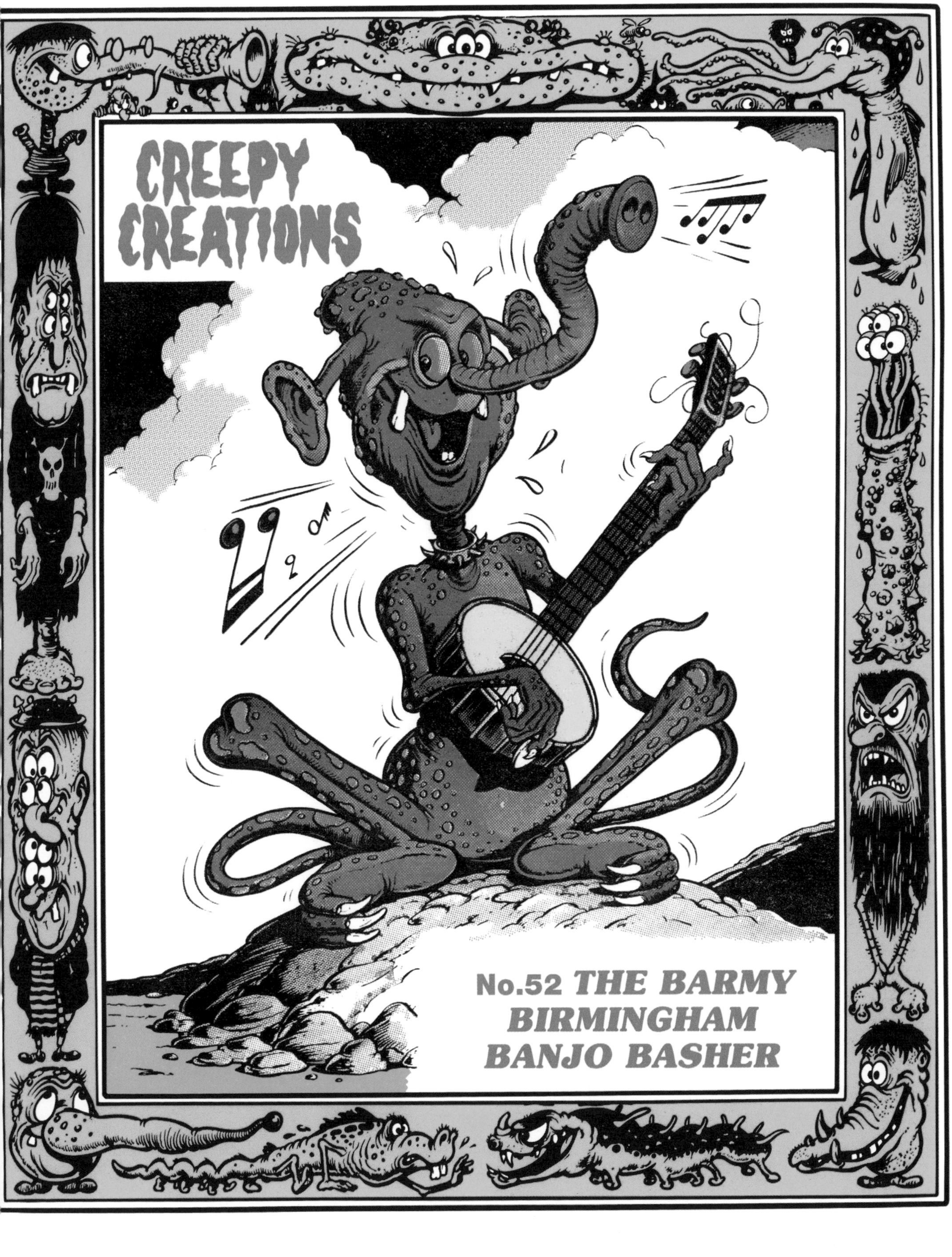
CREEPY CREATIONS
No.52 THE BARMY BIRMINGHAM BANJO BASHER

This crazy "monster piece" wins £1 for M. SQUIRE of BEXLEY HEATH

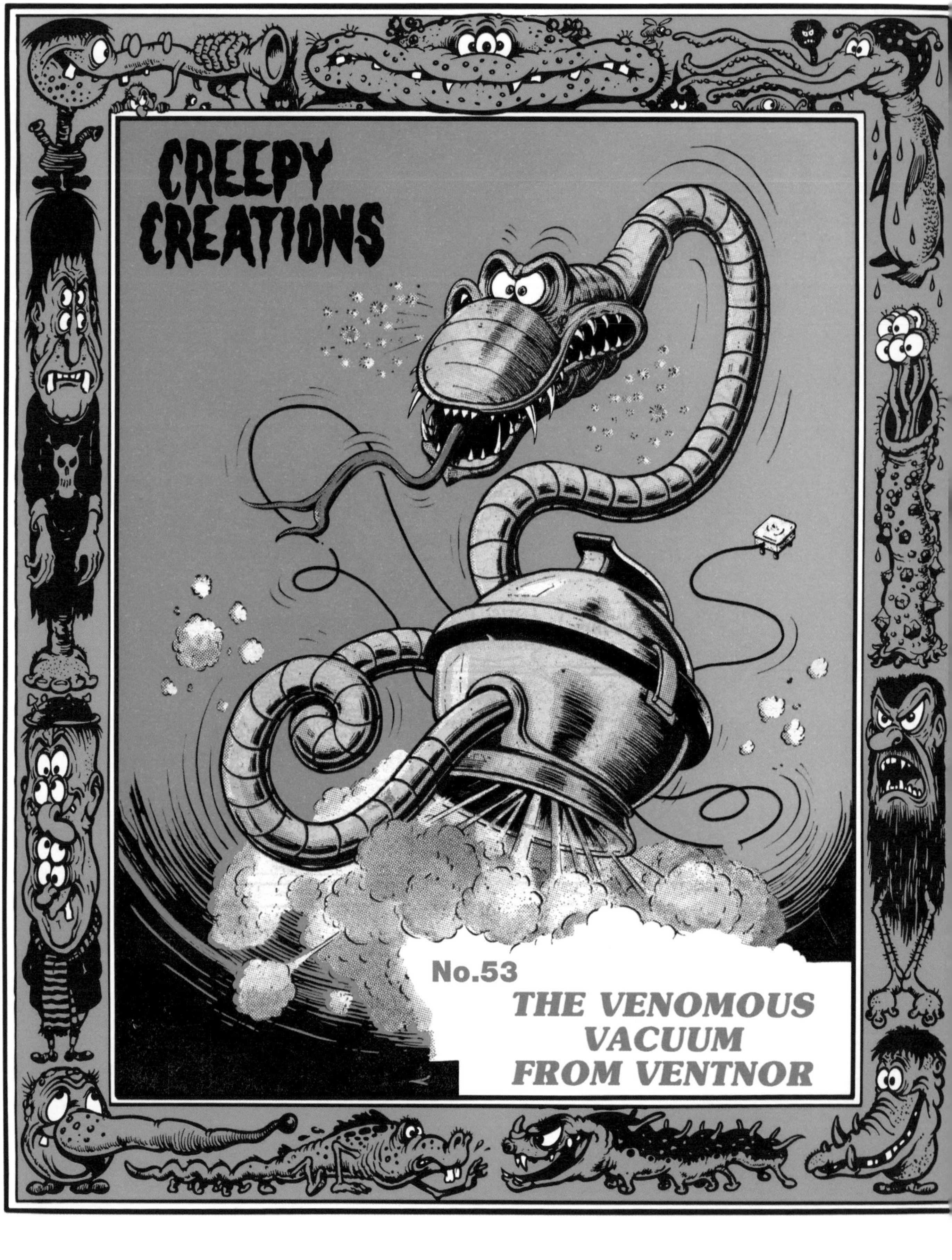
CREEPY CREATIONS
No.53
THE VENOMOUS VACUUM FROM VENTNOR

This crazy "monster piece" wins £1 for ALAN BLUNDELL of LINCOLN

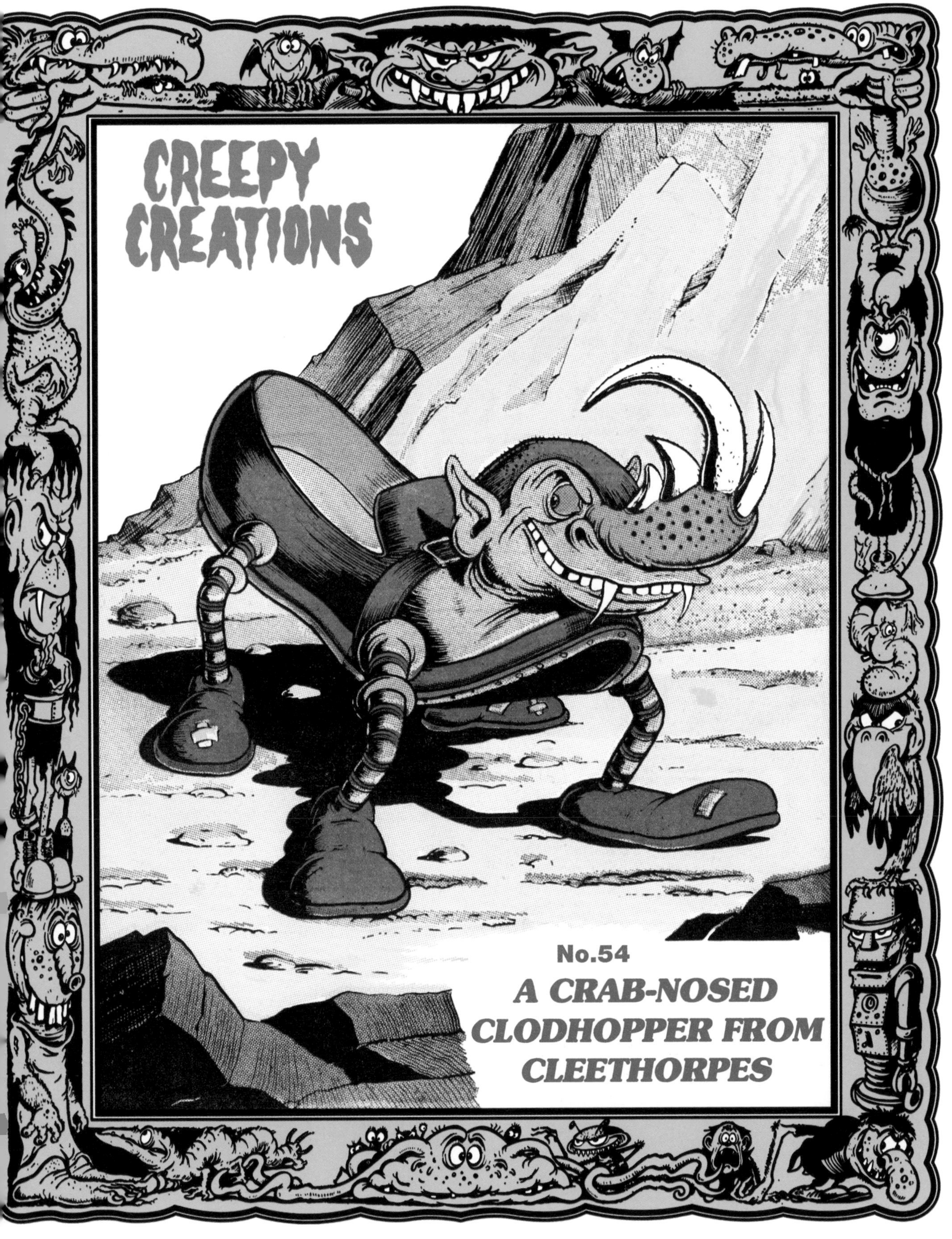
CREEPY CREATIONS
No.54
A CRAB-NOSED CLODHOPPER FROM CLEETHORPES

This crazy "monster piece" wins £1 for RICHARD DYSON of REDHILL

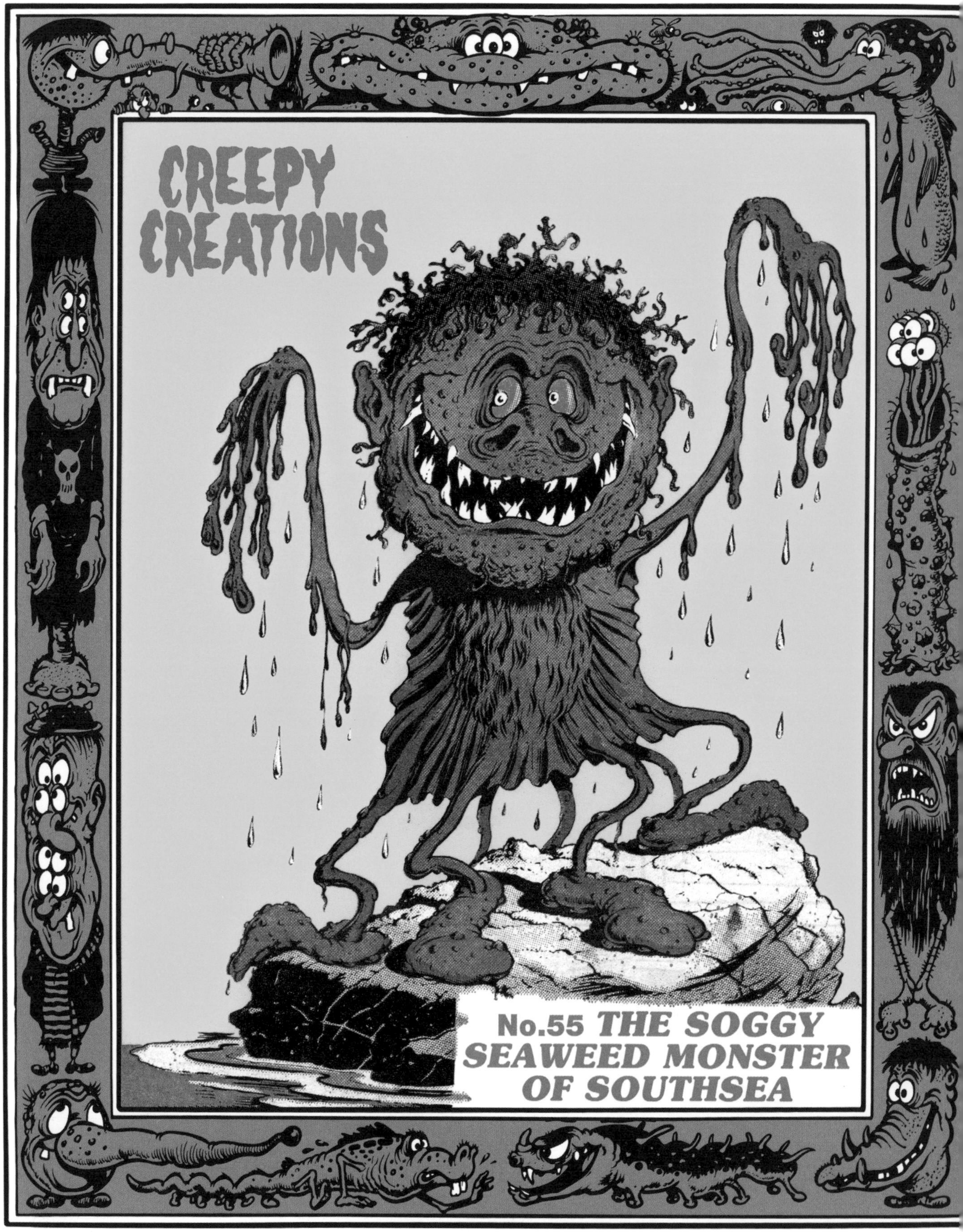
CREEPY CREATIONS
No.55 THE SOGGY SEAWEED MONSTER OF SOUTHSEA

This crazy "monster piece" wins £1 for A. CUTTILL of LEICESTER

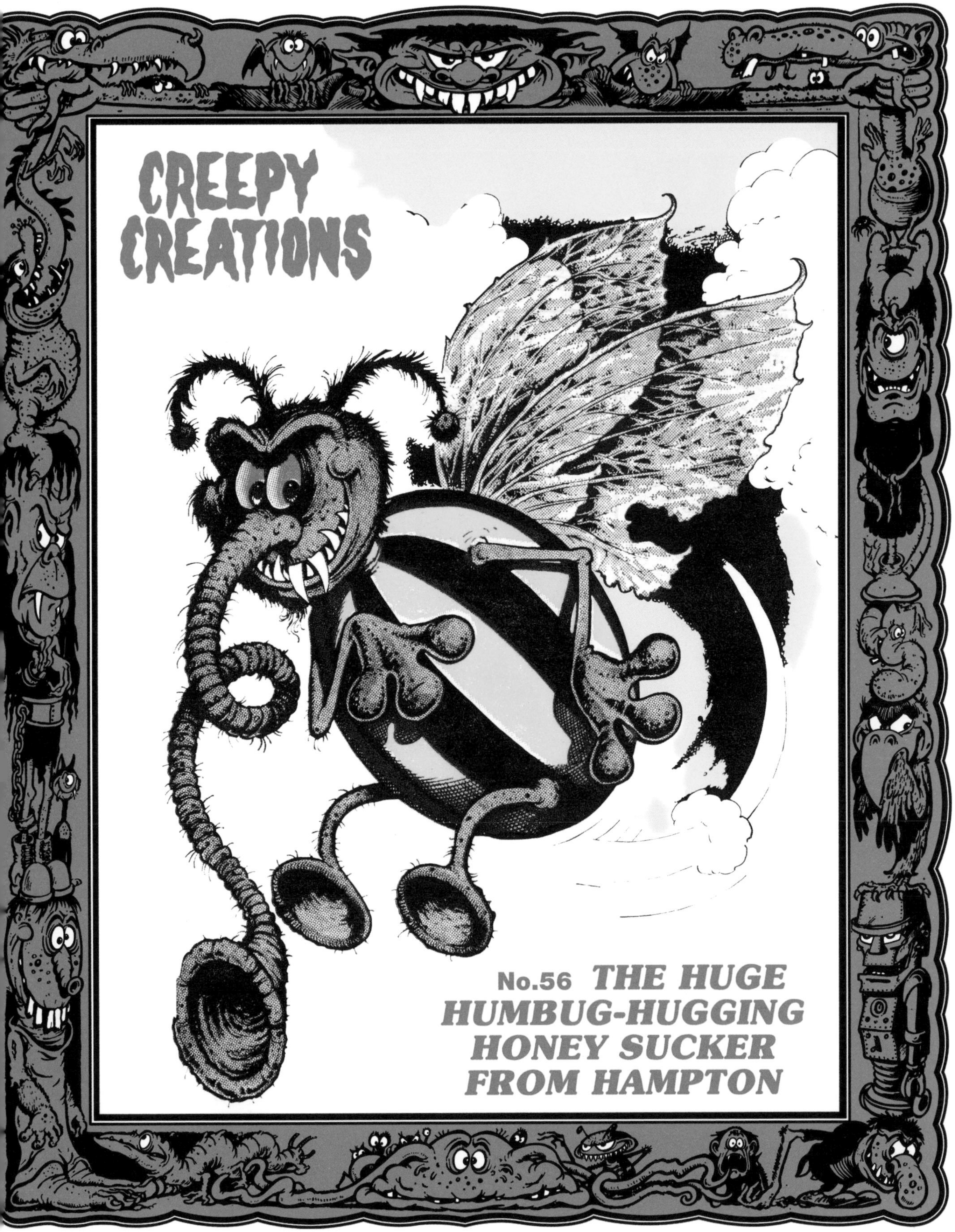
CREEPY CREATIONS
No.56 THE HUGE HUMBUG-HUGGING HONEY SUCKER FROM HAMPTON

This crazy "monster piece" wins £1 for LYNNE BISHOP of BRIGHTON

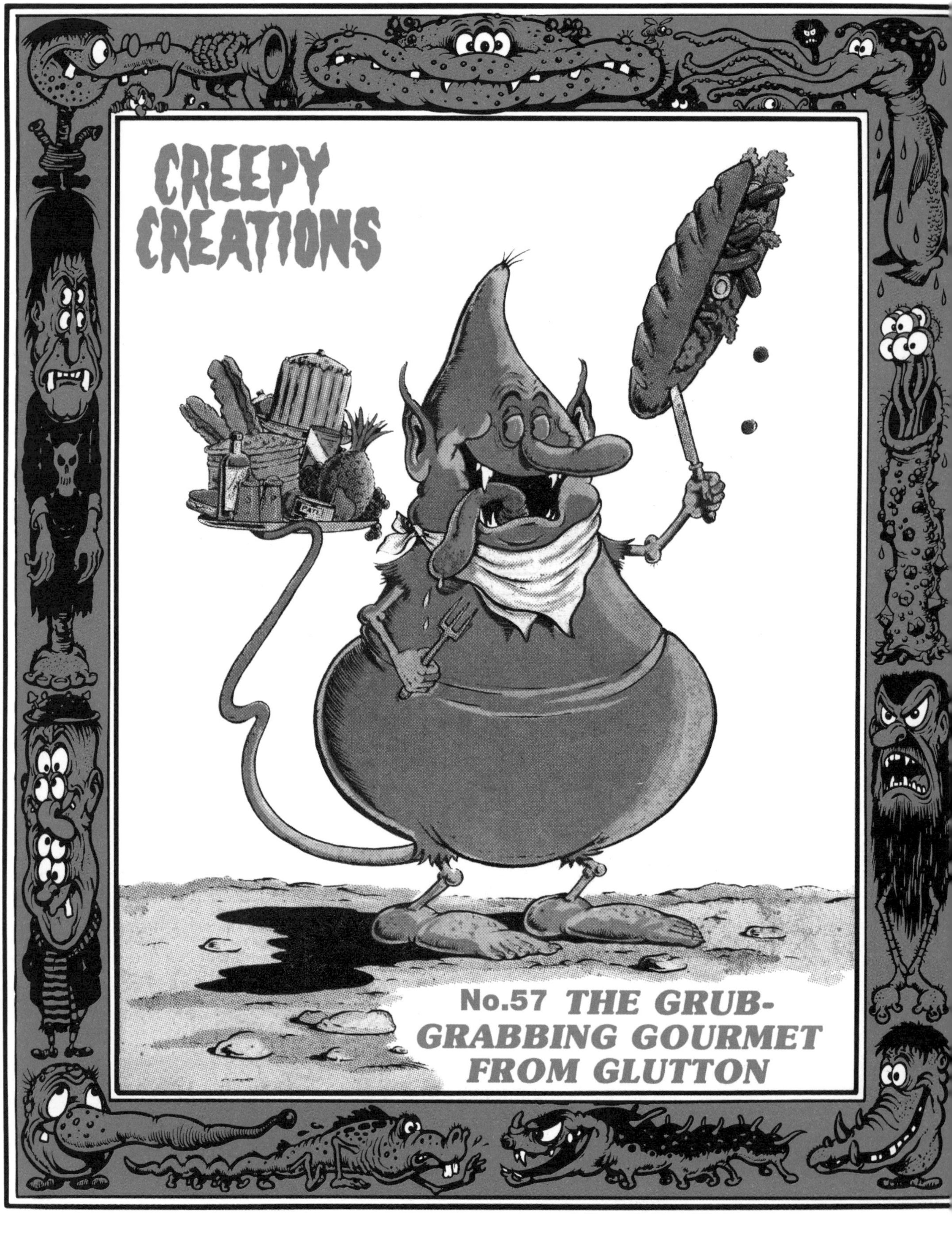
CREEPY CREATIONS
No.57 THE GRUB-GRABBING GOURMET FROM GLUTTON

This crazy "monster piece" wins £1 for ROBERT GEORGE of BLACKWOOD

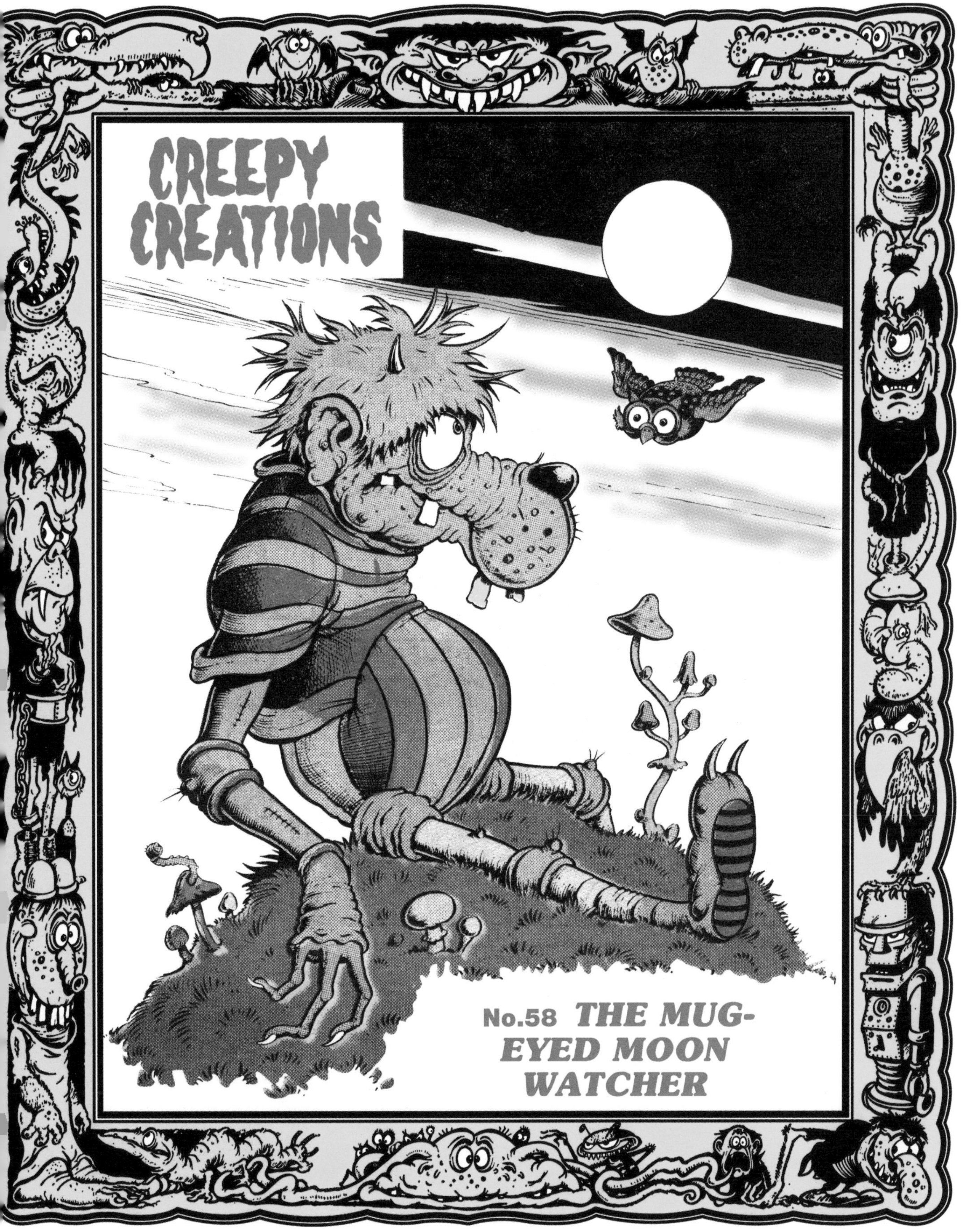
CREEPY CREATIONS
No.58 THE MUG-EYED MOON WATCHER

This crazy “monster piece” wins £1 for MARTIN PAUL of BARNSLEY

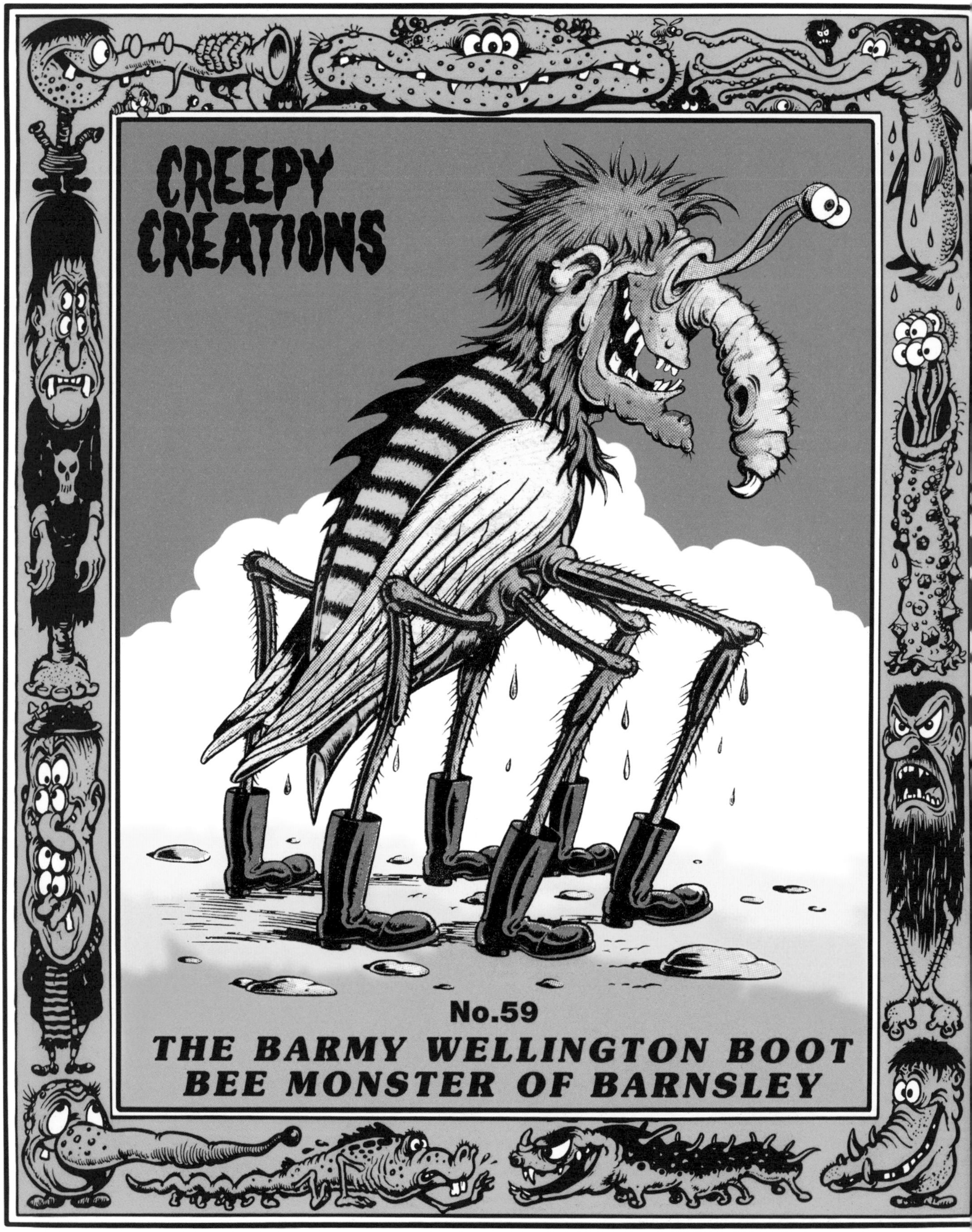
CREEPY CREATIONS
No.59
THE BARMY WELLINGTON BOOT BEE MONSTER OF BARNSLEY

This crazy "monster piece" wins £1 for STEVEN PARNELL of HACKNALL

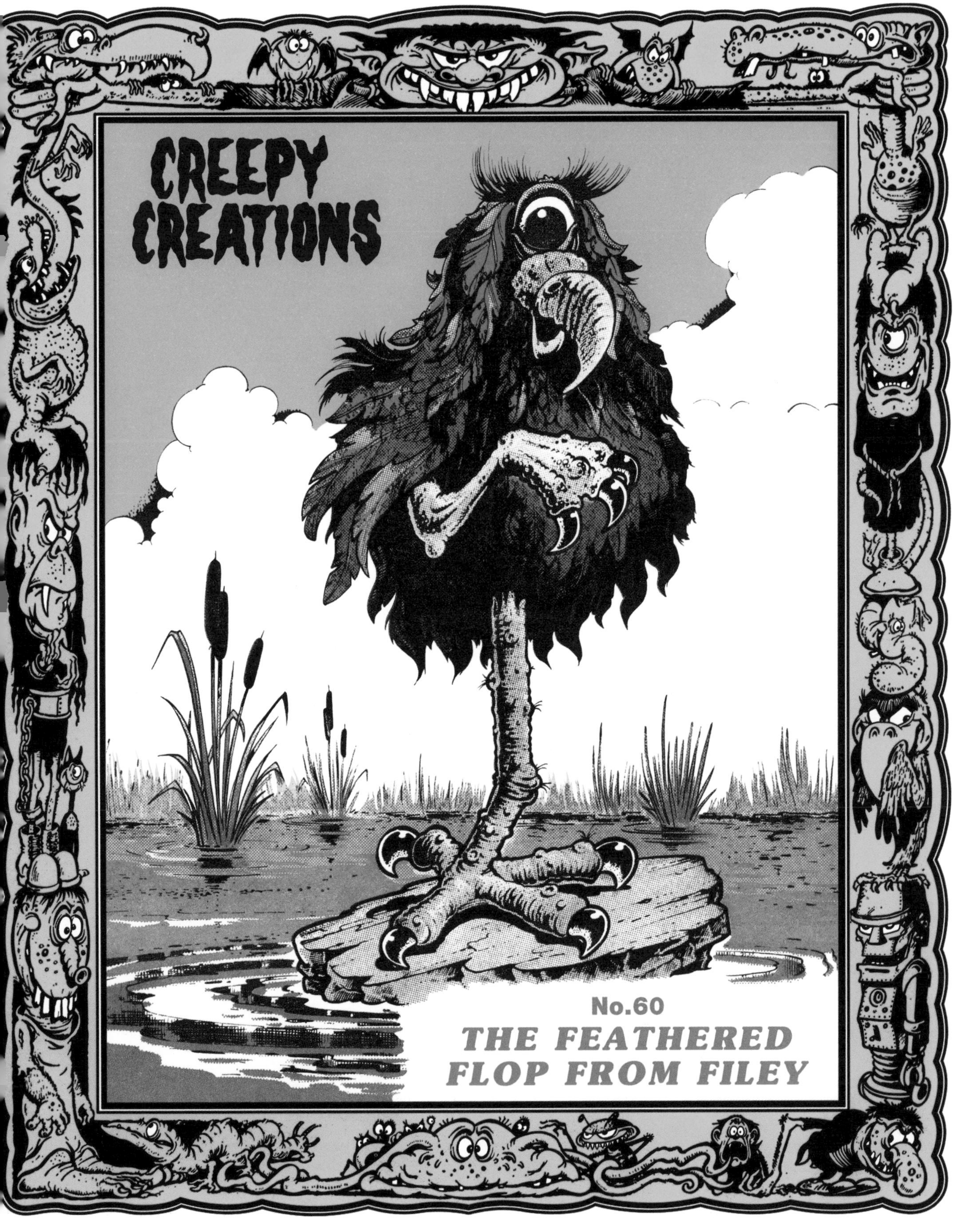
CREEPY CREATIONS
No.60
THE FEATHERED FLOP FROM FILEY

This crazy "monster piece" wins £1 for IAN JONES of EBBW VALE

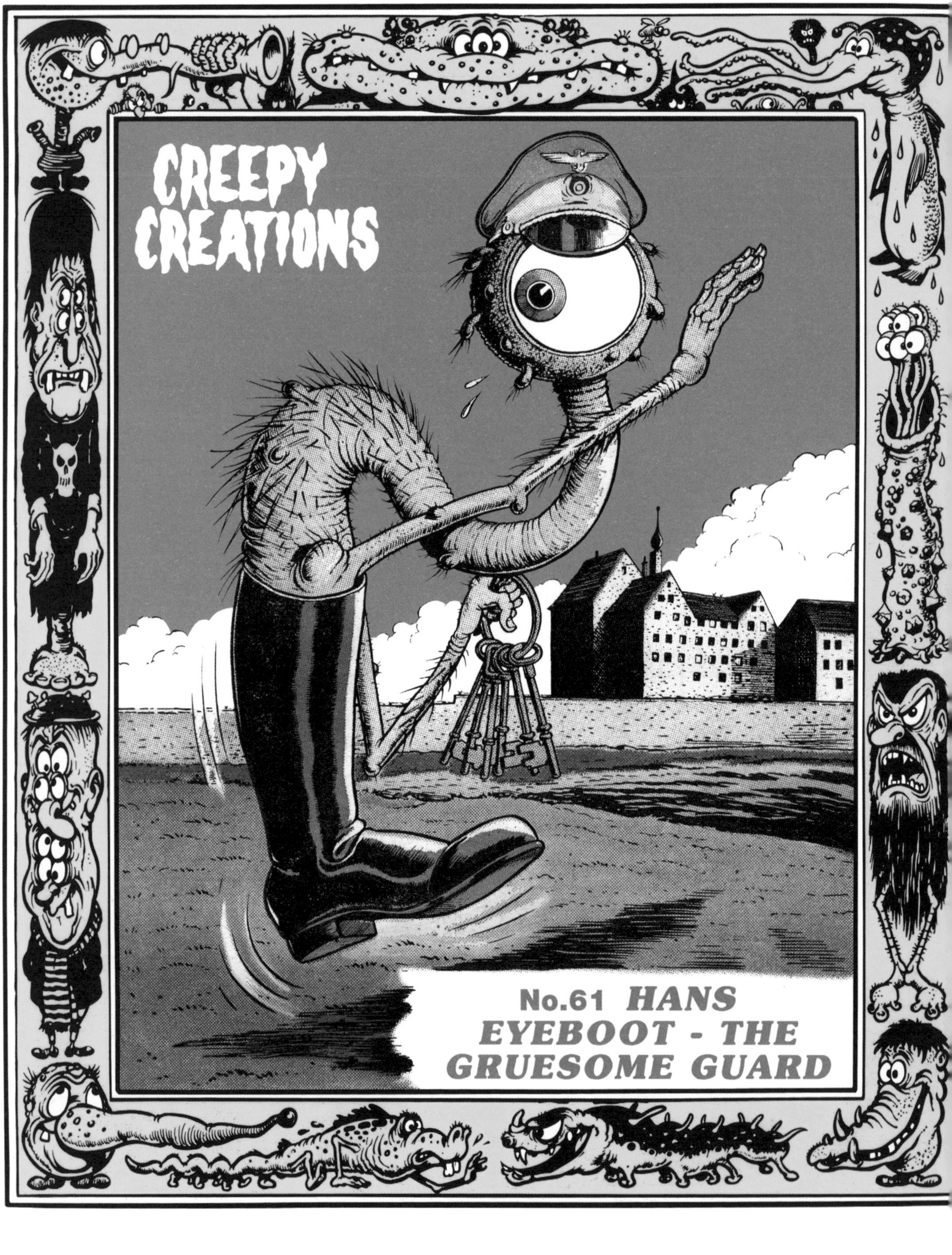
CREEPY CREATIONS
No.61 HANS EYEBOOT - THE GRUESOME GUARD

This crazy "monster piece" wins £1 for COLIN BIGGINS of BARROW-IN-FURNESS

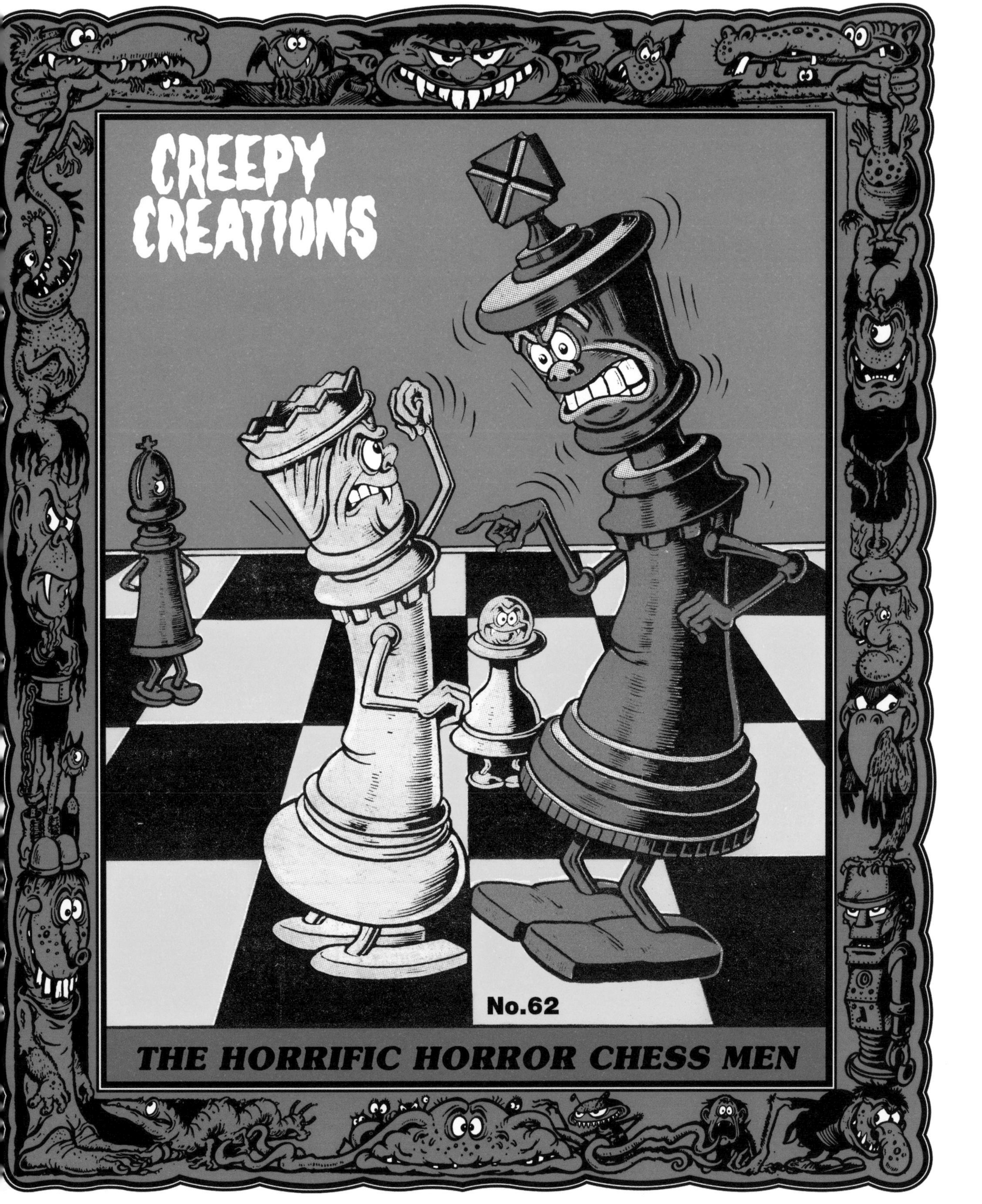

CREEPY CREATIONS
No.62
THE HORRIFIC HORROR CHESS MEN

This crazy "monster piece" wins £1 for ALAN BLUNDELL of LINCOLN

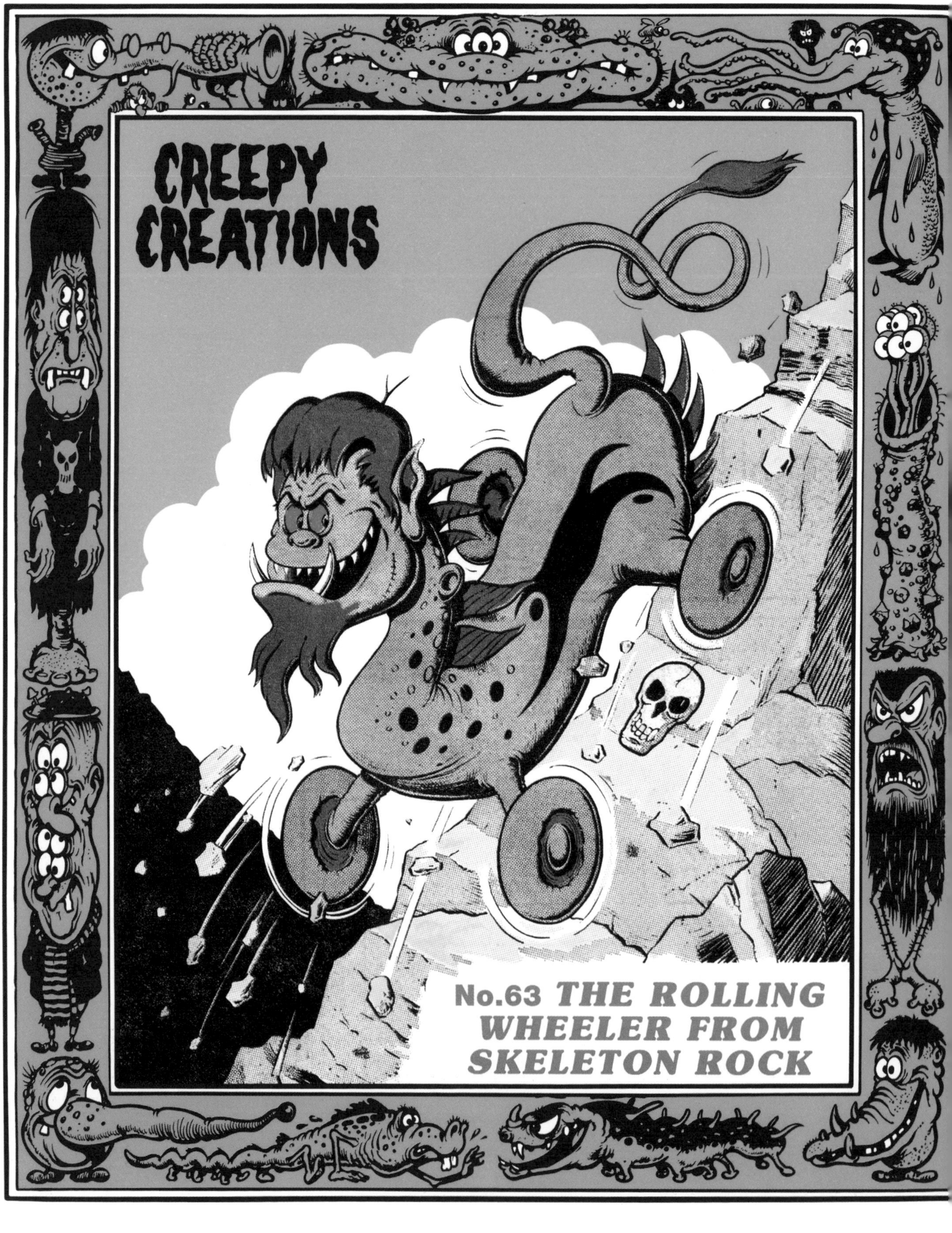
CREEPY CREATIONS
No.63 THE ROLLING WHEELER FROM SKELETON ROCK

This crazy “monster piece” wins £1 for RICHARD CORDEN of MANSFIELD

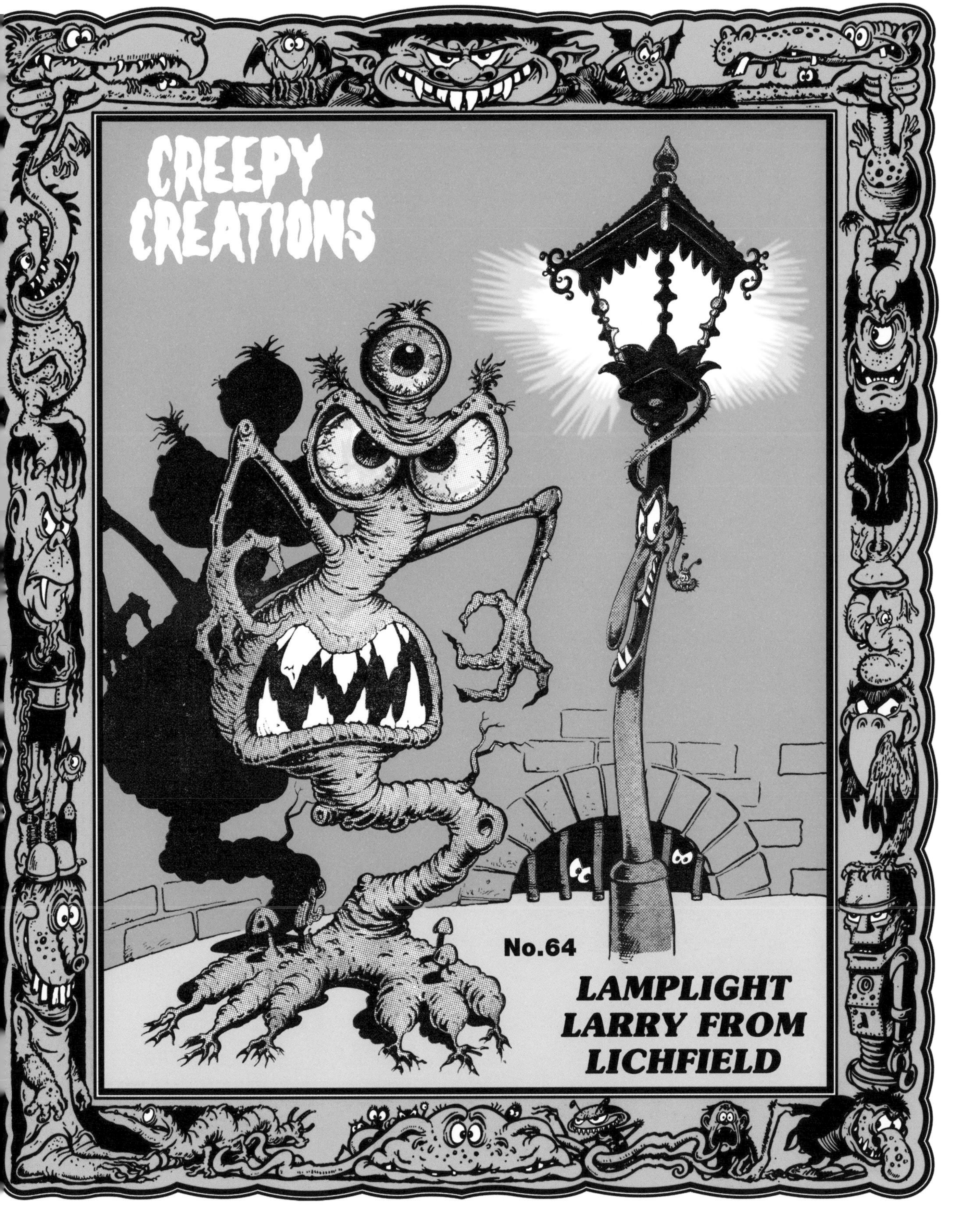
CREEPY CREATIONS
No.64
LAMPLIGHT LARRY FROM LICHFIELD

This crazy “monster piece” wins £1 for PAUL WORMULL of HAROLD HILL

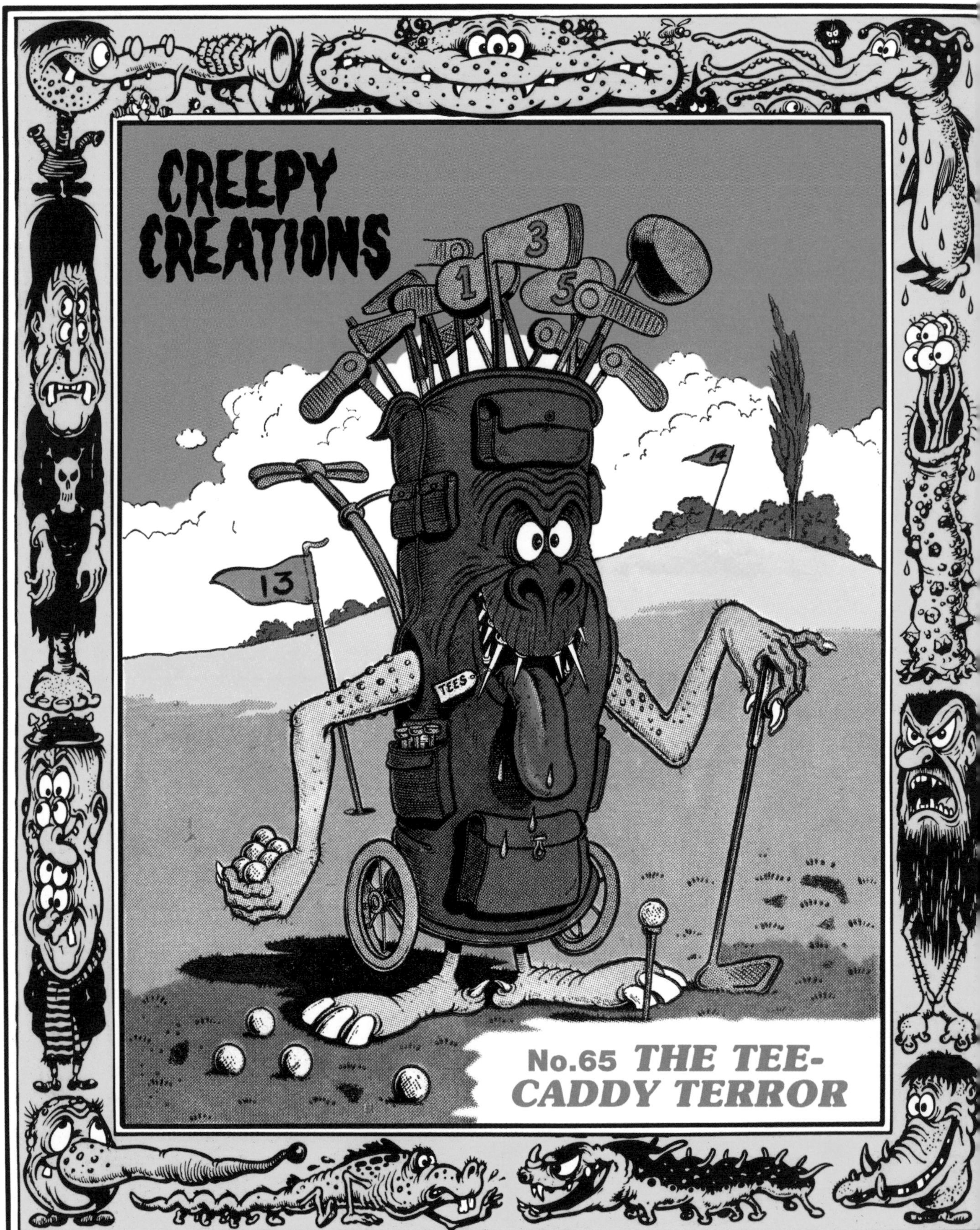
CREEPY CREATIONS
3
1
5
13
14
TEES
No.65 THE TEE-CADDY TERROR

This crazy "monster piece" wins £1 for MARK DAWSON of HAZLEMERE

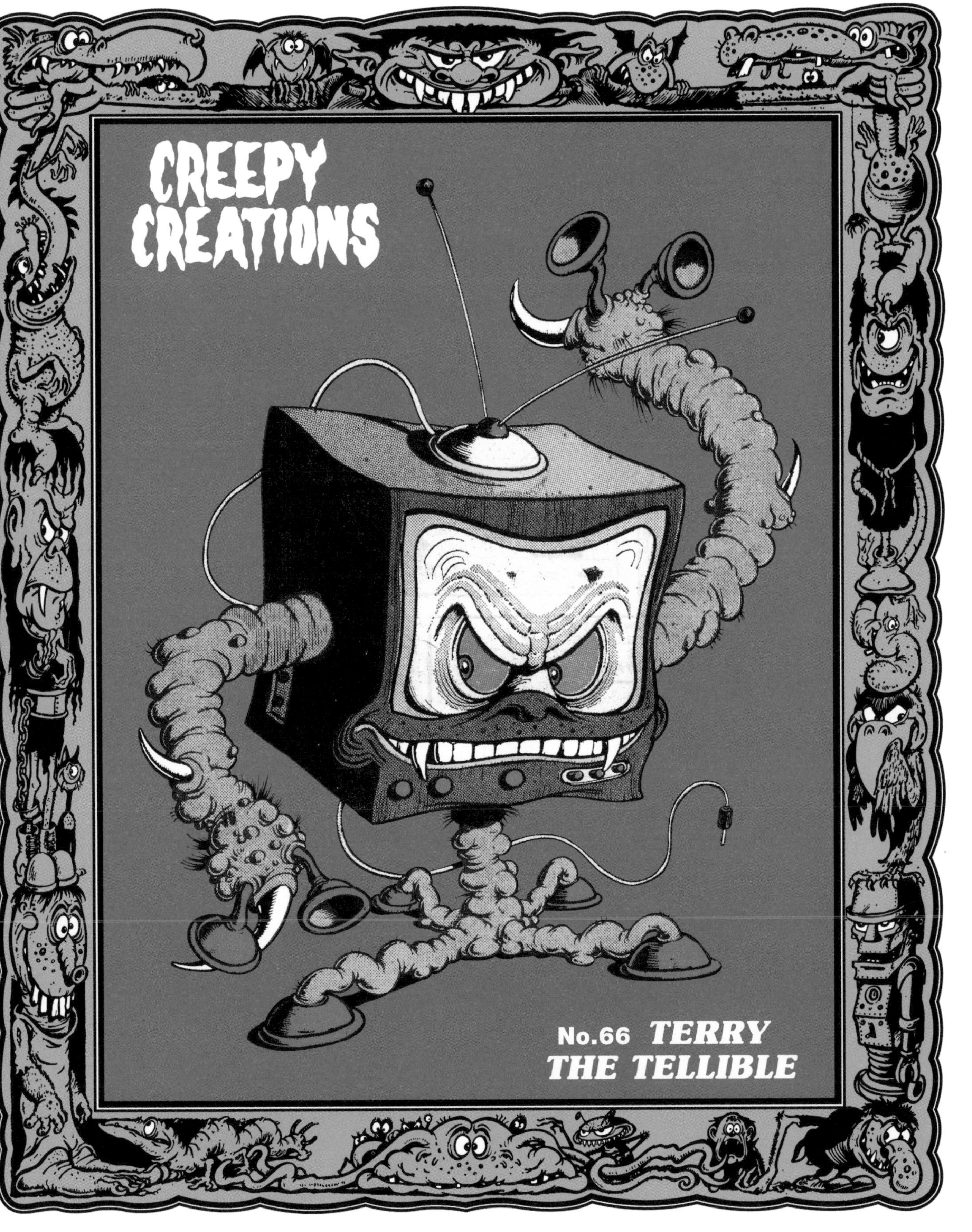
CREEPY CREATIONS
No.66 TERRY THE TELLIBLE

This crazy "monster piece" wins £1 for STEPHEN CHALK of WOOD GREEN

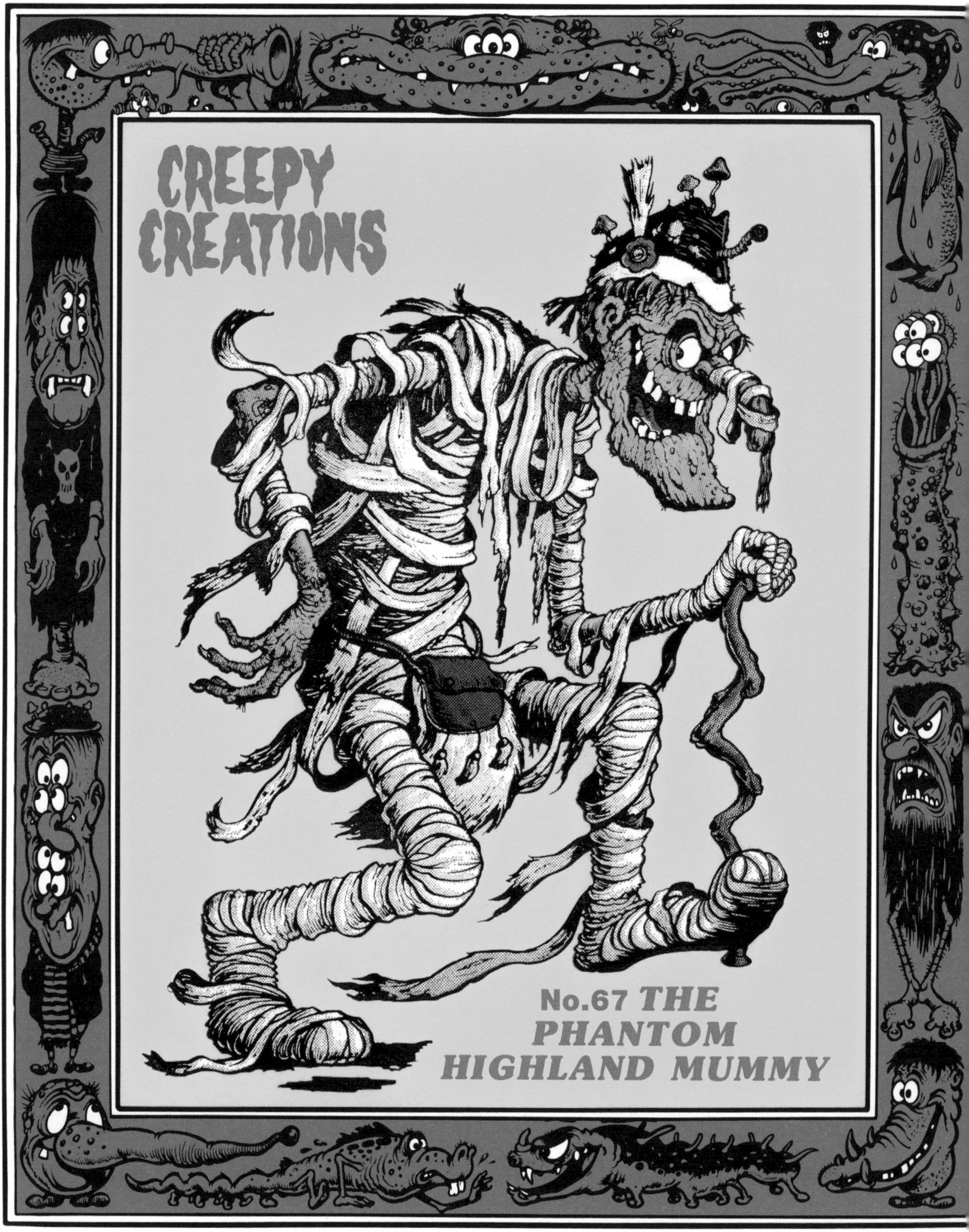
CREEPY CREATIONS
No.67 THE PHANTOM HIGHLAND MUMMY

This crazy "monster piece" wins £1 for ANDREW FORRESTER of MANSFIELD

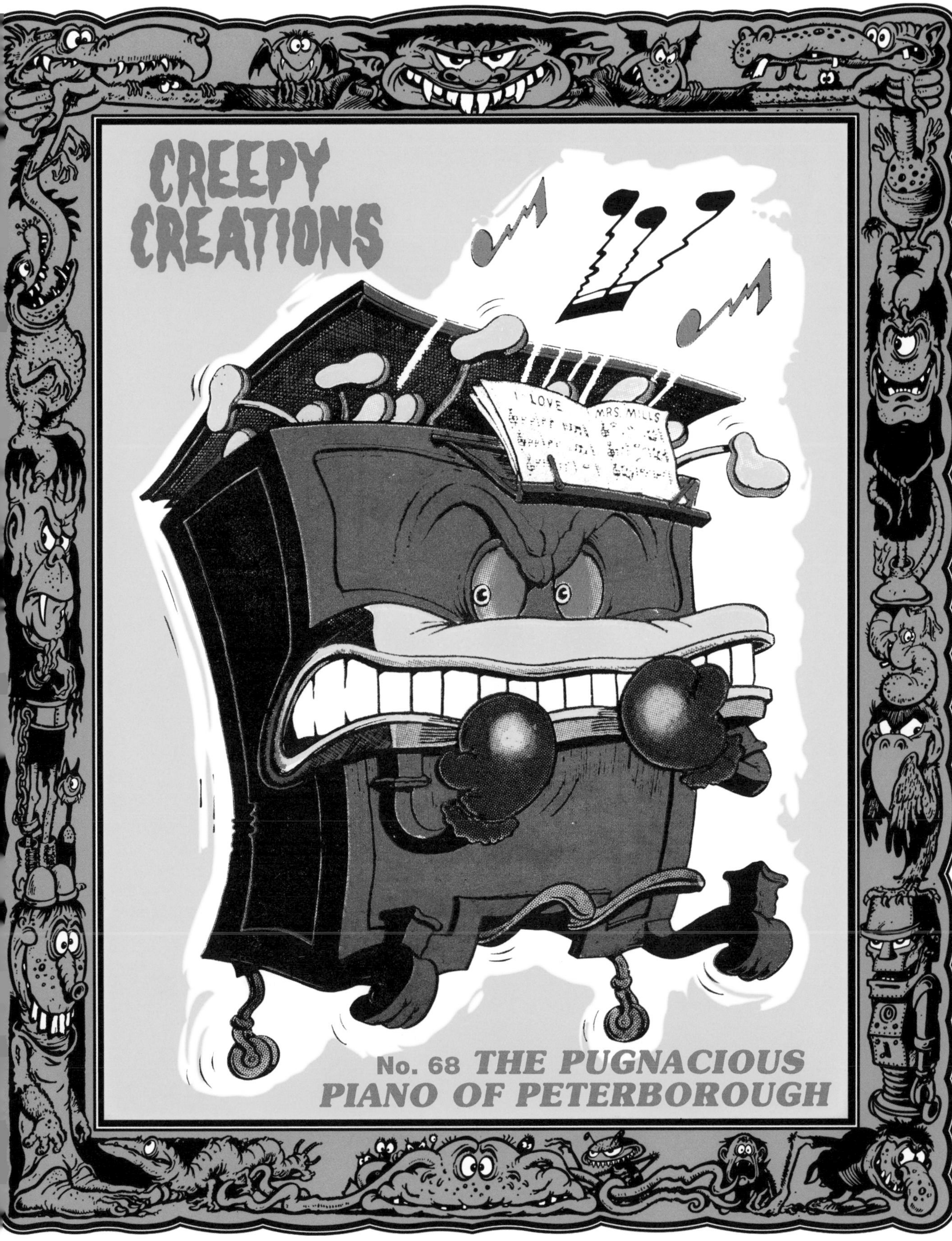
CREEPY CREATIONS
I LOVE MRS. MILLS
No. 68 THE PUGNACIOUS PIANO OF PETERBOROUGH

This crazy “monster piece” wins £1 for HARRIET BENNETT of MANCHESTER

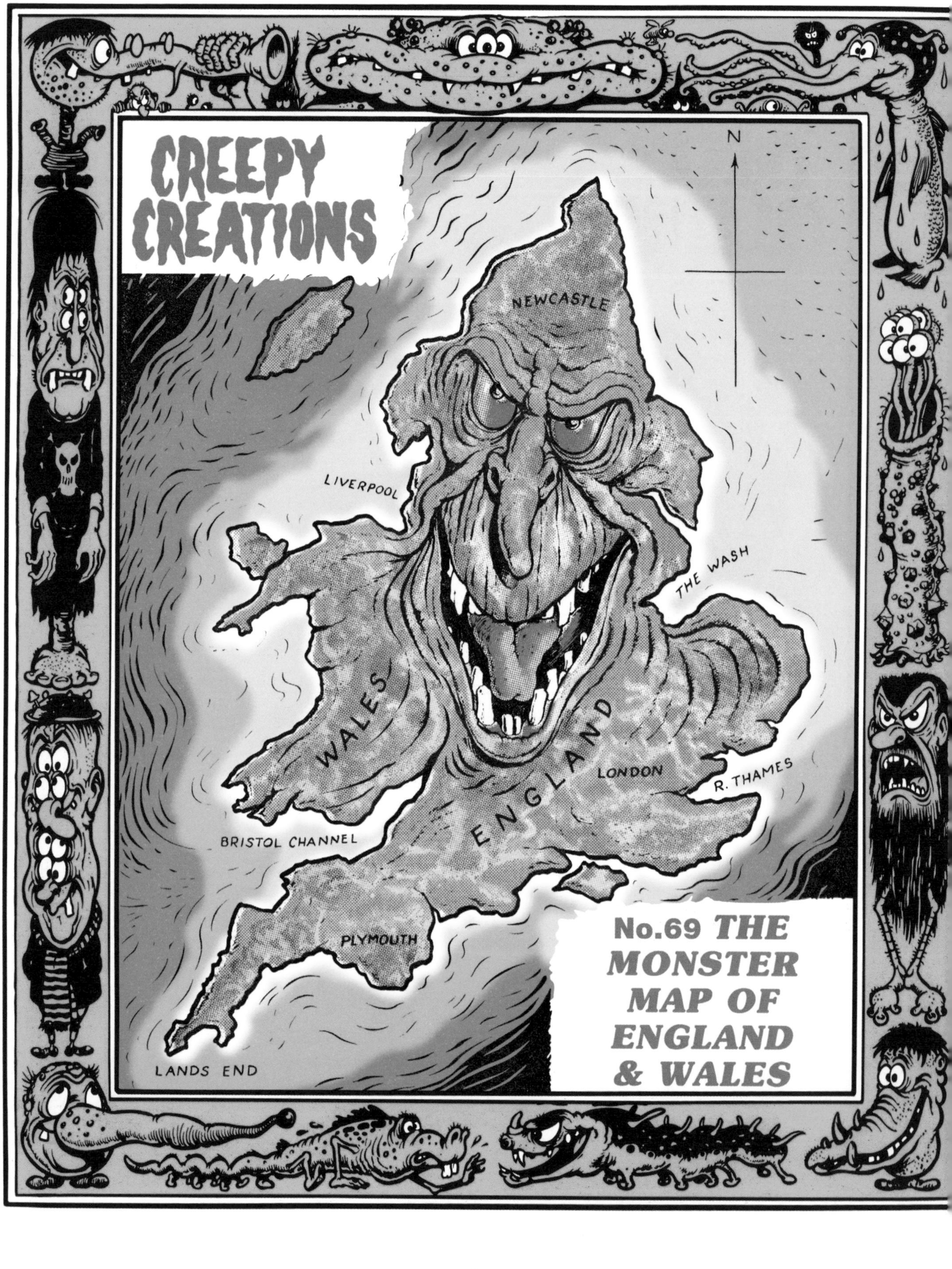
CREEPY CREATIONS
N
NEWCASTLE
LIVERPOOL
THE WASH
WALES
ENGLAND
LONDON
R. THAMES
BRISTOL CHANNEL
PLYMOUTH
LANDS END
No.69 THE MONSTER MAP OF ENGLAND & WALES

This crazy "monster piece" wins £1 for ANDREW STADDEN of RUSTINGTON

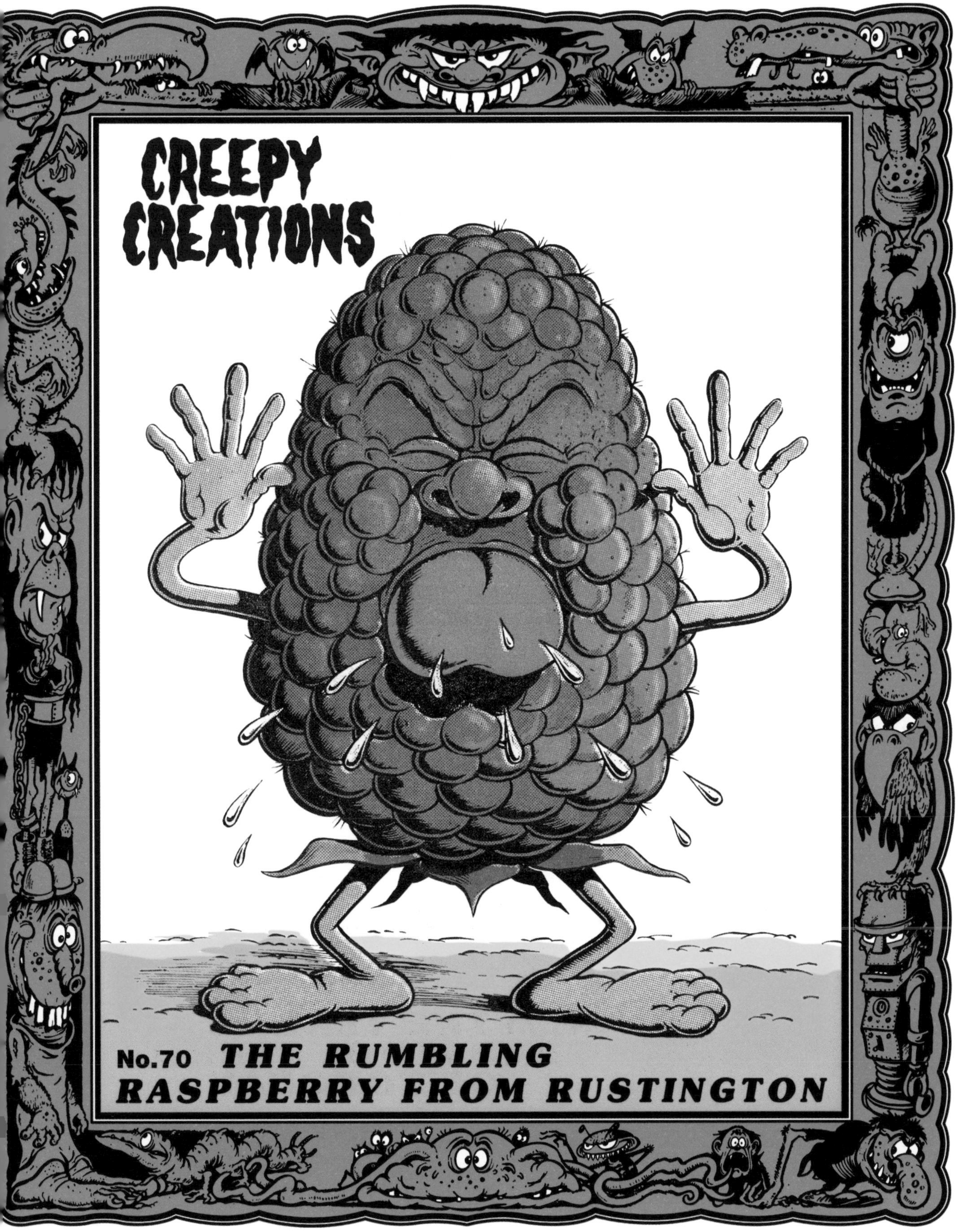
CREEPY CREATIONS
No.70 THE RUMBLING RASPBERRY FROM RUSTINGTON

This crazy "monster piece" wins £1 for ROBERT EARLE of HARROW

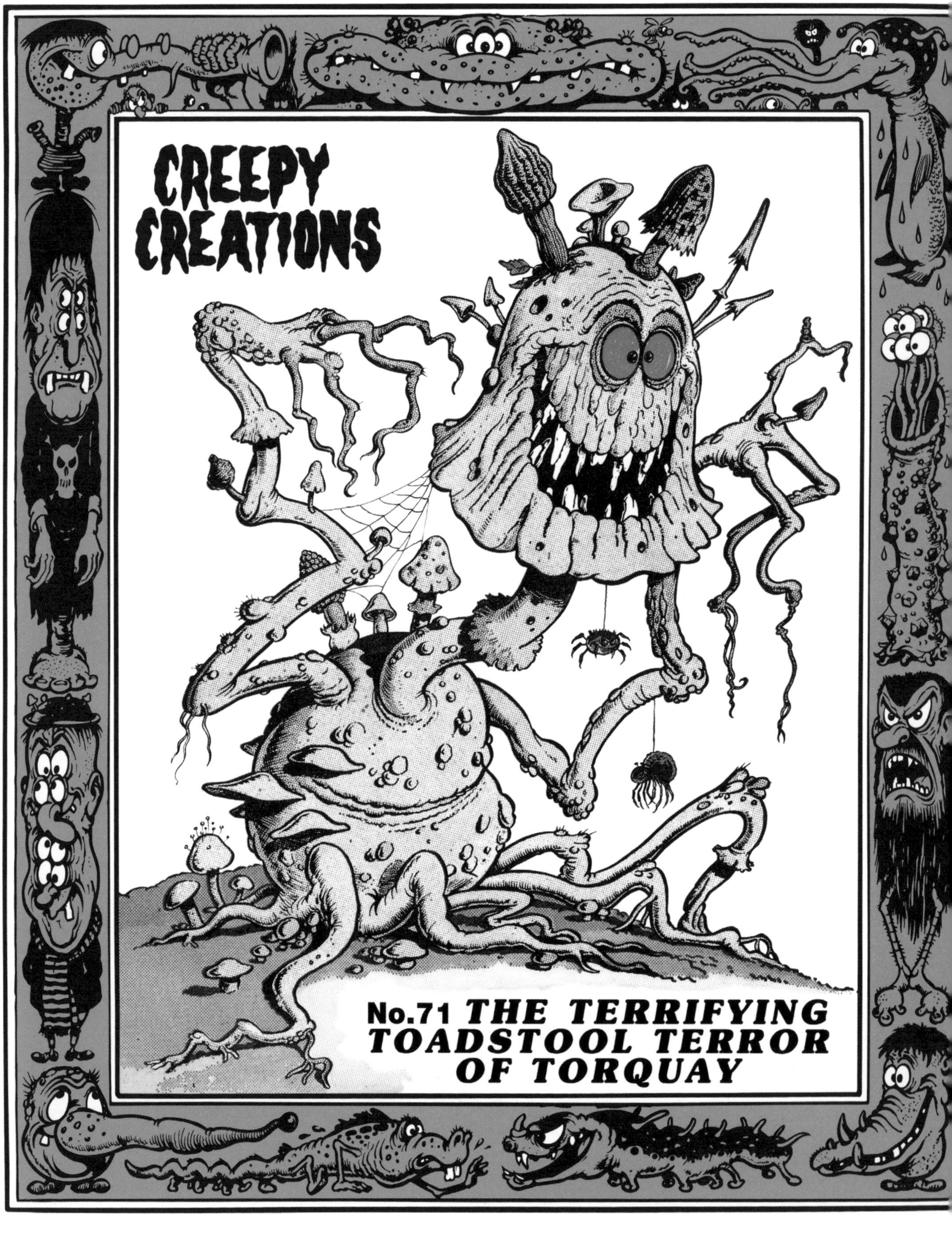
CREEPY CREATIONS
No.71 THE TERRIFYING TOADSTOOL TERROR OF TORQUAY

This crazy "monster piece" wins £1 for PAUL WILLIAMS of WIMBORNE

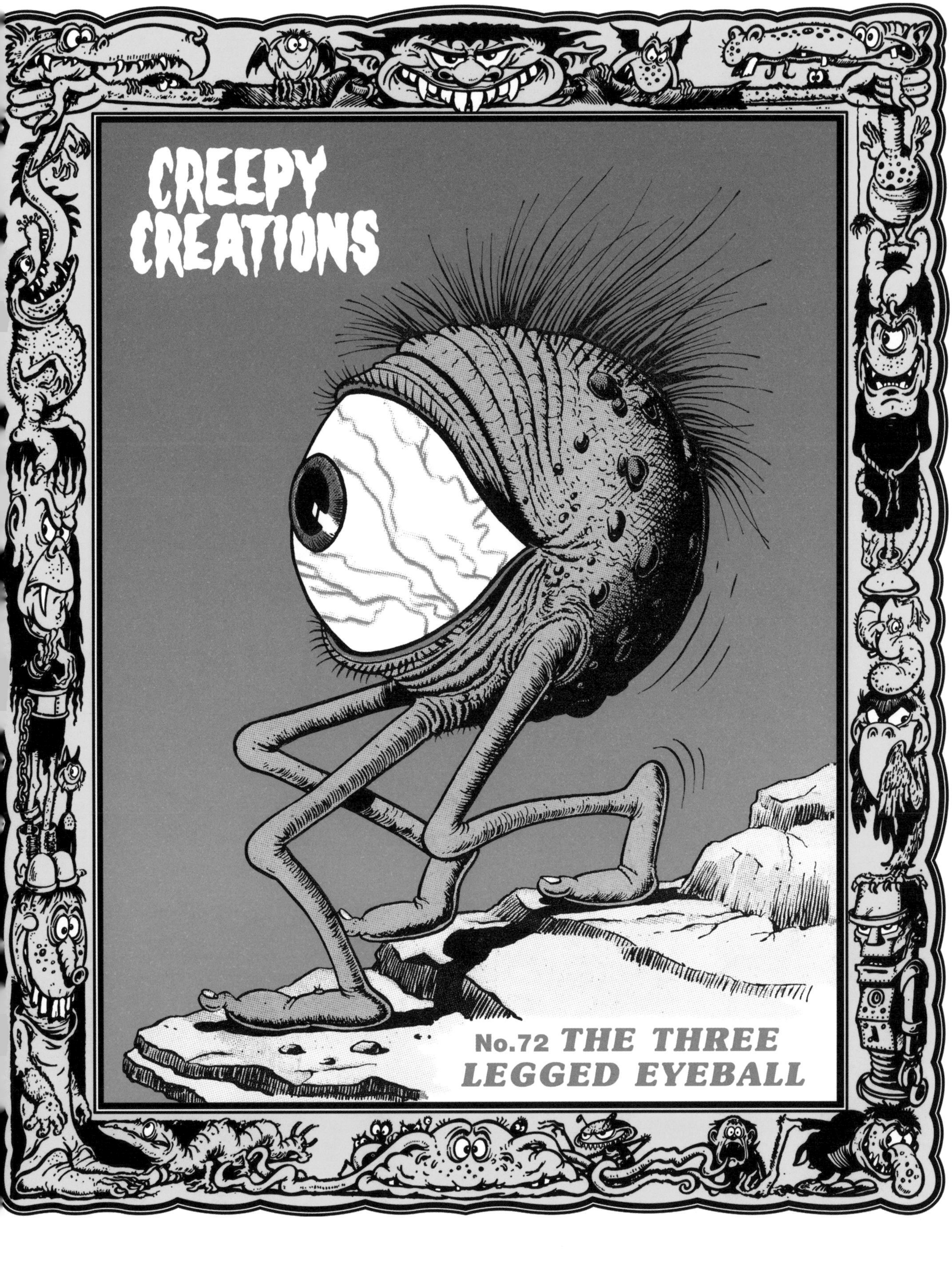
CREEPY CREATIONS
No.72 THE THREE LEGGED EYEBALL

This crazy "monster piece" wins £1 for CHERIE HOGBIE of DARLINGTON

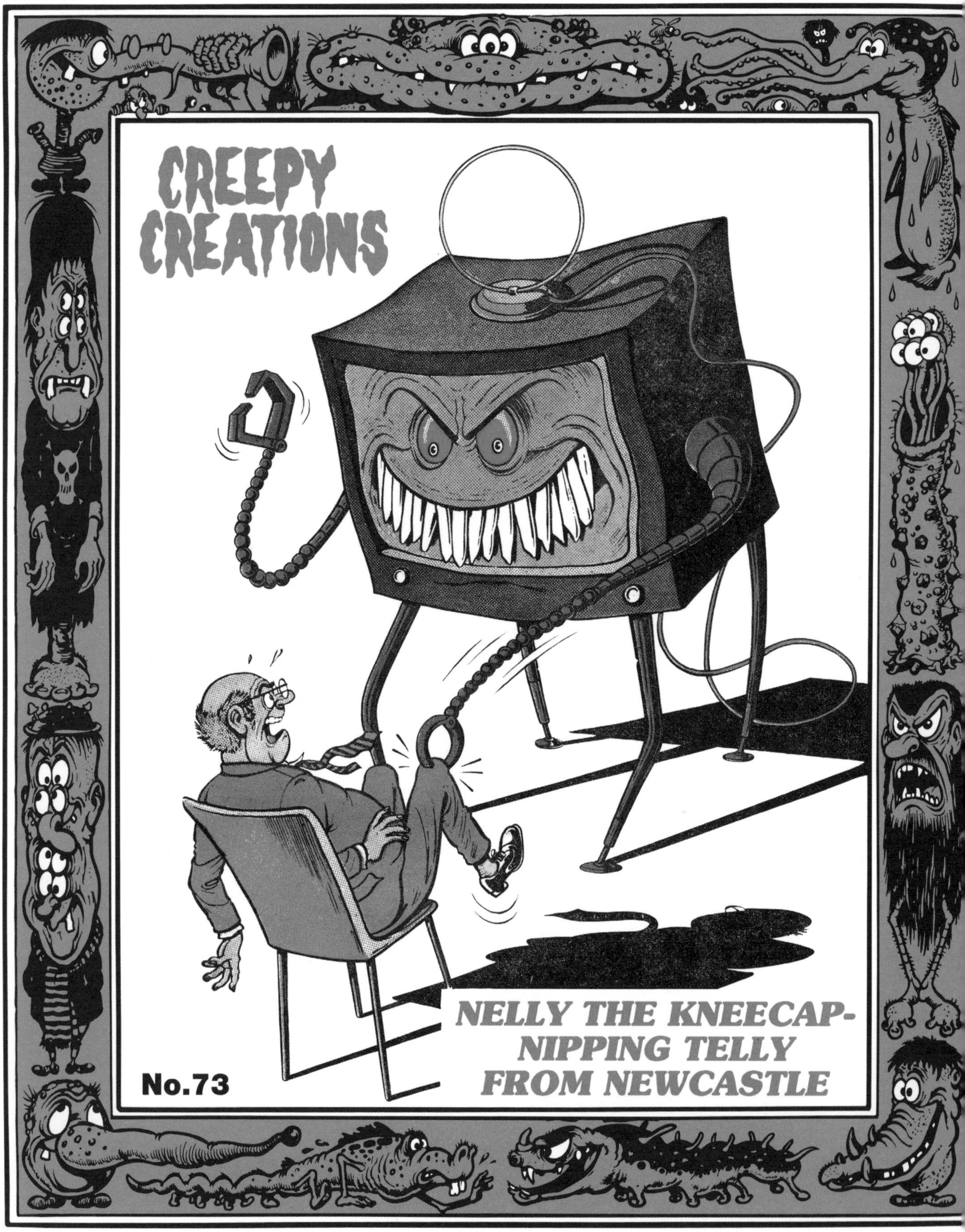
CREEPY CREATIONS
NELLY THE KNEECAP-NIPPING TELLY FROM NEWCASTLE
No.73

This crazy "monster piece" wins £1 for MANDY SMITH of OLD HATFIELD

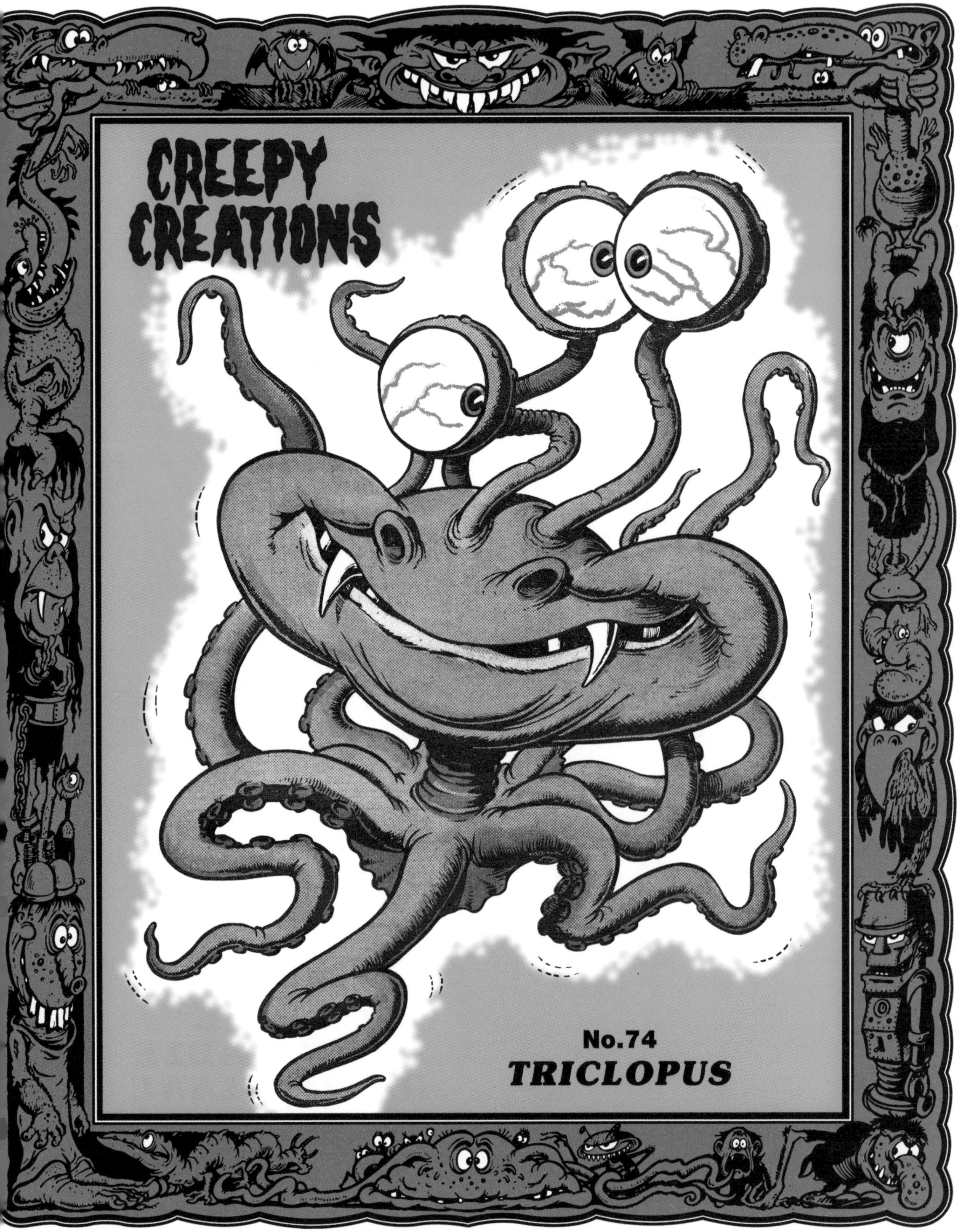
CREEPY CREATIONS
No.74
TRICLOPUS

This crazy "monster piece" wins £1 for DAVID YOUNG of BIRMINGHAM

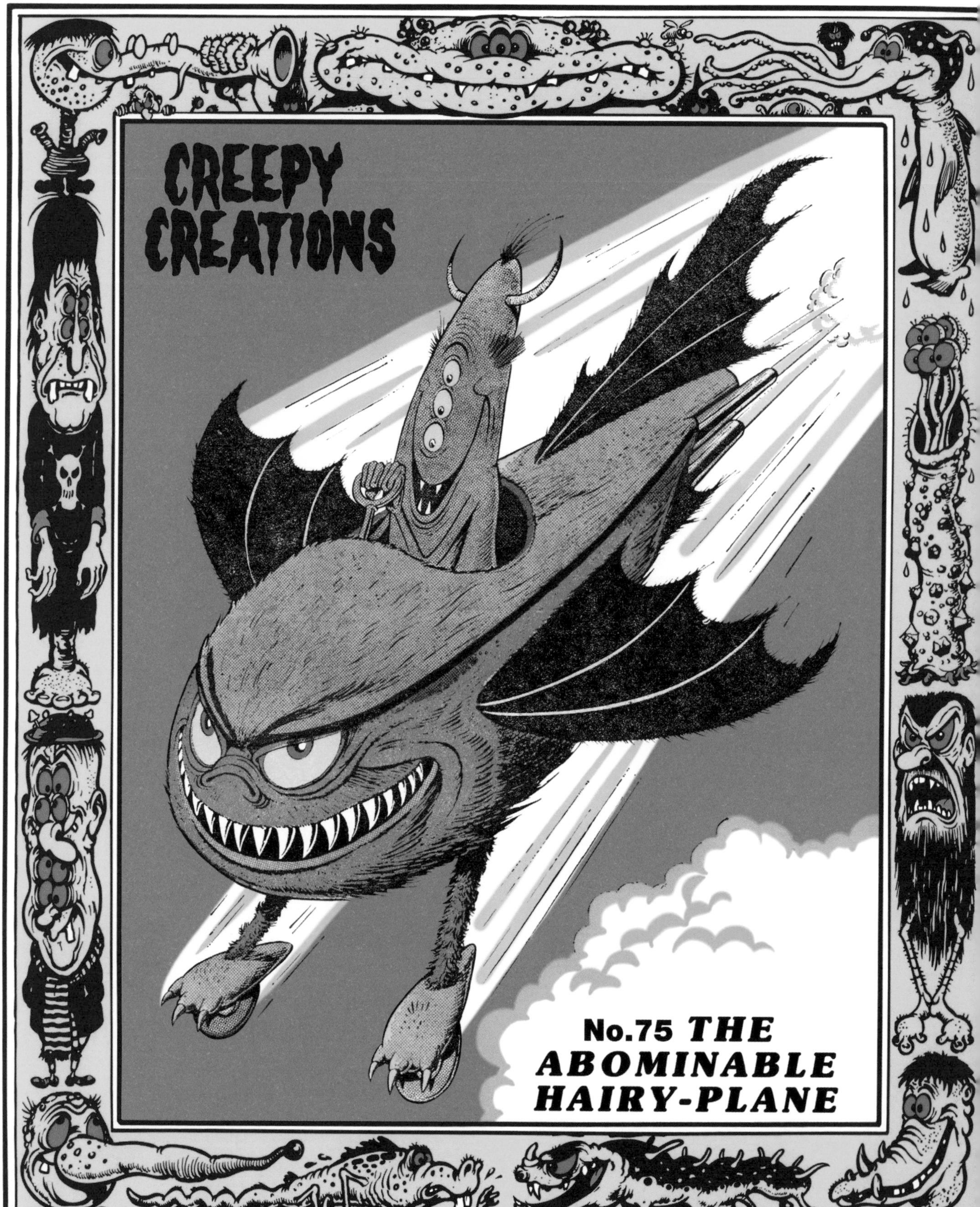
CREEPY CREATIONS
No.75 THE ABOMINABLE HAIRY-PLANE

This crazy “monster piece” wins £1 for LOUISE EDWARDS of CHELSEA

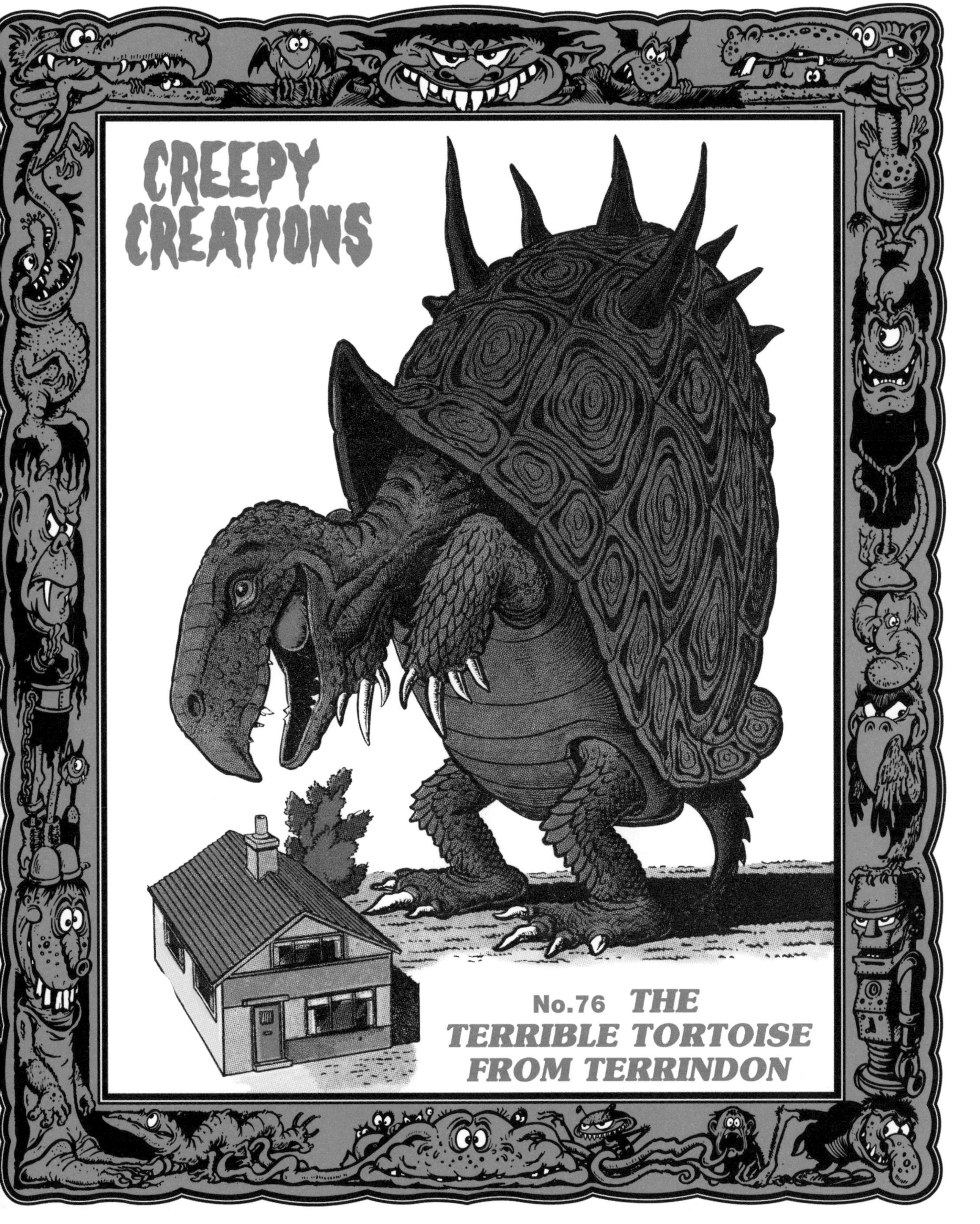
CREEPY CREATIONS
No.76 THE TERRIBLE TORTOISE FROM TERRINDON

This crazy "monster piece" wins £1 for NIGEL MELBOURNE of ALVASTON

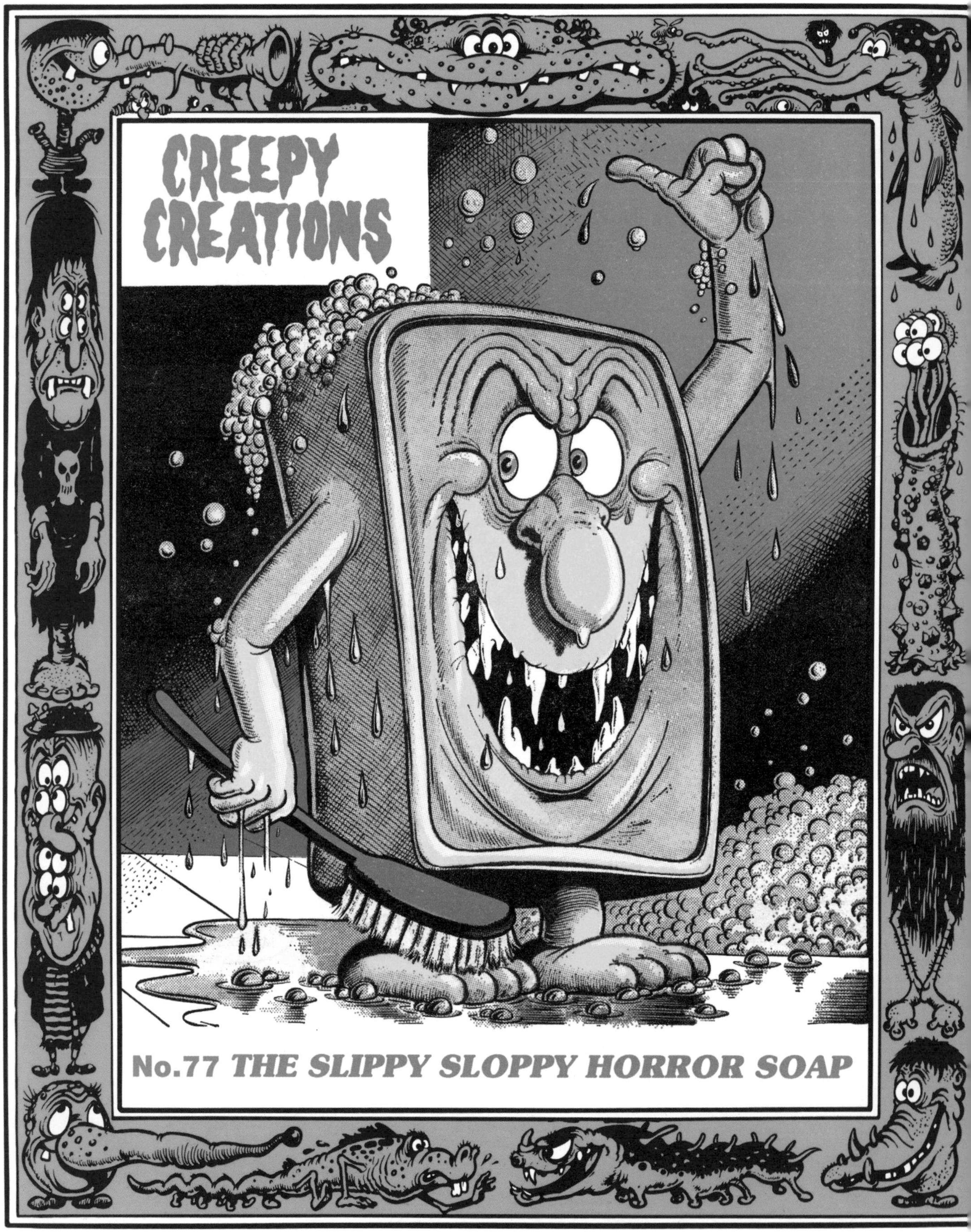
CREEPY CREATIONS
No.77 THE SLIPPY SLOPPY HORROR SOAP

This crazy "monster piece" wins £1 for ANDREW CSANYI of COVENTRY

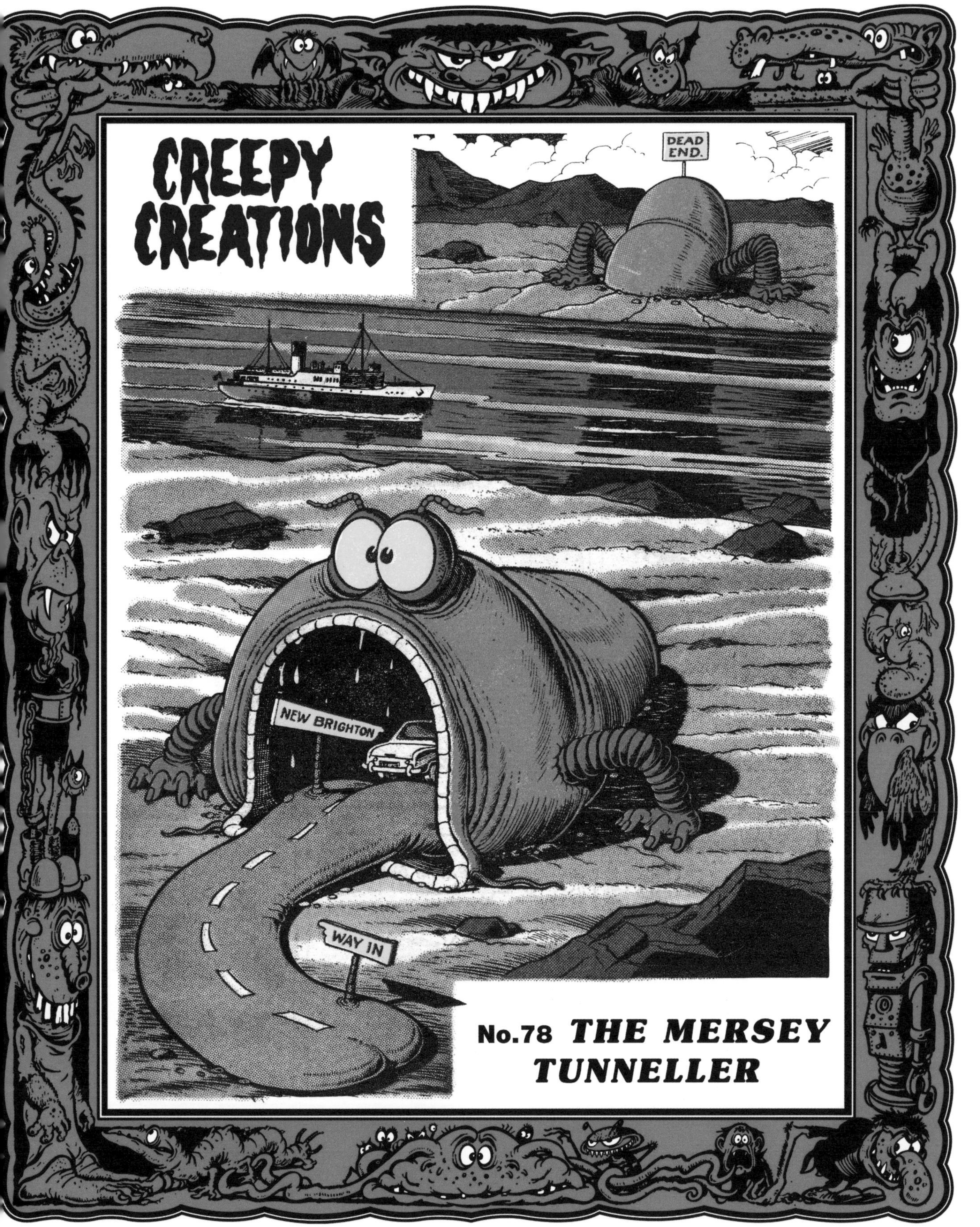
CREEPY CREATIONS
DEAD END.
NEW BRIGHTON
WAY IN
No.78 THE MERSEY TUNNELLER

This crazy "monster piece" wins £1 for LOUISE SCULLION of HELENSBURGH

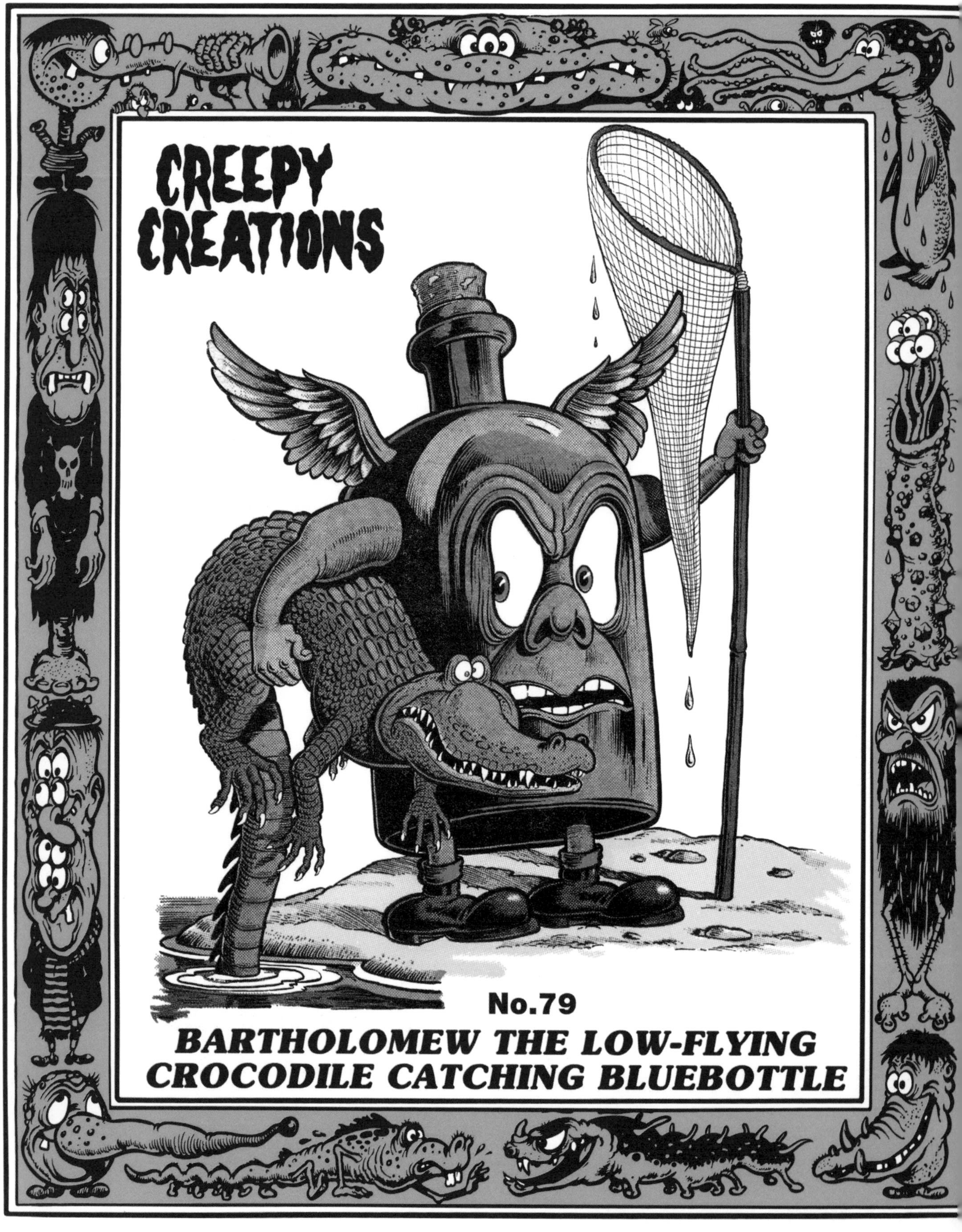
CREEPY CREATIONS
No.79
BARTHOLOMEW THE LOW-FLYING CROCODILE CATCHING BLUEBOTTLE

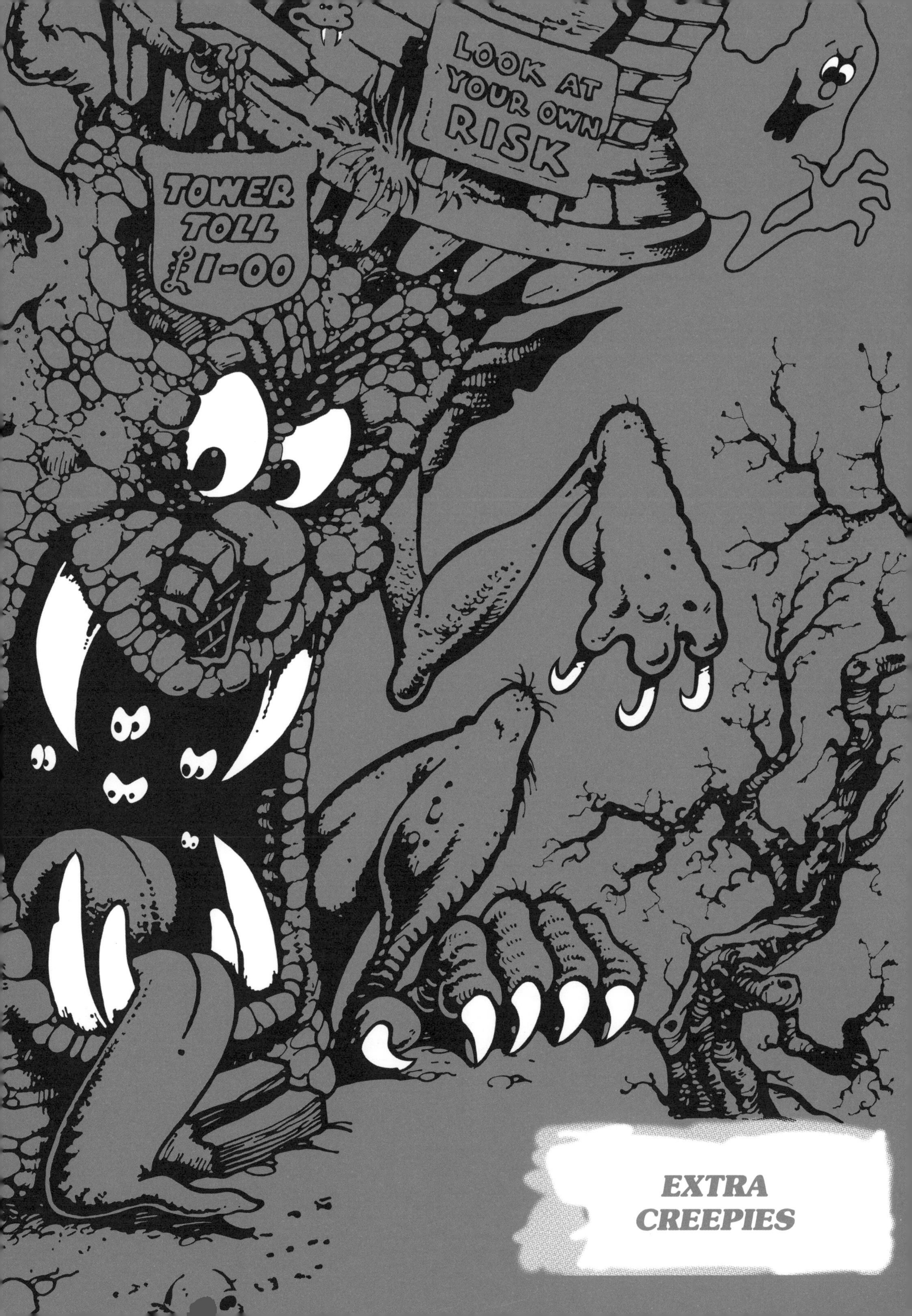
LOOK AT YOUR OWN RISK
TOWER TOLL £1-00

EXTRA CREEPIES

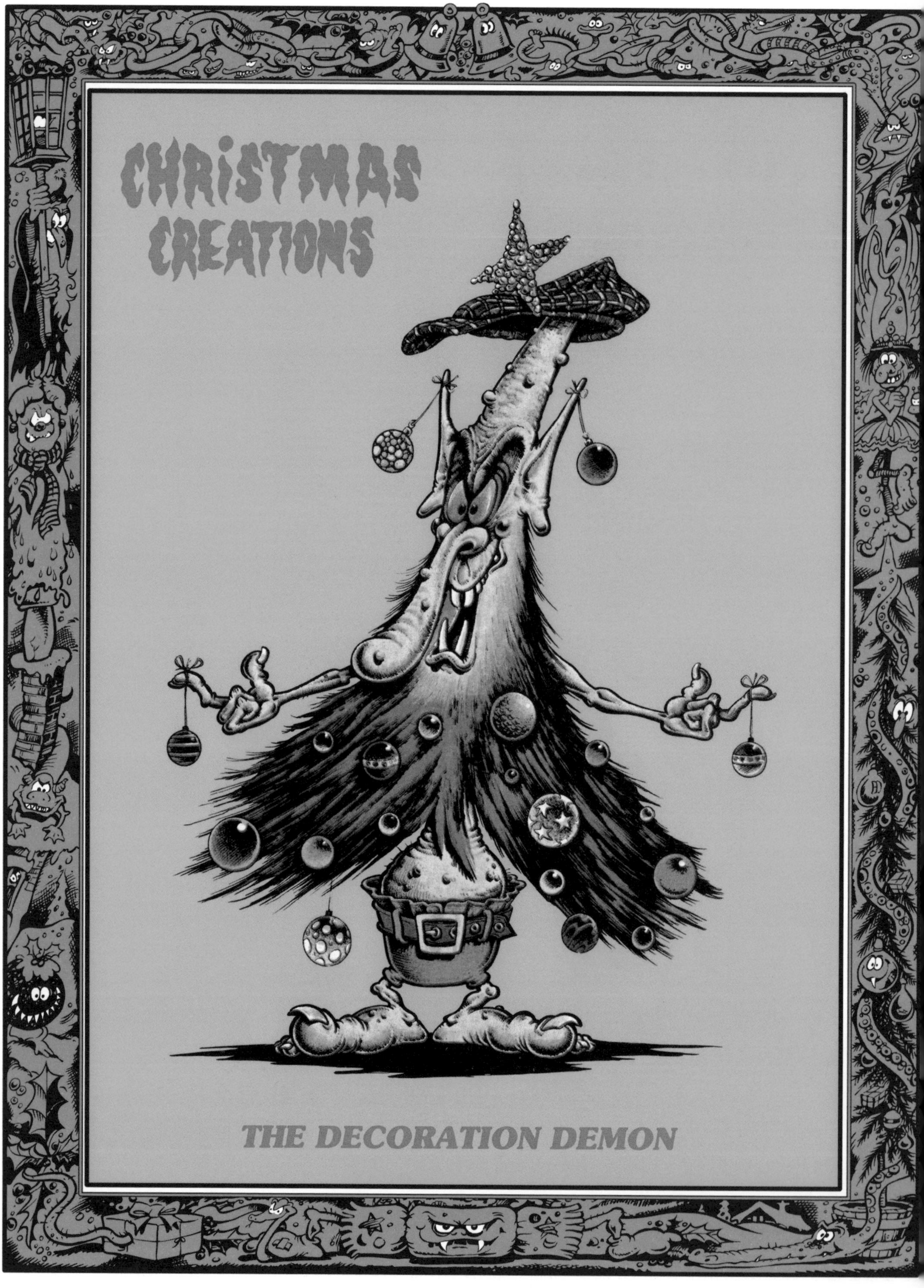
CHRISTMAS
CREATIONS
THE DECORATION DEMON

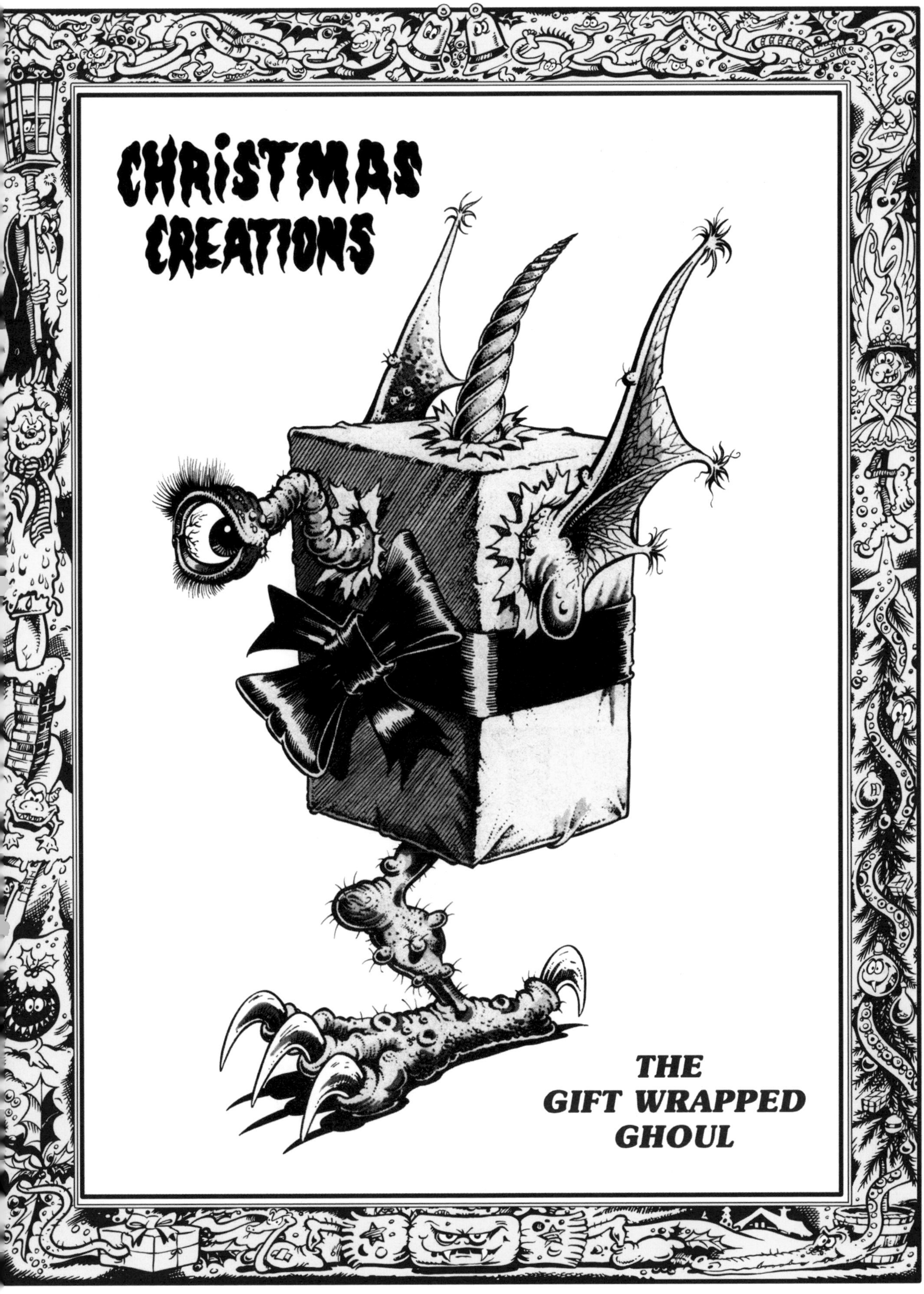
CHRISTMAS CREATIONS
THE GIFT WRAPPED GHOUL

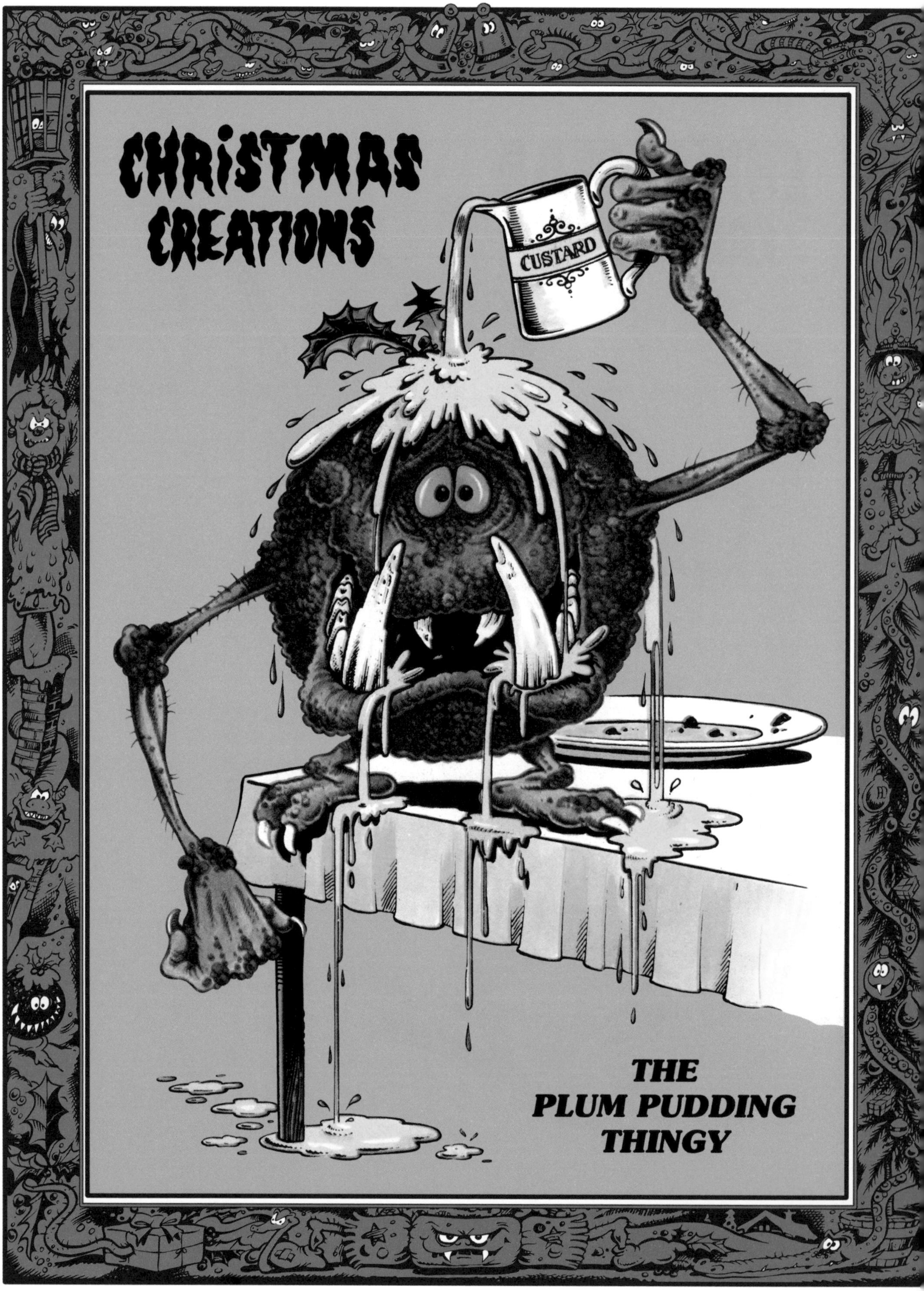
CHRISTMAS CREATIONS
CUSTARD
THE PLUM PUDDING THINGY

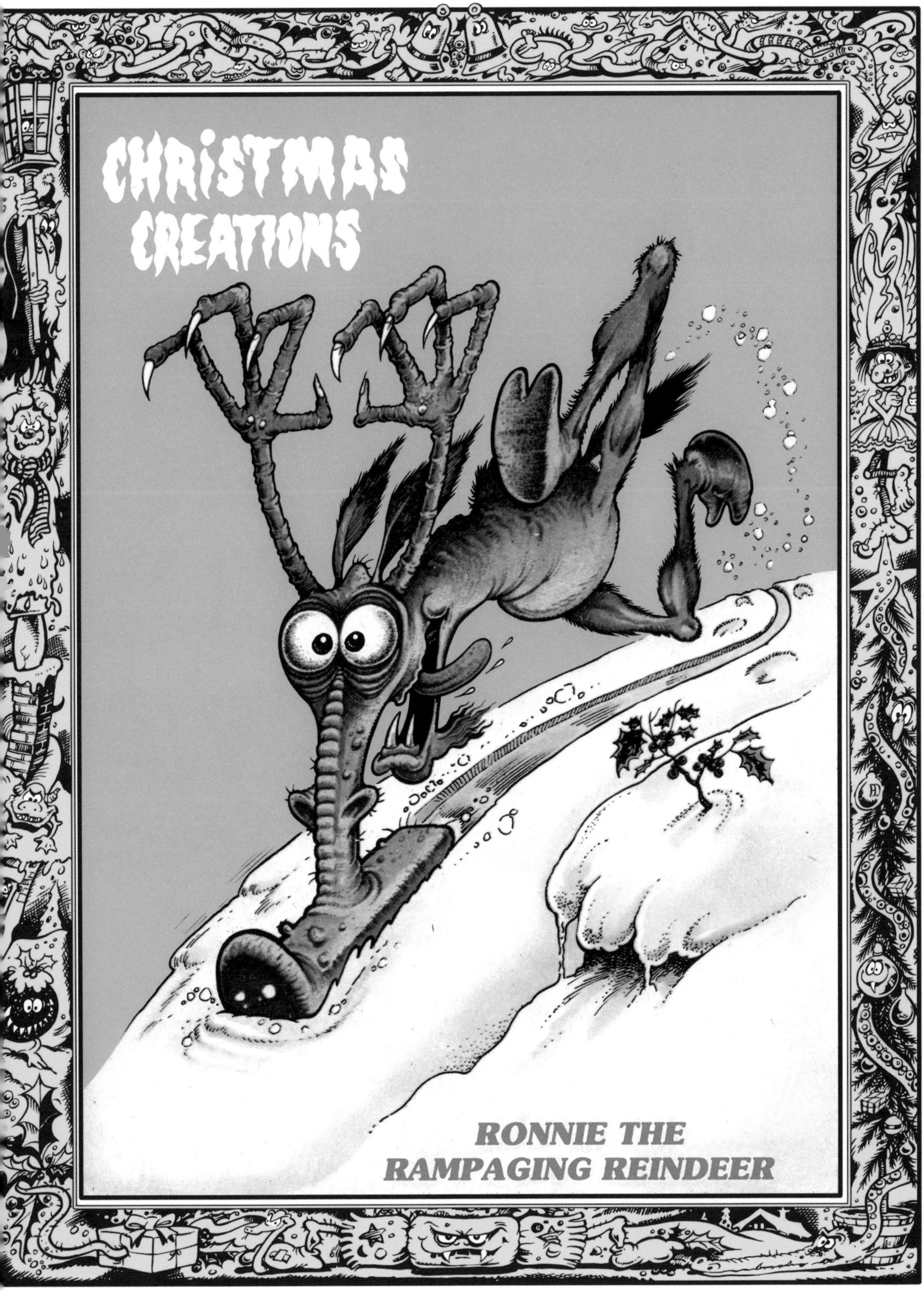
CHRISTMAS CREATIONS
RONNIE THE RAMPAGING REINDEER

CREEPY CREATIONS

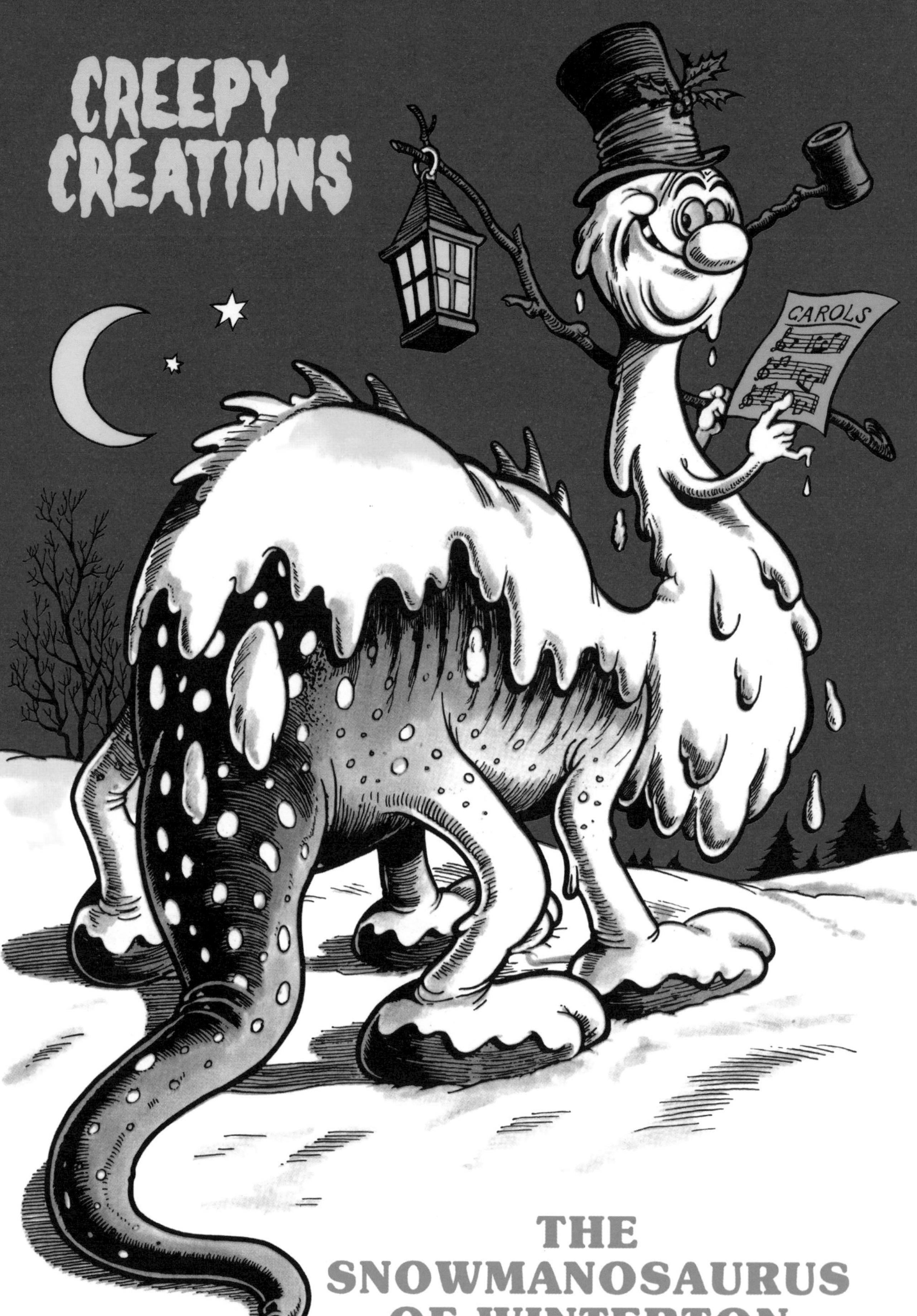
CAROLS

THE SNOWMANOSAURUS OF WINTERTON

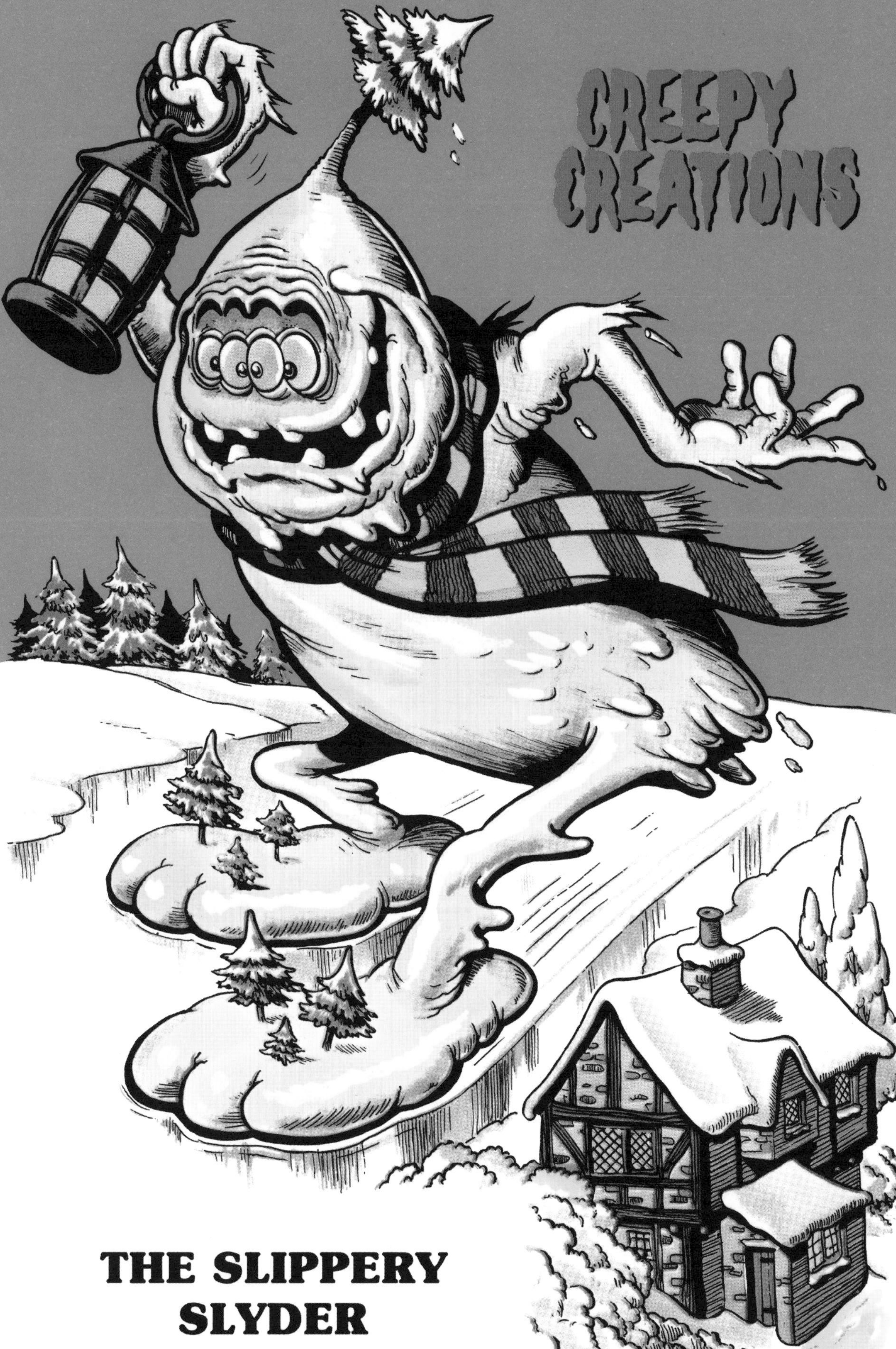
CREEPY CREATIONS

THE SLIPPERY SLYDER OF SLEDMERE

The CREEPY CREATIONS

JANUARY

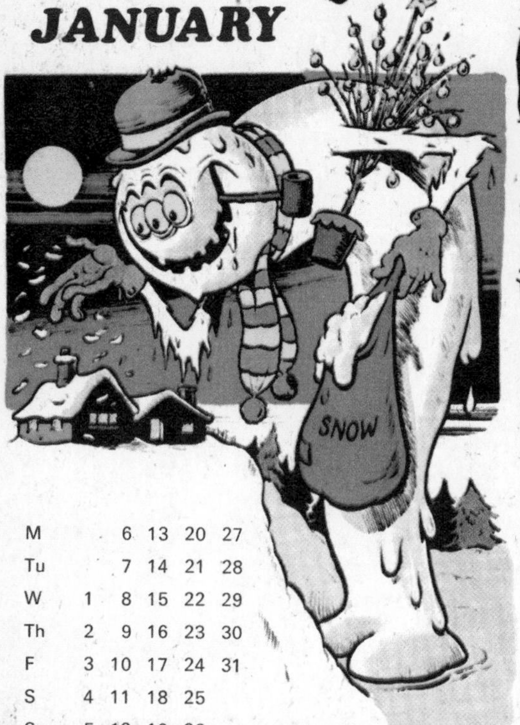
SNOW

M		6	13	20	27
Tu		7	14	21	28
W	1	8	15	22	29
Th	2	9	16	23	30
F	3	10	17	24	31
S	4	11	18	25	
Su	5	12	19	26	

FEBRUARY

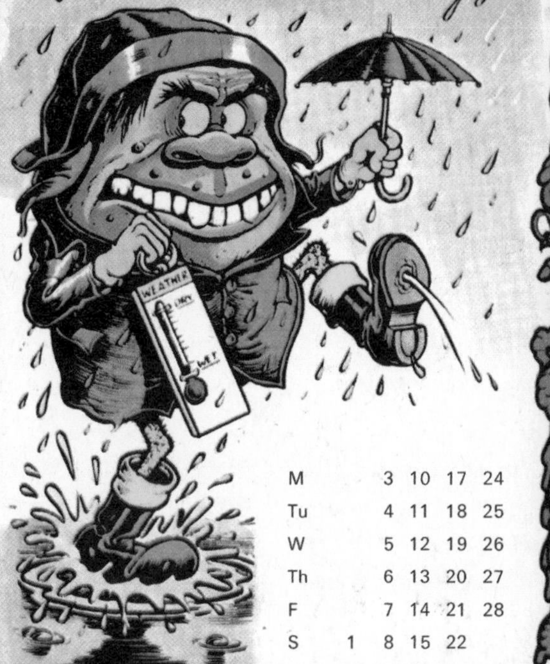

M		3	10	17	24
Tu		4	11	18	25
W		5	12	19	26
Th		6	13	20	27
F		7	14	21	28
S	1	8	15	22	
Su	2	9	16	23	

MARCH

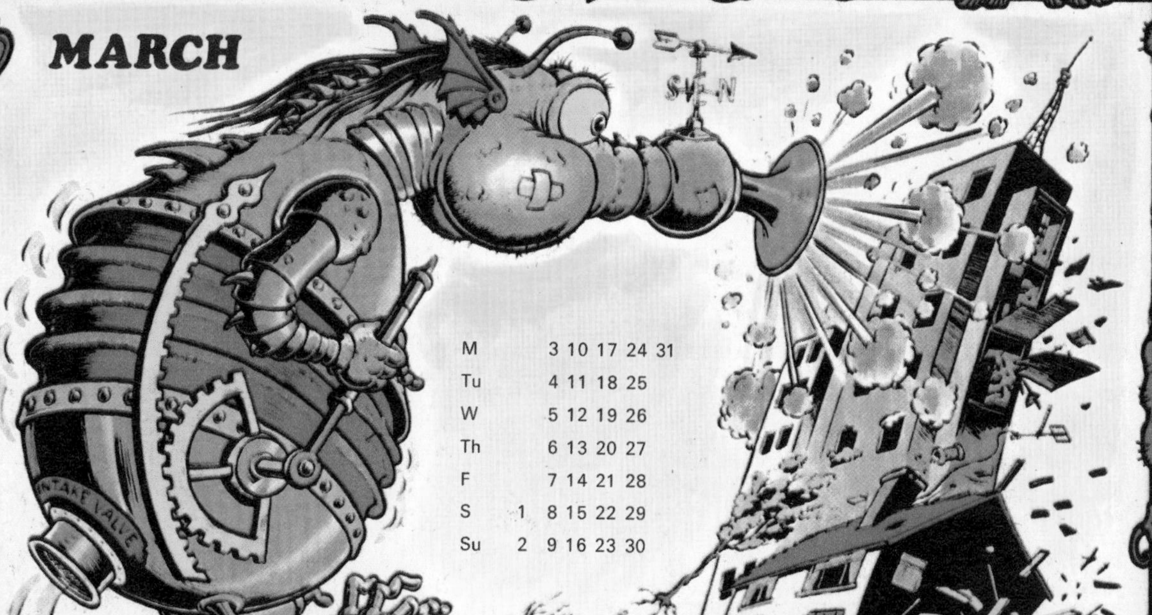
INTAKE VALVE

M		3	10	17	24	31
Tu		4	11	18	25	
W		5	12	19	26	
Th		6	13	20	27	
F		7	14	21	28	
S	1	8	15	22	29	
Su	2	9	16	23	30	

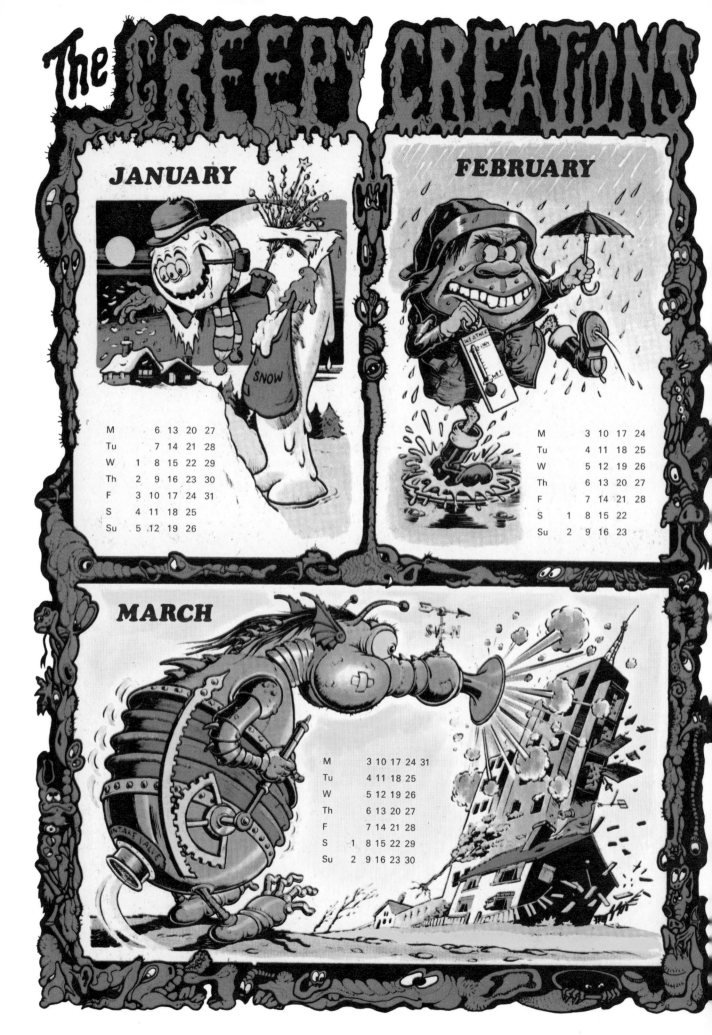

CALENDAR·1975

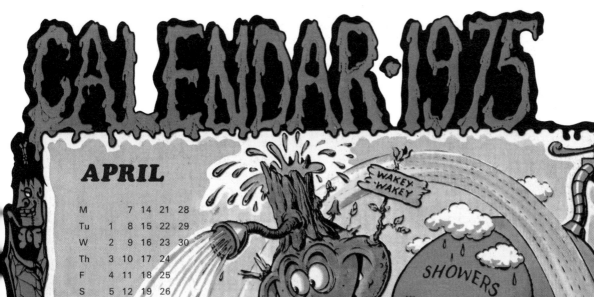

APRIL

M		7	14	21	28
Tu	1	8	15	22	29
W	2	9	16	23	30
Th	3	10	17	24	
F	4	11	18	25	
S	5	12	19	26	
Su	6	13	20	27	

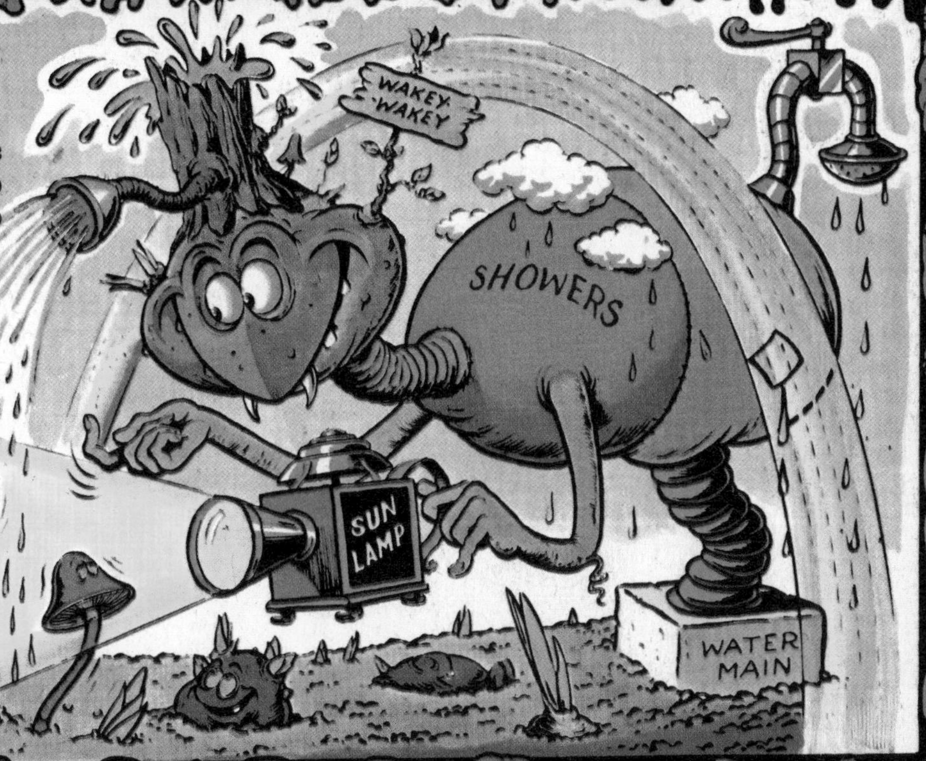
WAKEY-WAKEY
SHOWERS
YAWN
SUN LAMP
WATER MAIN

MAY

M		5	12	19	26
Tu		6	13	20	27
W		7	14	21	28
Th	1	8	15	22	29
F	2	9	16	23	30
S	3	10	17	24	31
Su	4	11	18	25	

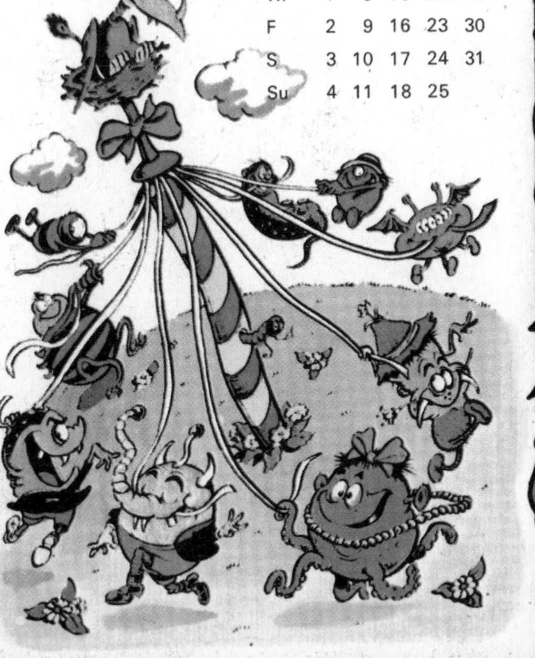

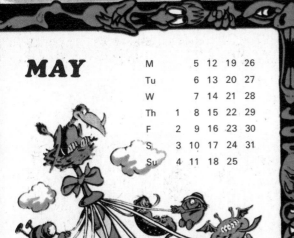

JUNE

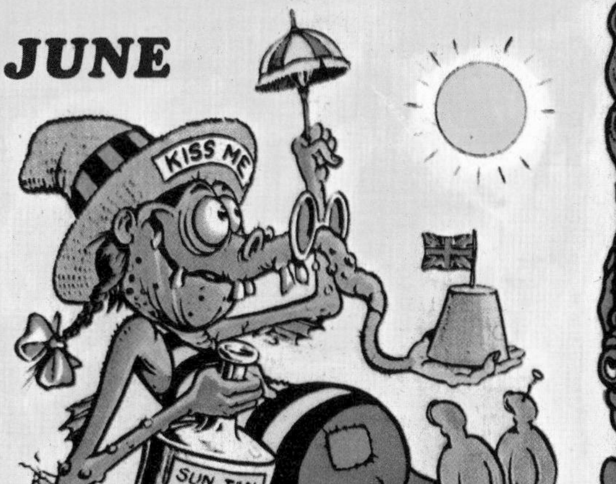
KISS ME
SUN TAN OIL

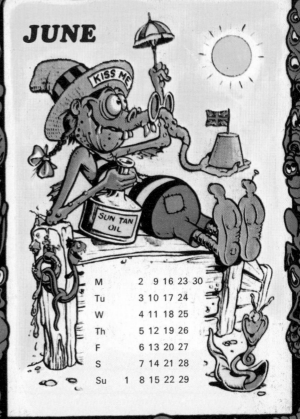

M		2	9	16	23	30
Tu		3	10	17	24
W		4	11	18	25
Th		5	12	19	26
F		6	13	20	27
S		7	14	21	28
Su	1	8	15	22	29

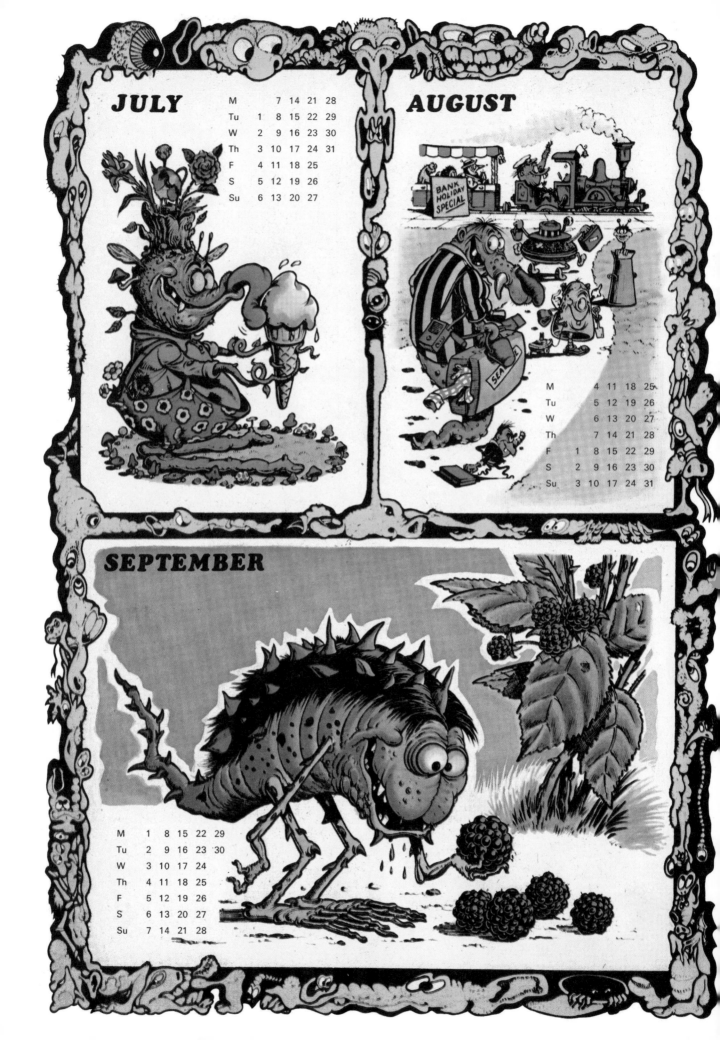

JULY

M		7	14	21	28
Tu	1	8	15	22	29
W	2	9	16	23	30
Th	3	10	17	24	31
F	4	11	18	25	
S	5	12	19	26	
Su	6	13	20	27	

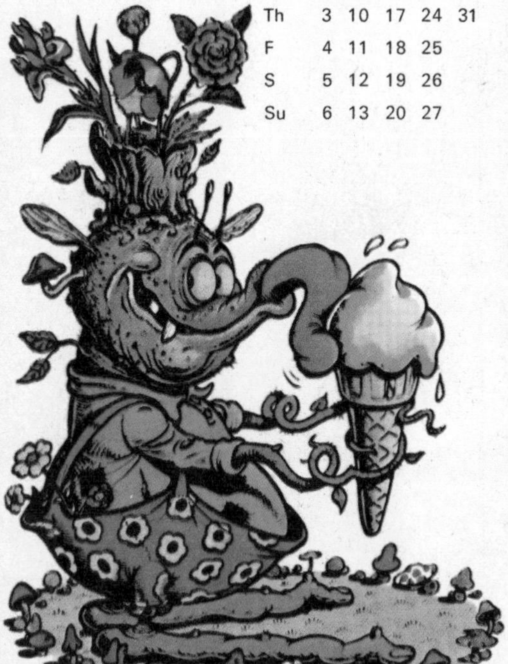

AUGUST

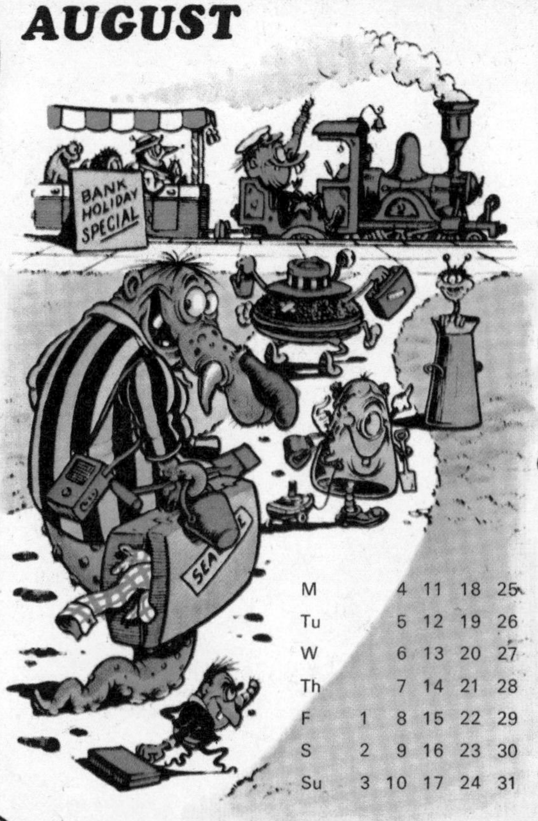
BANK HOLIDAY SPECIAL

M		4	11	18	25
Tu		5	12	19	26
W		6	13	20	27
Th		7	14	21	28
F	1	8	15	22	29
S	2	9	16	23	30
Su	3	10	17	24	31

SEPTEMBER

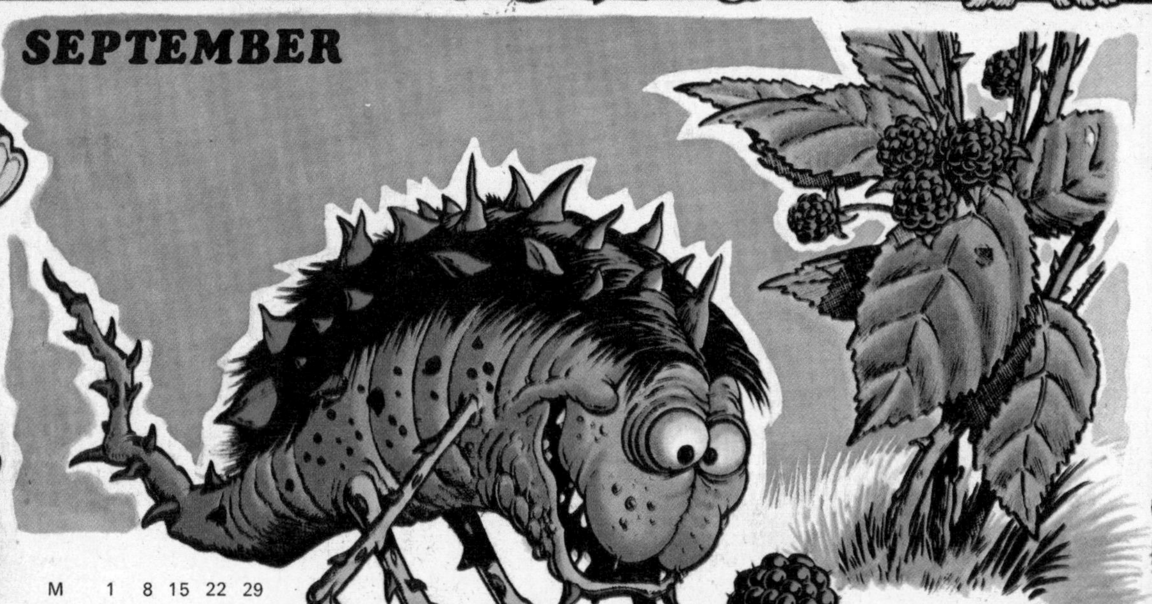

M	1	8	15	22	29
Tu	2	9	16	23	30
W	3	10	17	24	
Th	4	11	18	25	
F	5	12	19	26	
S	6	13	20	27	
Su	7	14	21	28	

OCTOBER

M		6	13	20	27
Tu		7	14	21	28
W	1	8	15	22	29
Th	2	9	16	23	30
F	3	10	17	24	31
S	4	11	18	25	
Su	5	12	19	26	

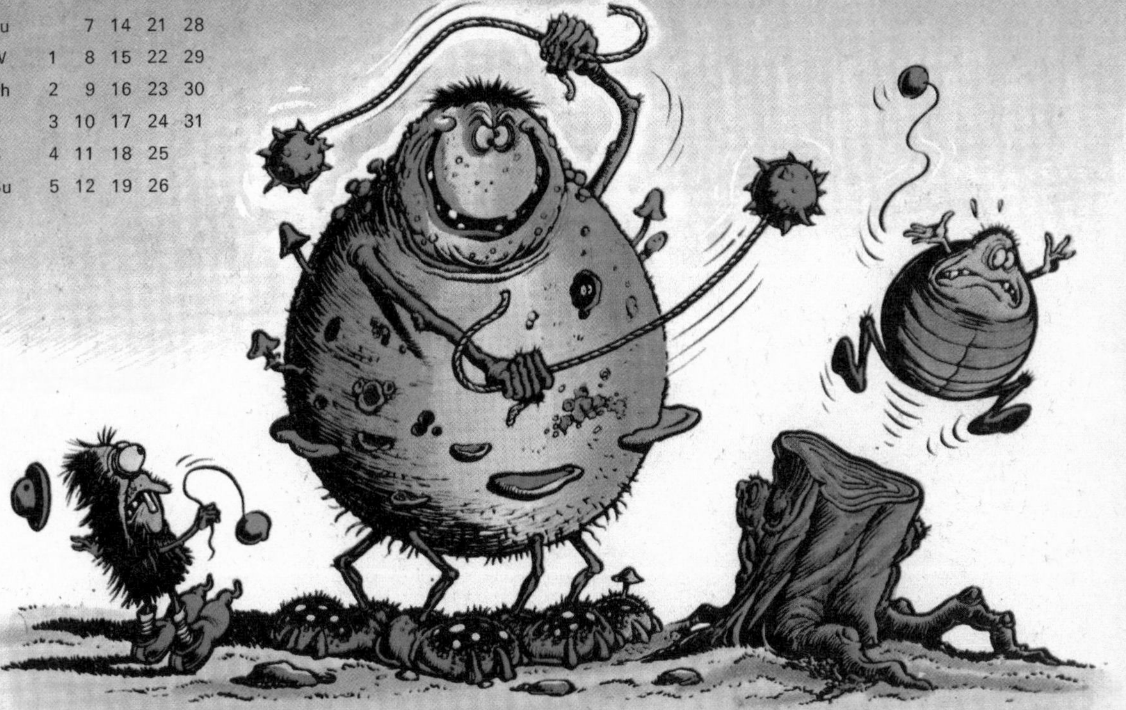

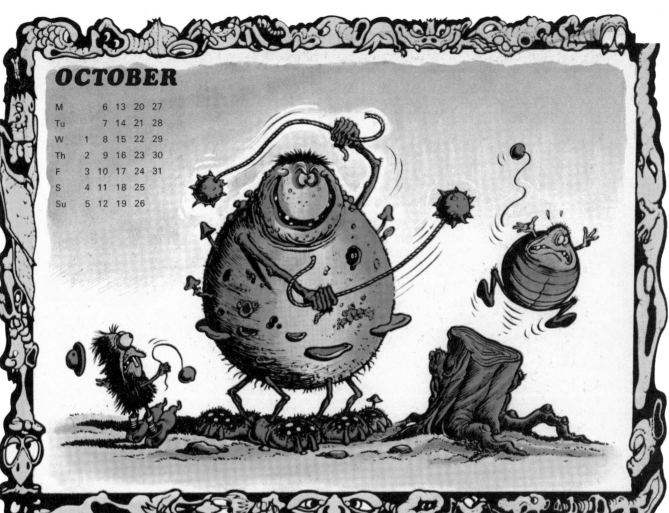

NOVEMBER

M		3	10	17	24
Tu		4	11	18	25
W		5	12	19	26
Th		6	13	20	27
F		7	14	21	28
S	1	8	15	22	29
Su	2	9	16	23	30

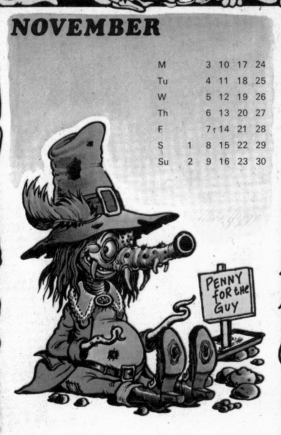

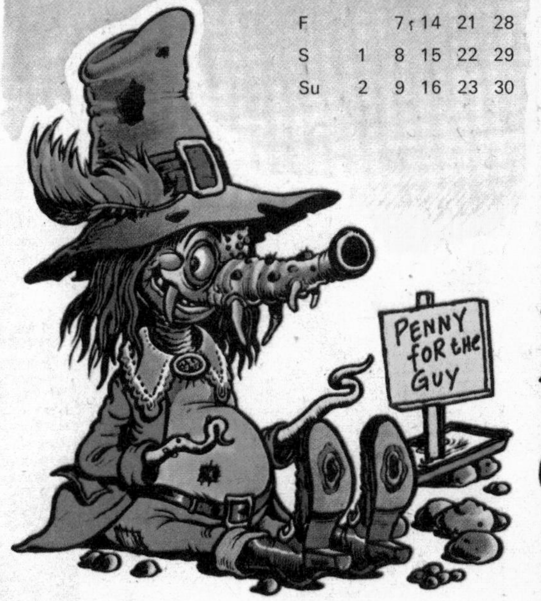
PENNY FOR the GUY

DECEMBER

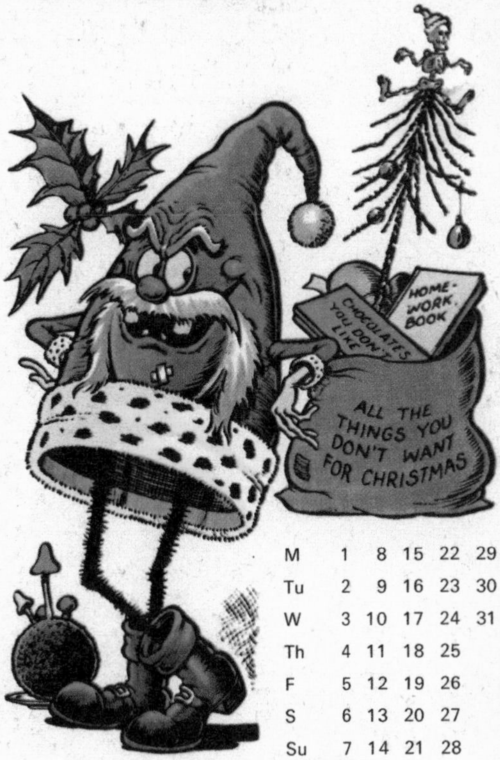
HOME-WORK BOOK
CHOCOLATES YOU DON'T LIKE
ALL THE THINGS YOU DON'T WANT FOR CHRISTMAS

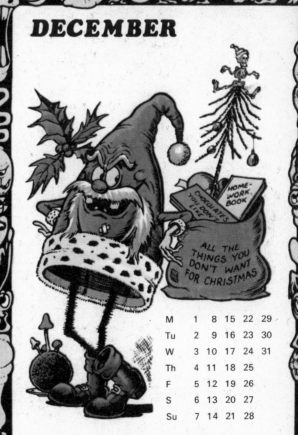

M	1	8	15	22	29
Tu	2	9	16	23	30
W	3	10	17	24	31
Th	4	11	18	25	
F	5	12	19	26	
S	6	13	20	27	
Su	7	14	21	28	

MINI MONSTER

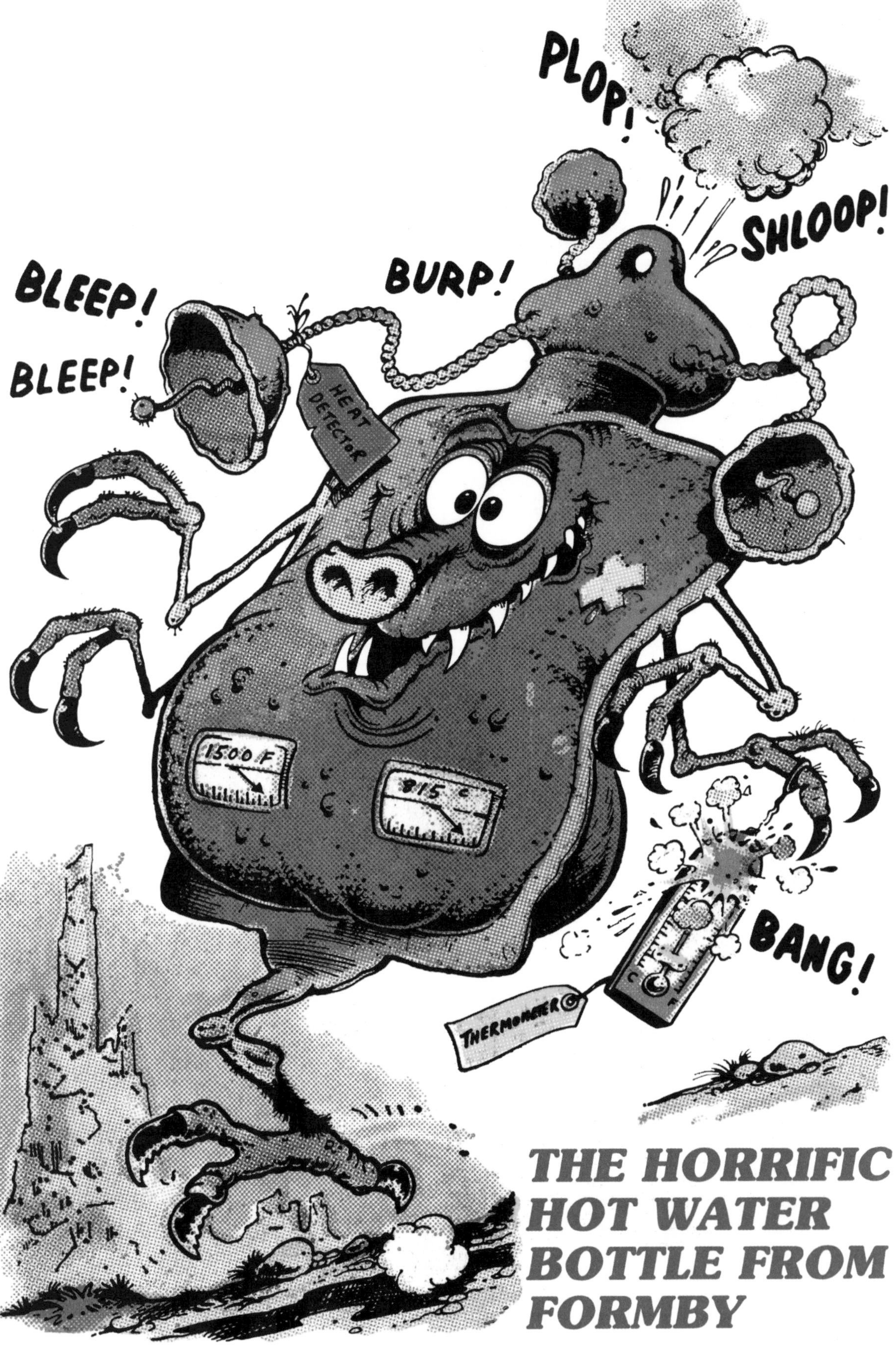
PLOP!
SHLOOP!
BURP!
BLEEP!
BLEEP!
HEAT DETECTOR
1500 F
815 C
BANG!
THERMOMETER

THE HORRIFIC HOT WATER BOTTLE FROM FORMBY

MINI MONSTER

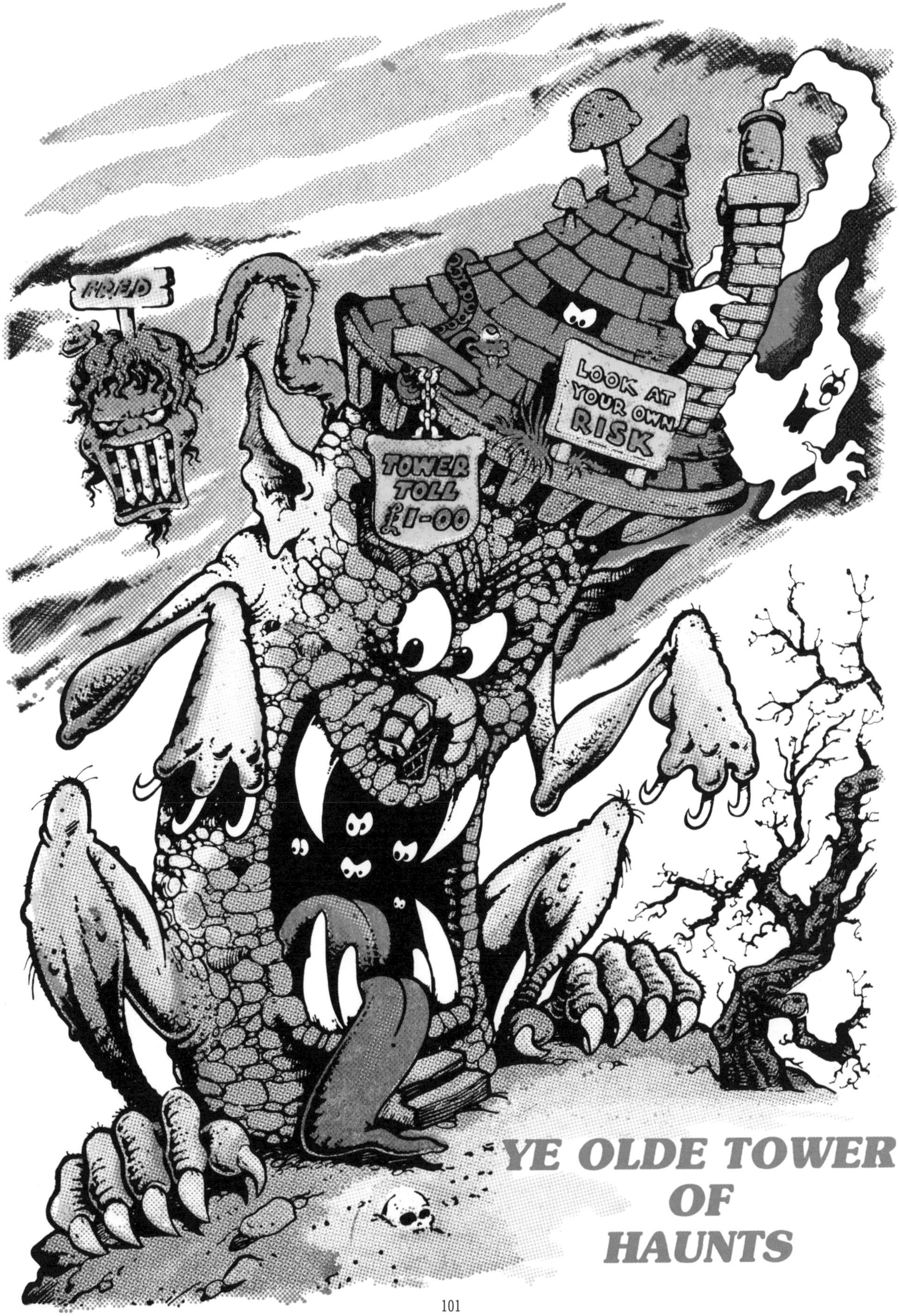
FRED
LOOK AT YOUR OWN RISK
TOWER TOLL £1-00
YE OLDE TOWER OF HAUNTS

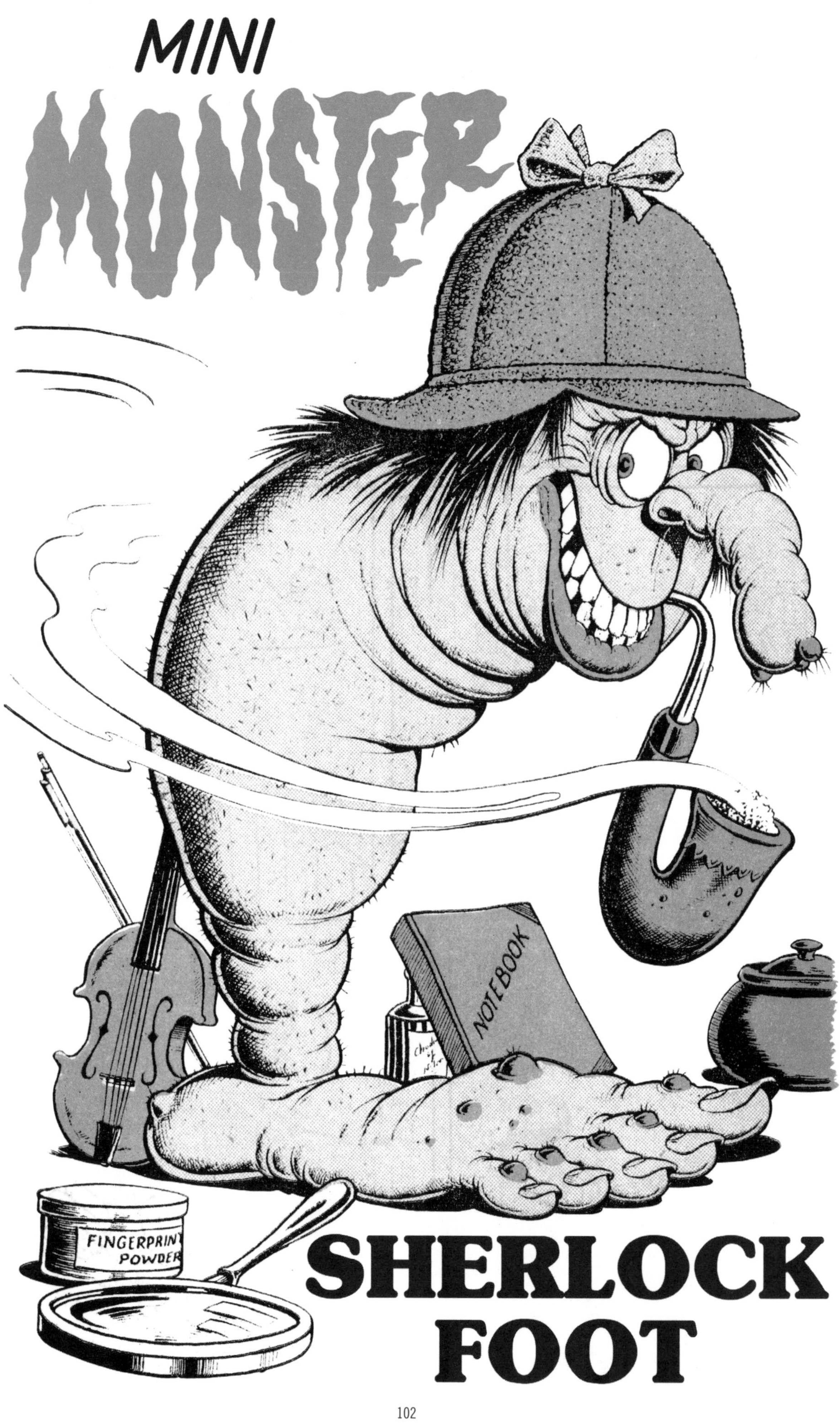
MINI
MONSTER
NOTEBOOK
FINGERPRINT POWDER
SHERLOCK FOOT

MINI MONSTER

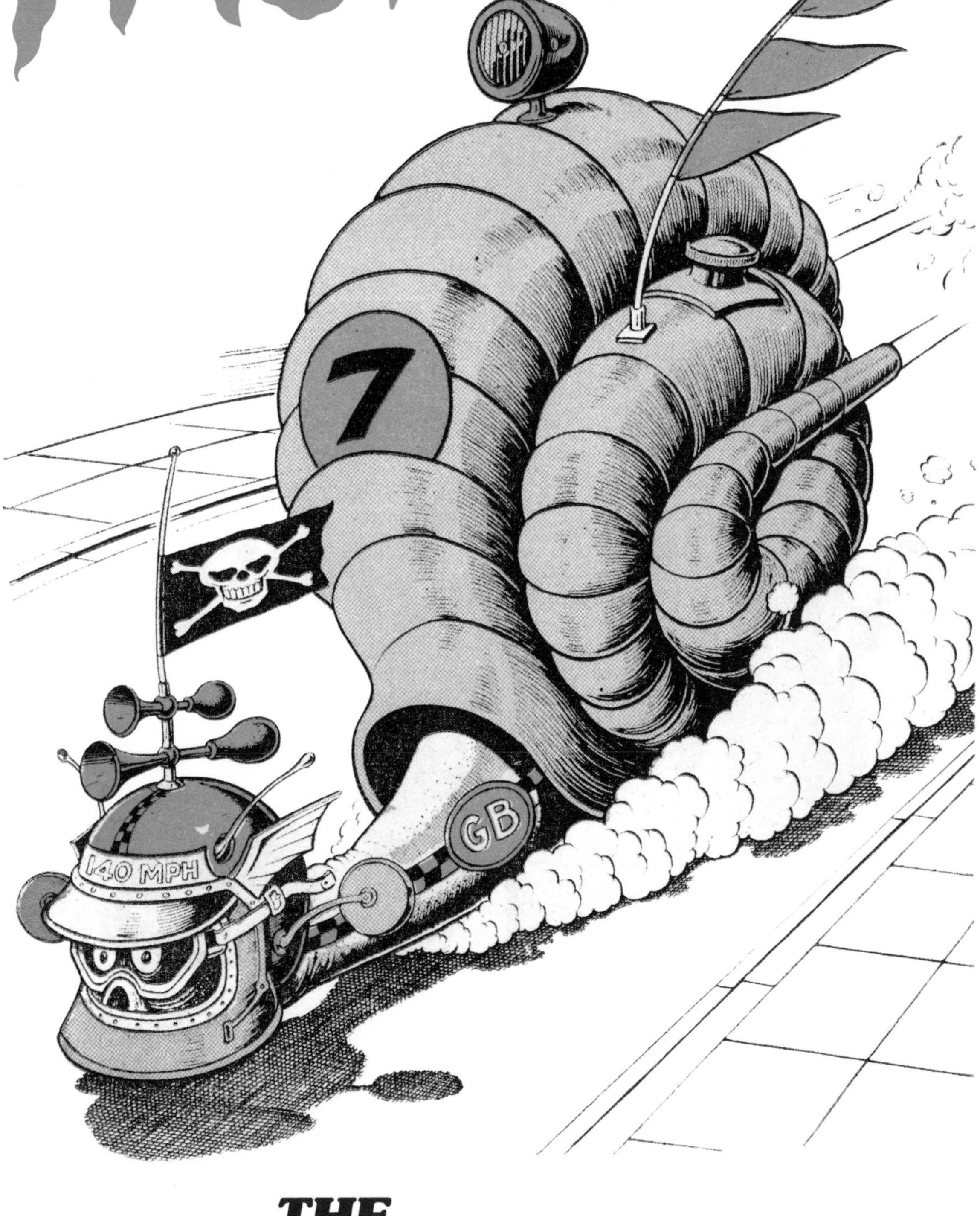
7
140 MPH
GB

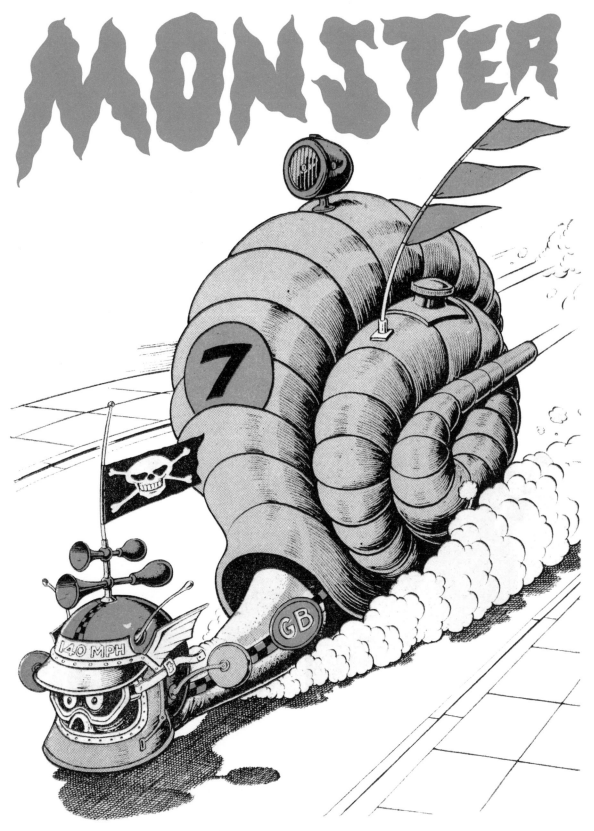

THE JET-PROPELLED SNAILMOBILE

YOUR HORRORSCOPE

AQUARIUS

(Jan 20 – Feb 18) Don't let big things get on top of you . . . dinosaurs can be very heavy! Beware of going out with were-wolves, they are known to be change-able!

PISCES

(Feb 19 – Mar 20) You may be invited to a ghoul friend's party. Should be a scream.

ARIES

(Mar 21 – Apr 20) Be kind to elderly tarant-ulas. Unlucky colour: Black with soggy green spots!

TAURUS

(Apr 21 – May 20) Red is your lucky colour – but not on picnics. Try not to get into rows with abominable snowmen.

GEMINI

(May 21 – Jun 20) Keep in good spirits. Lock bad spirits in a coal shed: An old friend is dying to see you. Unlucky number for burglars: 999!

CANCER

(Jun 21 – July 20) You may be feeling the pinch this week. Don't lose your head in a crisis. If you do, make sure you've some glue to stick it back on.

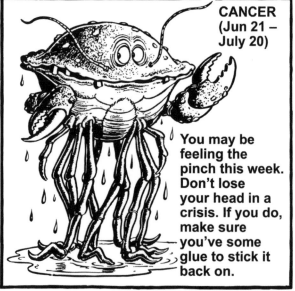

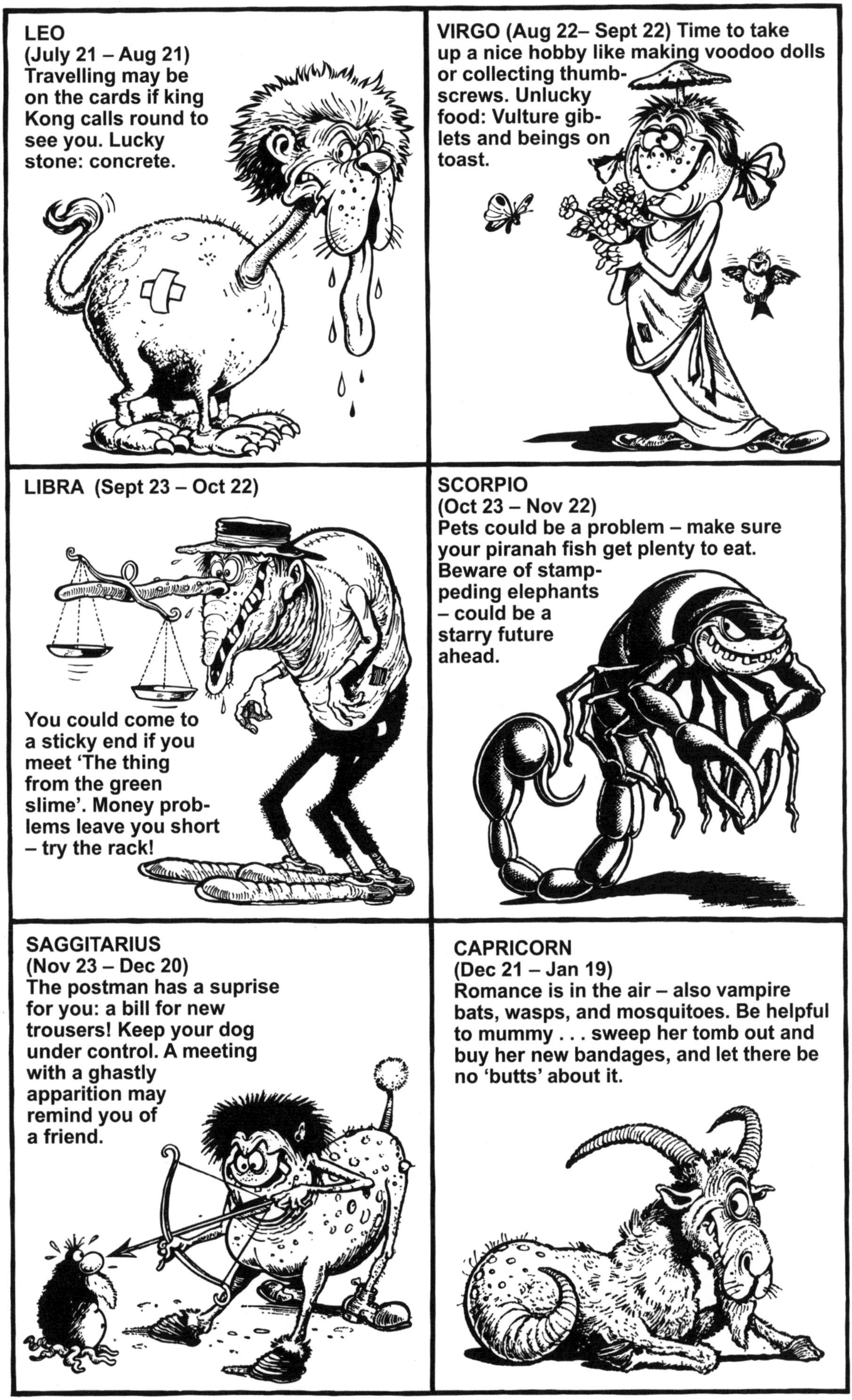
LEO
(July 21 – Aug 21)
Travelling may be on the cards if king Kong calls round to see you. Lucky stone: concrete.
VIRGO (Aug 22– Sept 22) Time to take up a nice hobby like making voodoo dolls or collecting thumb-screws. Unlucky food: Vulture gib-lets and beings on toast.
LIBRA (Sept 23 – Oct 22)
You could come to a sticky end if you meet 'The thing from the green slime'. Money prob-lems leave you short – try the rack!
SCORPIO
(Oct 23 – Nov 22)
Pets could be a problem – make sure your piranah fish get plenty to eat. Beware of stamp-peding elephants – could be a starry future ahead.
SAGGITARIUS
(Nov 23 – Dec 20)
The postman has a suprise for you: a bill for new trousers! Keep your dog under control. A meeting with a ghastly apparition may remind you of a friend.
CAPRICORN
(Dec 21 – Jan 19)
Romance is in the air – also vampire bats, wasps, and mosquitoes. Be helpful to mummy . . . sweep her tomb out and buy her new bandages, and let there be no 'butts' about it.

COMING IN 2019

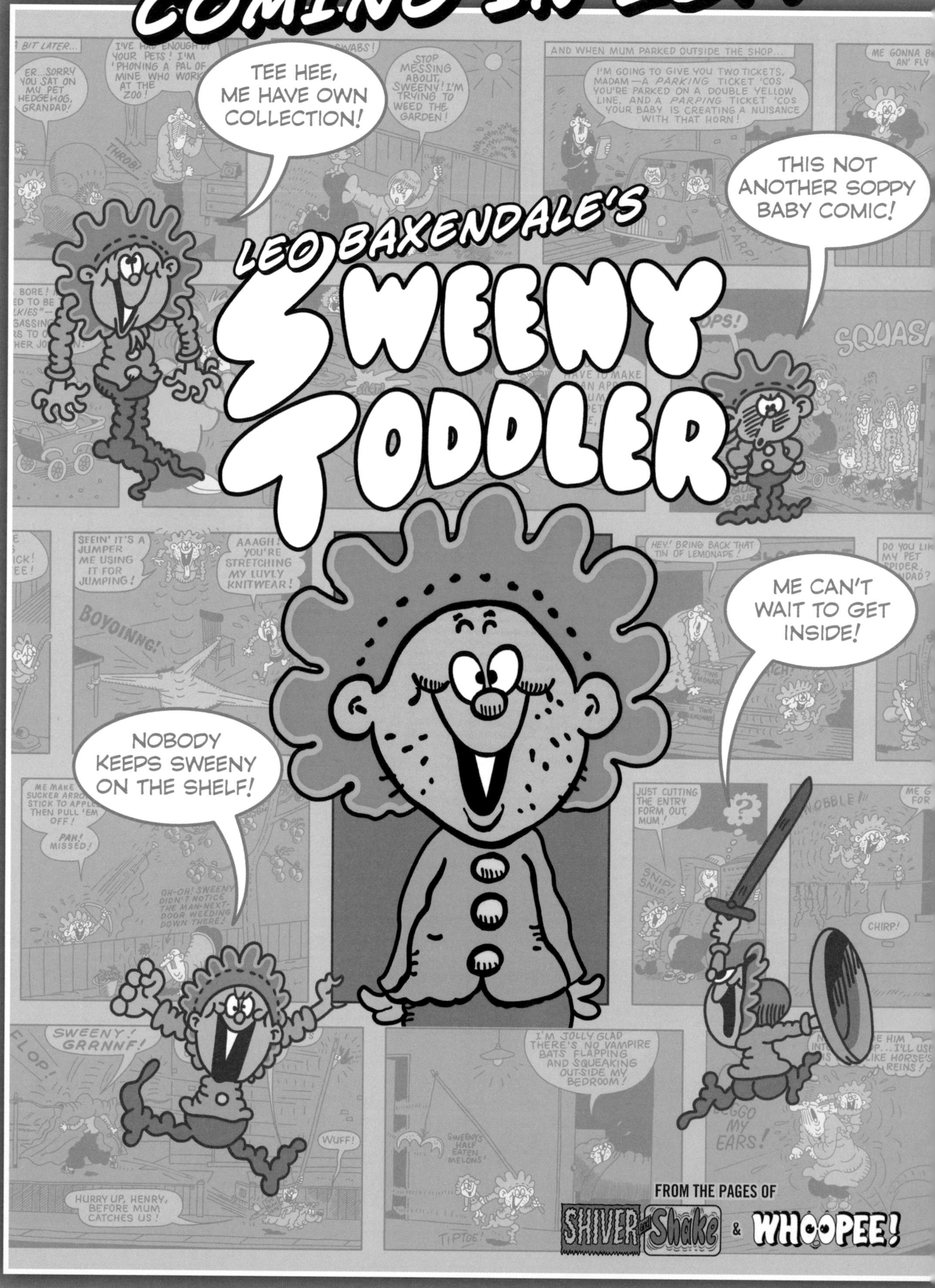

LEO BAXENDALE'S
SWEENY TODDLER
TEE HEE, ME HAVE OWN COLLECTION!
THIS NOT ANOTHER SOPPY BABY COMIC!
ME CAN'T WAIT TO GET INSIDE!
NOBODY KEEPS SWEENY ON THE SHELF!
FROM THE PAGES OF
SHIVER and Shake & WHOOPEE!

There's something fishy going on here ... stop awhile and 'pond-er'!

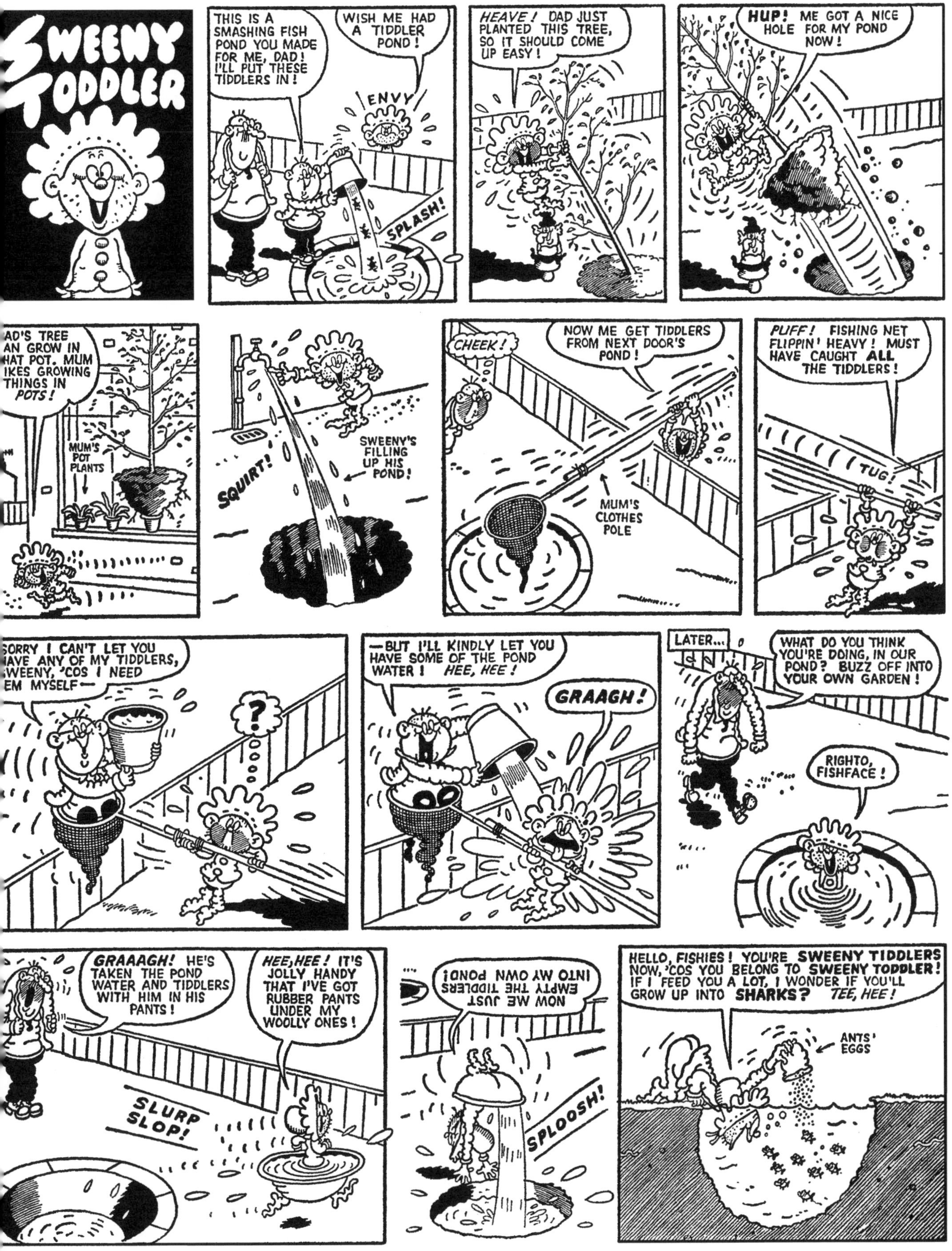
SWEENY TODDLER
THIS IS A SMASHING FISH POND YOU MADE FOR ME, DAD! I'LL PUT THESE TIDDLERS IN!
WISH ME HAD A TIDDLER POND!
ENVY
SPLASH!
HEAVE! DAD JUST PLANTED THIS TREE, SO IT SHOULD COME UP EASY!
HUP! ME GOT A NICE HOLE FOR MY POND NOW!
AD'S TREE AN GROW IN HAT POT. MUM IKES GROWING THINGS IN POTS!
MUM'S POT PLANTS
SQUIRT!
SWEENY'S FILLING UP HIS POND!
CHEEK!
NOW ME GET TIDDLERS FROM NEXT DOOR'S POND!
MUM'S CLOTHES POLE
PUFF! FISHING NET FLIPPIN' HEAVY! MUST HAVE CAUGHT ALL THE TIDDLERS!
TUG!
SORRY I CAN'T LET YOU HAVE ANY OF MY TIDDLERS, SWEENY, 'COS I NEED EM MYSELF—
?
—BUT I'LL KINDLY LET YOU HAVE SOME OF THE POND WATER! HEE, HEE!
GRAAGH!
LATER...
WHAT DO YOU THINK YOU'RE DOING, IN OUR POND? BUZZ OFF INTO YOUR OWN GARDEN!
RIGHTO, FISHFACE!
GRAAAGH! HE'S TAKEN THE POND WATER AND TIDDLERS WITH HIM IN HIS PANTS!
HEE, HEE! IT'S JOLLY HANDY THAT I'VE GOT RUBBER PANTS UNDER MY WOOLLY ONES!
SLURP SLOP!
NOW ME JUST EMPTY THE TIDDLERS INTO MY OWN POND!
SPLOOSH!
HELLO, FISHIES! YOU'RE SWEENY TIDDLERS NOW, 'COS YOU BELONG TO SWEENY TODDLER! IF I FEED YOU A LOT, I WONDER IF YOU'LL GROW UP INTO SHARKS? TEE, HEE!
ANTS' EGGS

Sweeny's in good shape this week ... he tries to be a model child!

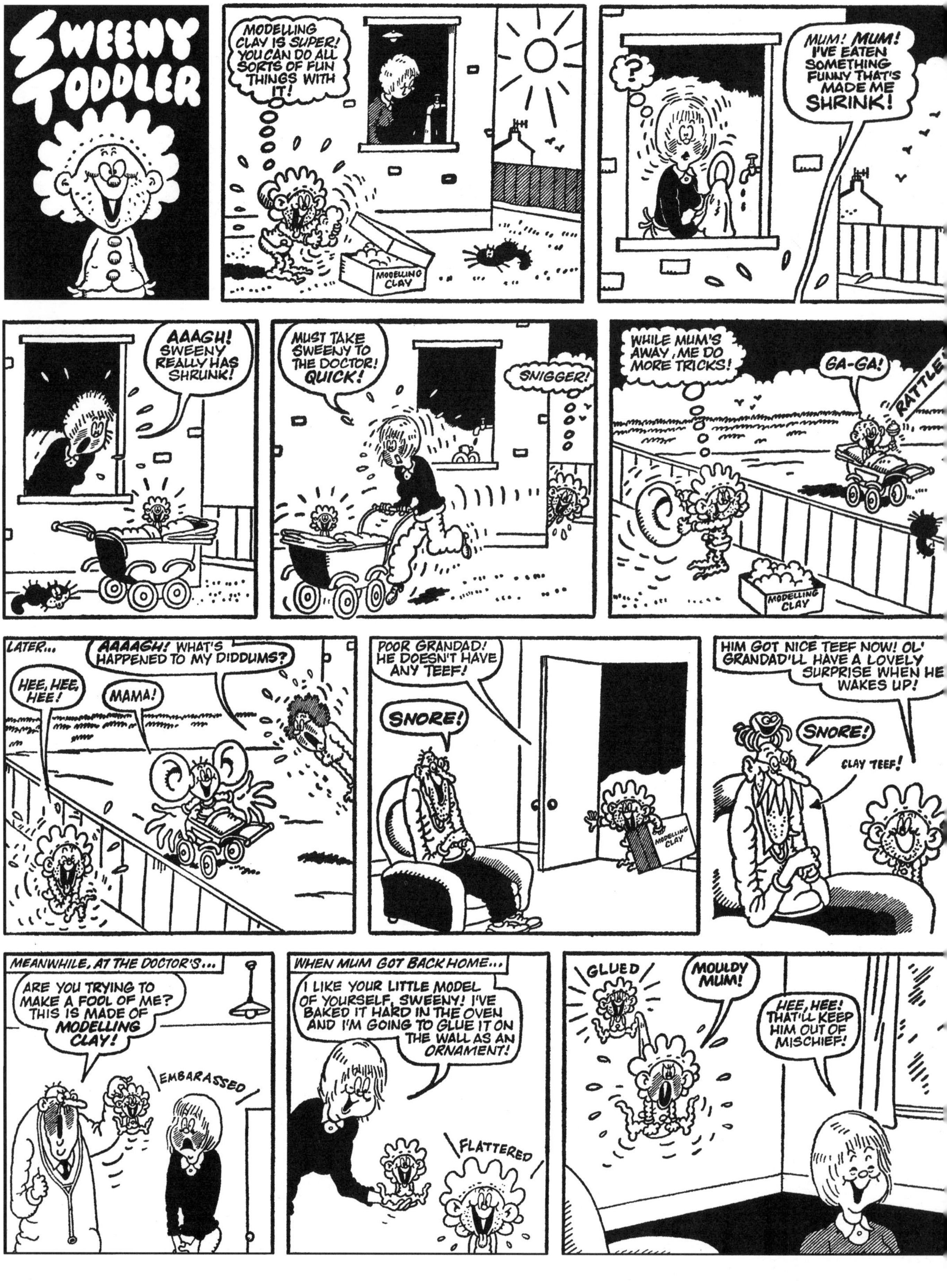
SWEENY TODDLER
MODELLING CLAY IS SUPER! YOU CAN DO ALL SORTS OF FUN THINGS WITH IT!
MODELLING CLAY
?
MUM! MUM! I'VE EATEN SOMETHING FUNNY THAT'S MADE ME SHRINK!
AAAGH! SWEENY REALLY HAS SHRUNK!
MUST TAKE SWEENY TO THE DOCTOR! QUICK!
SNIGGER!
WHILE MUM'S AWAY, ME DO MORE TRICKS!
GA-GA!
RATTLE
MODELLING CLAY
LATER...
AAAAGH! WHAT'S HAPPENED TO MY DIDDUMS?
HEE, HEE, HEE!
MAMA!
POOR GRANDAD! HE DOESN'T HAVE ANY TEEF!
SNORE!
MODELLING CLAY
HIM GOT NICE TEEF NOW! OL' GRANDAD'LL HAVE A LOVELY SURPRISE WHEN HE WAKES UP!
SNORE!
CLAY TEEF!
MEANWHILE, AT THE DOCTOR'S...
ARE YOU TRYING TO MAKE A FOOL OF ME? THIS IS MADE OF MODELLING CLAY!
EMBARASSED
WHEN MUM GOT BACK HOME...
I LIKE YOUR LITTLE MODEL OF YOURSELF, SWEENY! I'VE BAKED IT HARD IN THE OVEN AND I'M GOING TO GLUE IT ON THE WALL AS AN ORNAMENT!
FLATTERED
GLUED
MOULDY MUM!
HEE, HEE! THAT'LL KEEP HIM OUT OF MISCHIEF!

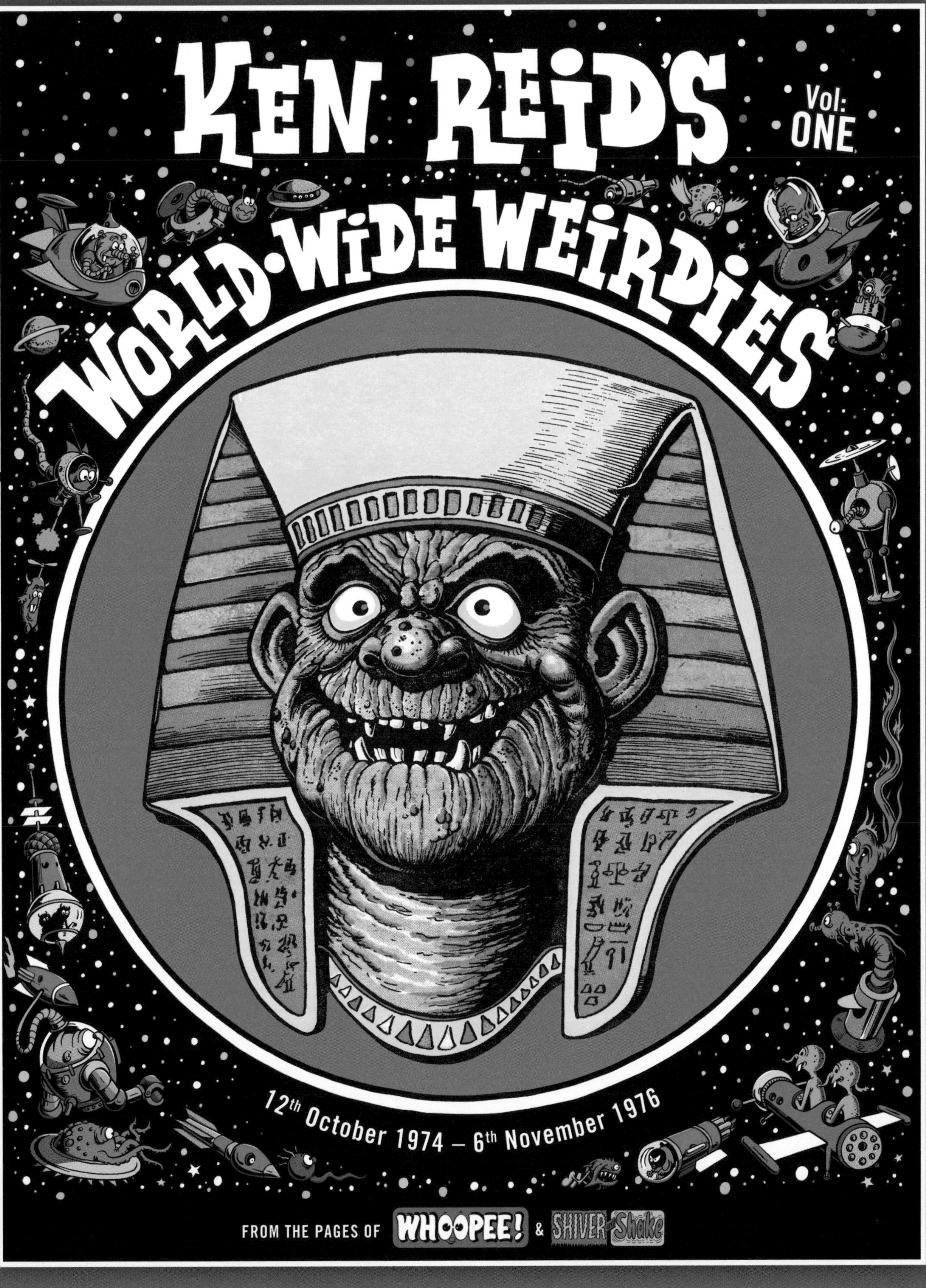
KEN REID'S
Vol: ONE
WORLD·WIDE WEIRDIES
12th October 1974 – 6th November 1976
FROM THE PAGES OF WHOOPEE! & SHIVER and Shake

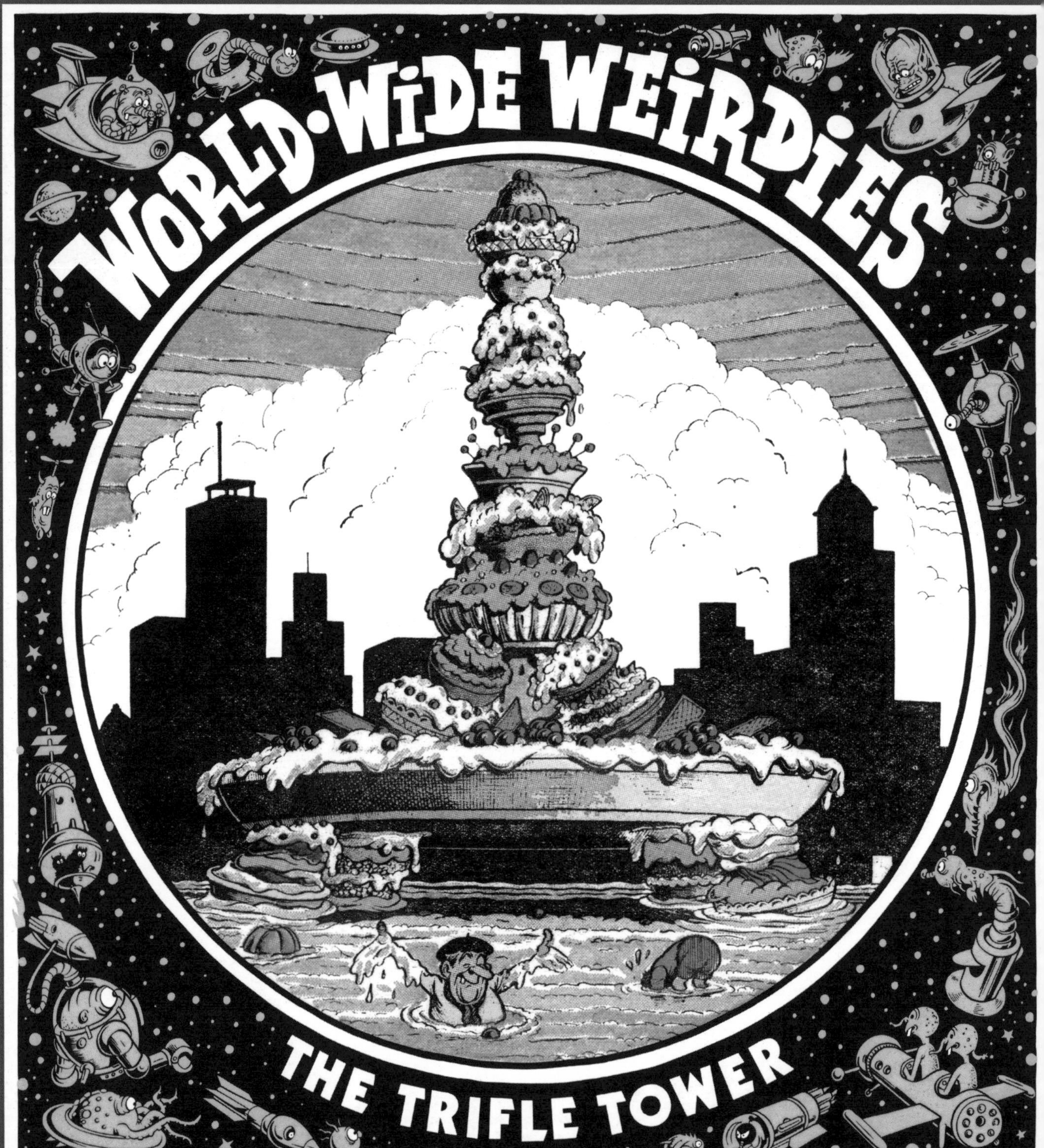
WORLD-WIDE WEIRDIES
THE TRIFLE TOWER

AVAILABLE FROM
ALL GOOD BOOK STORES
IN 2019!

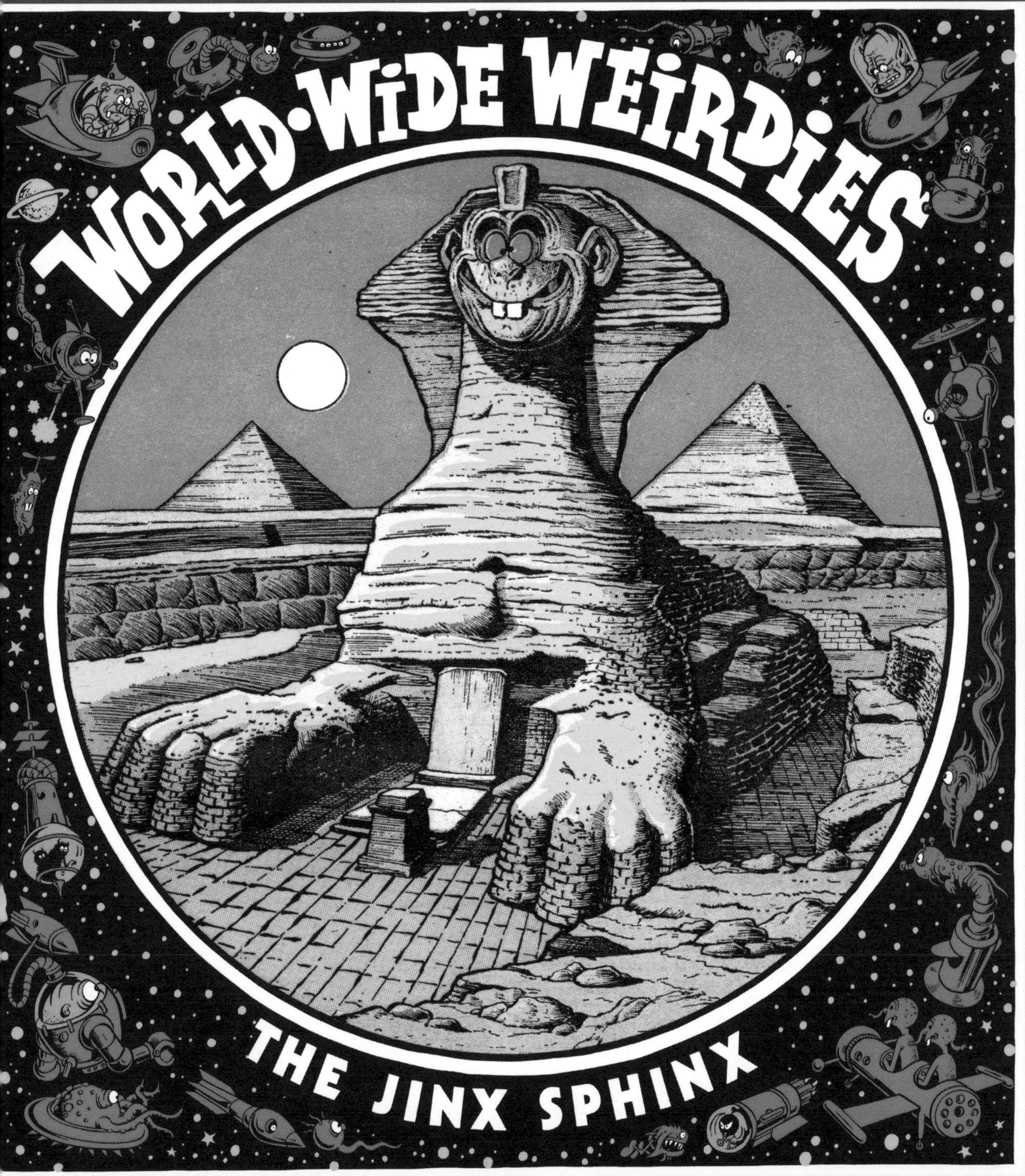
WORLD·WIDE WEIRDIES
THE JINX SPHINX

TREASURY OF BRITISH COMICS

KEN REID

OFTEN CITED AS one of Britain's greatest comic book illustrators, **Ken Reid** was born in Manchester in 1919. An avid artist from an early age, Ken was constantly drawing, even when confined to bed for six months after developing a tubercular hip at the age of nine.

After leaving school at the age of thirteen, he won a scholarship to Salford Art School. His father, who had always offered Ken a tremendous amount of encouragement, became his agent and got his son an interview over at the **Manchester Evening News**. Ken submitted several strip ideas for the children's section of the newspaper, which led to them commissioning *The Adventures of Fudge the Elf*. Originally appearing in 1938, Fudge's adventures were published right the way through to 1962, only stopping in 1941 during WWII until 1946 when Reid was de-mobbed.

In the 1950's, Ken was courted by Scottish publishers D.C.Thomson (his brother-in-law, Bill Holroyd was already working for them), where he starting working on a new strip for **The Beano** called *Roger the Dodger*. Grandpa, Jonah and other strips followed in **The Dandy**. Then in the 1960's, Ken and another member of the British comics royalty – Leo Baxendale, left the company to work for Odhams Press on the new titles **Smash and Wham!** A major draw for Ken was that he was being allowed to both write and illustrate for these titles. It was at Odhams on such strips as *Frankie Stein, The Nervs* and *Dare-a-Day Davy* that Ken really got to show off his skill at drawing the beautifully grotesque that he would later become synonymous with. *Dare-a-Day Davy* was particularly great. About a schoolboy who could never say no to a challenge, readers were encouraged to send in a dare and if selected would be paid a pound for their contribution. This led to 86 strips including a Marvel crossover (of sorts) with Nick Fury and an unpublished episode featuring Frankenstein that ended up in the pages of **Weird Fantasy** magazine.

In the 1970s, Ken created his most popular character working for IPC. First published in the pages of **Jet**, *Faceache* became an instant fan favourite. The adventures of Ricky Rubberneck and his malleable mush ran through **Jet** and into **Buster** when the two titles merged. *Faceache* was a strip that Ken both wrote and illustrated (though Ian Mennell wrote two of the early instalments). In 1978, Ken's brilliance was recognised when he was presented with two awards by the Society of Strip Illustration – Cartoonist of the Year and Humorous Script Writer of the Year.

His great work continued through to the next decade where he worked on strips such as *Robot Smith, Martha's Monster Make-Up* and *Tom Horror's World*. He passed away on 2nd February 1987 whilst working on a page of *Faceache*.

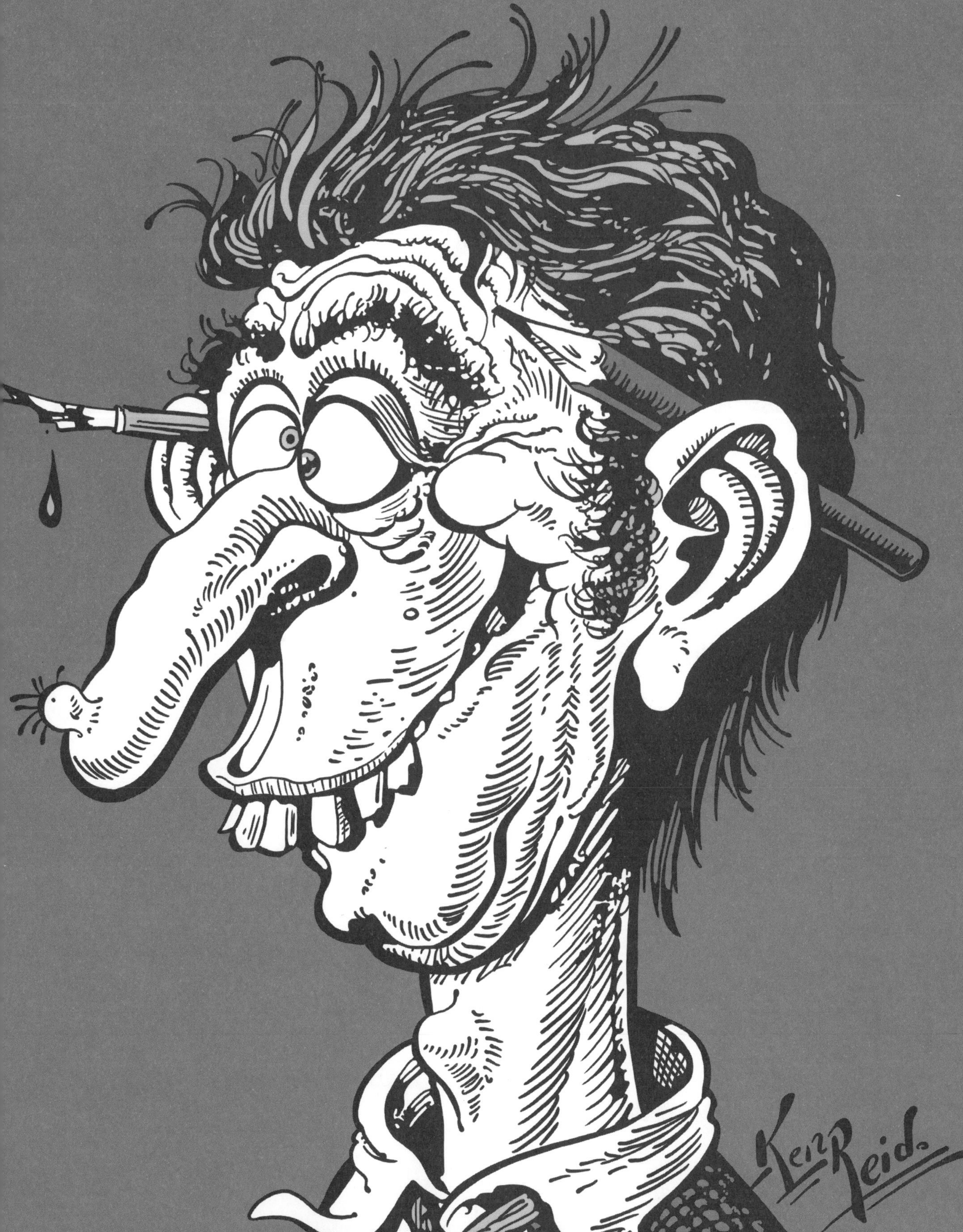
Ken Reid.

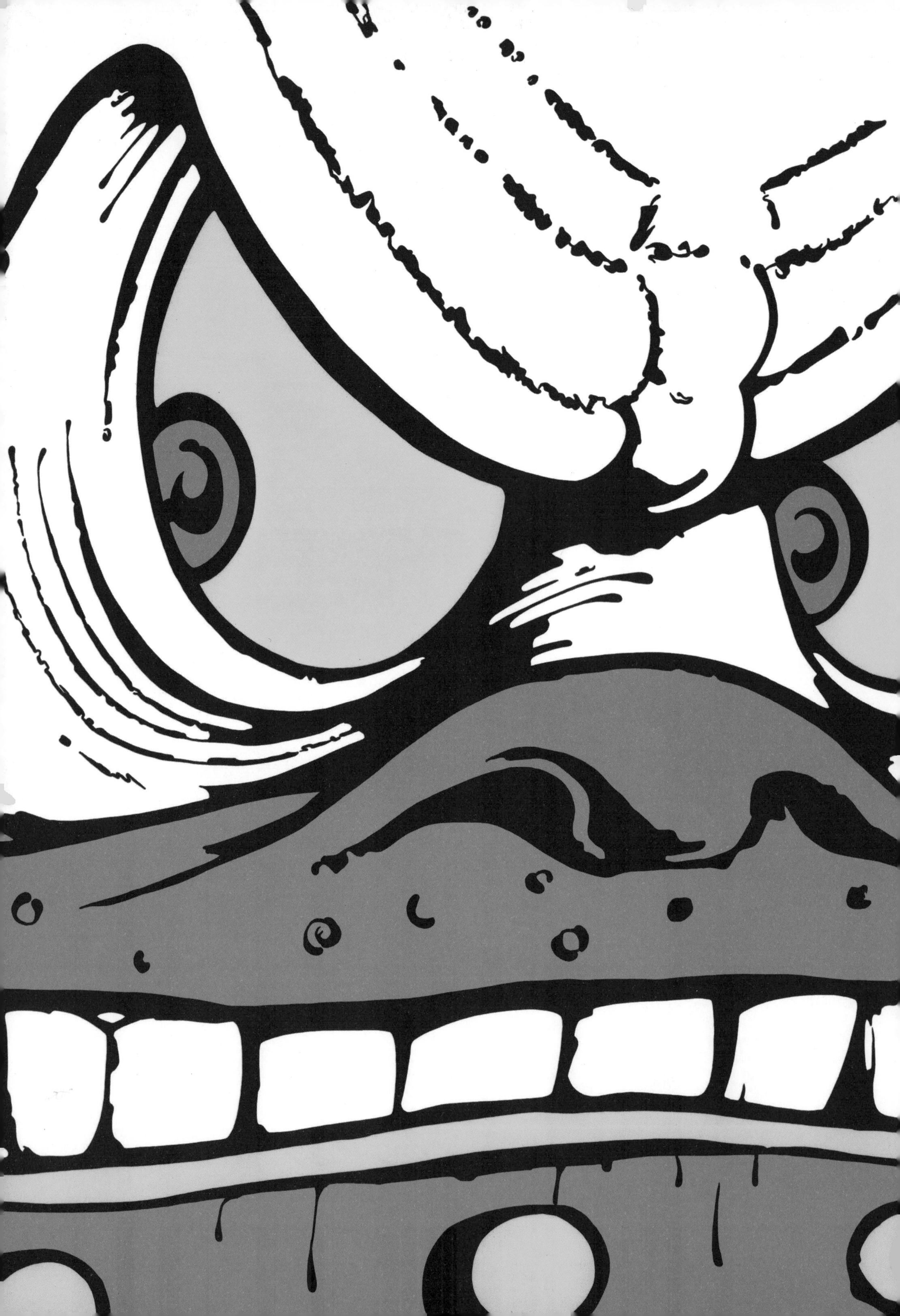